Lecture Notes in Computer Science   11553

Commenced Publication in 1973
Founding and Former Series Editors:
Gerhard Goos, Juris Hartmanis, and Jan van Leeuwen

Alessio Malizia · Stefano Valtolina ·
Anders Morch · Alan Serrano ·
Andrew Stratton (Eds.)

End-User Development

7th International Symposium, IS-EUD 2019
Hatfield, UK, July 10–12, 2019
Proceedings

 Springer

Editors
Alessio Malizia
University of Hertfordshire
Hatfield, UK

Stefano Valtolina
University of Milan
Milan, Italy

Anders Morch
University of Oslo
Oslo, Norway

Alan Serrano
Brunel University London
Uxbridge, UK

Andrew Stratton
University of Sheffield
Sheffield, UK

ISSN 0302-9743 ISSN 1611-3349 (electronic)
Lecture Notes in Computer Science
ISBN 978-3-030-24780-5 ISBN 978-3-030-24781-2 (eBook)
https://doi.org/10.1007/978-3-030-24781-2

LNCS Sublibrary: SL2 – Programming and Software Engineering

This Springer imprint is published by the registered company Springer Nature Switzerland AG
The registered company address is: Gewerbestrasse 11, 6330 Cham, Switzerland

Preface

This volume is the proceedings of IS-EUD 2019, the 7th International Symposium on End-User Development, held at the College Lane Campus, University of Hertfordshire, UK, during July 10–12, 2019. Software developers cannot easily anticipate idiosyncratic needs of end-users that are not always known at the time software is designed and developed, but rather emerge during the use of systems and services, as this use is embedded in practice in a specific context. End-user development is a field that aims to empower end-users who are not necessarily experts in software development, to create their own software to address their specific needs. End-user development is an interdisciplinary field that traditionally relates to areas such as human–computer interaction, psychology of programming, and empirical studies in software engineering. Technological trends like ubiquitous computing, tangible and embodied interaction, and the Internet of Things have renewed interest in end-user development for diverse audiences looking into industrial design, online communities, open innovation, and crowdsourcing.

IS-EUD is a biannual event that gathers researchers interested in extending their knowledge about how to design end-user development technologies and to provide scientific accounts of phenomena surrounding end-user development practices. IS-EUD cuts across application areas such as ubiquitous and wearable computing, online communities, domotics, robotics, games, etc.

IS-EUD 2019 invited contributions focused on applications of EUD in smart environments. Indeed, end-users are called on to become end-user developers of systems that encompass a variety of software and hardware components, such as smart homes, smartphones, smartwatches, interactive displays, as well as any other interactive device available in an Internet of Things setting. One of the main application of such systems is smart environments that become modular systems in which humans are embedded. Also, cloud computing and artificial intelligence (AI) are enabling smart environments, and promise to make them increasingly common in many parts of our lives: smart homes, transportation, health care, smart factories, and consumer products are only a few of the most talked about outcomes. In this symposium, we discussed progress in research around end-user development through, or towards, methods, socio-technical environments, intelligent agents, as well as the most effective end-user programming paradigms for smart environments. Papers and submissions in all categories addressed this specific theme together with topics that have been traditionally covered by the broader themes of end-user development, such as domain specific tools, spreadsheets, educational applications, and end-user aspects.

IS-EUD 2019 collected research contributions as papers, short papers, and work-in-progress papers, which described:

- New, simple, and efficient environments for end-user development
- New processes and methods for designing open-ended solutions and empowering users to cover the last mile of software development

- Case studies and design implications on challenges and practices of end-user development and user creativity
- Theoretical concepts and foundations for the field of end-user development
- Internet of Things solutions to support end-user development in daily life
- AI technologies and infrastructures for end-user development
- Methods, tools, and studies of end-user development for enabling smart environments

The paper track received 26 submissions of full and short papers, of which we accepted nine full papers and eight short papers after a rigorous double-blind review process.

The program was opened and closed by two invited keynote speakers, in areas where end-user development is becoming increasingly interesting: learning through play strategies and games and visual effects.

Siddhart Muthyala (Product and Interaction Designer at LEGO) gave a lecture on learning through play and the crucial role play has in shaping learning and development in children and adults. He presented insight into LEGO's inner thinking and creative work process.

Peter Richardson (Full Professor at University of Hertfordshire) discussed strategies for supporting users in designing impact visual effects in immersive film and television technologies.

We are happy to sustain the tradition of high-quality papers reporting on advances in this specialized field of human–computer interaction. This preface was written in anticipation of an energizing and inspiring event, with a rich program that aspired to fuel further research in end-user development for the symposium attendants as well as the broader readership of this volume.

May 2019

Stefano Valtolina
Anders Morch
Alessio Malizia
Alan Serrano
Andrew Stratton

Organization

General Chair

Alessio Malizia   University of Hertfordshire, UK

Program Chairs

Stefano Valtolina   Universitá degli Studi di Milano, Italy
Anders Morch   University of Oslo, Norway

Short Paper Chairs

Alan Serrano   Brunel University London, UK
Andrew Stratton   University of Sheffield, UK

Work in Progress Chairs

Monica Maceli   Pratt Institute, School of Information, NY, USA
Chris Crawford   University of Alabama, USA

Demos Chairs

Giuseppe Destefanis   Brunel University London, UK
Barbara Rita Barricelli   Universitá degli Studi di Milano, Italy

Workshop Chairs

Daniela Fogli   University of Brescia, Italy
Alan Chamberlain   University of Nottingham, UK

Doctoral Consortium Chairs

Silvio Carta   University of Hertfordshire, UK
David Bell   Brunel University London, UK

Proceedings Chair

Tommaso Turchi   University of Hertfordshire, UK

Publicity Chairs

Vito Gentile   Universitá degli Studi di Palermo, Italy
Elisa Rubegni   University of Lincoln, UK

Local Arrangements Chairs

David Tree   University of Hertfordshire, UK
Rubem Barbosa-Hughes   University of Hertfordshire, UK

Program Committee

Jose Abdelnour Nocera   University of West London, UK
Carmelo Ardito   University of Bari Aldo Moro, Italy
Rubem Barbosa-Hughes   University of Hertfordshire, UK
Barbara Rita Barricelli   University of Milan, Italy
Elefelious Getachew Belay   University of Milan, Italy
Andrea Bellucci   Universidad Carlos III de Madrid, Spain
Paolo Bottoni   Sapienza University of Rome, Italy
Paolo Buono   University of Bari Aldo Moro, Italy
Silvio Carta   University of Hertfordshire, UK
Elena Casiraghi   University of Milan, Italy
Alan Chamberlain   University of Nottingham, Italy
Torkil Clemmensen   CBS, Denmark
Chris Crawford   University of Alabama, USA
Boris De Ruyter   Philips Research, The Netherlands
Clarisse de Souza   PUC-Rio, Brazil
Giuseppe Desolda   University of Bari Aldo Moro, Italy
Giuseppe Destefanis   Brunel University London, UK
Ines Di Loreto   UTT - Université de Technologie de Troyes, France
Simone Diniz Junqueira   PUC-Rio, Brazil
  Barbosa
Daniela Fogli   University of Brescia, Italy
Rosella Gennari   Free University of Bozen-Bolzano, Italy
Vito Gentile   University of Palermo, Italy
Fatme Hachem   University of Milan, Italy
Thomas Herrmann   University of Bochum, Germany
Rosa Lanzilotti   University of Bari Aldo Moro, Italy
Catherine Letondal   ENAC, France
Angela Locoro   Carlo Cattaneo University - LIUC, Italy
Thomas Ludwig   University of Siegen, Germany
Monica Maceli   Pratt Institute, USA
Alessio Malizia   University of Hertfordshire, UK
Panos Markopoulos   Eindhoven University of Technology, The Netherlands
Maristella Matera   Politecnico di Milano, Italy
Alessandra Melonio   Free University of Bozen-Bolzano, Italy

Contents

Challenges of Traditional Usability Evaluation in End-User Development

Daniel Rough$^{(\boxtimes)}$ and Aaron Quigley

School of Computer Science, University of St Andrews, St Andrews, Scotland, UK
{djr53,aquigley}@st-andrews.ac.uk

Abstract. End-user development (EUD) research has yielded a variety of novel environments and techniques, often accompanied by lab-based usability studies that test their effectiveness in the completion of representative real-world tasks. While lab studies play an important role in resolving frustrations and demonstrating the potential of novel tools, they are insufficient to accurately determine the acceptance of a technology in its intended context of use, which is highly dependent on the diverse and dynamic requirements of its users, as we show here. As such, usability in the lab is unlikely to represent usability in the field. To demonstrate this, we first describe the results of a think-aloud usability study of our EUD tool "Jeeves", followed by two case studies where Jeeves was used by psychologists in their work practices. Common issues in the artificial setting were seldom encountered in the real context of use, which instead unearthed new usability issues through unanticipated user needs. We conclude with considerations for usability evaluation of EUD tools that enable development of software for other users, including planning for collaborative activities, supporting developers to evaluate their own tools, and incorporating longitudinal methods of evaluation.

Keywords: End-user development · Usability · Case studies

1 Introduction

Creating end-user development (EUD) tools that support users in their working practices is a significant challenge, compounded by the difficulty in evaluating their success in doing so. In the deployment of any novel technology in a professional environment, intended users' interactions with this technology depend on organisational factors, including other individuals with whom communication and collaboration take place, or existing technology used in working practices. As such, EUD tools are intended to address this difficulty of anticipating the needs of end-users in advance, by providing the flexibility to adapt software to their context-specific needs.

Given the contextual influences of EUD in practice, it is somewhat surprising that a prevalence of lab-based usability studies in the evaluation of EUD is contrasted by the lack of research into their real-world utility [23], a disparity recognised within HCI as a whole [8]. EUD evaluations are largely focused

A. Malizia et al. (Eds.): IS-EUD 2019, LNCS 11553, pp. 1–17, 2019.
https://doi.org/10.1007/978-3-030-24781-2_1

on the programming paradigm and how users' mental models of programming tasks affect the usability of particular paradigms. However, successful deployment of EUD tools requires knowledge of who the potential end-users are, what their goals and motivations are, and how such tools could fit within their current working practices. In this regard, Mehandjiev et al. highlight a lack of *"necessary knowledge of how to deal with problems and conflicts which are likely to emerge from the formalization of EUD"* [14]. A recent review by Barricelli et al. explicates the breadth of EUD research and the contexts in which it is applied [1], from personal web mashups to complex industry-standard software. Thus, an EUD tool's ease-of-use is contingent not only on the development paradigm, but on the domain in which it is employed, its users, and other external conditions.

In this paper, we show that the external variables pertaining to ease-of-use cannot be resolutely determined for EUD, posing a challenge to lab-based evaluation. We discuss the issues and related requirements emerging from a lab-based think-aloud usability study of *Jeeves*, our EUD tool. Following this, two case studies are described where Jeeves was employed by psychology researchers to address their own research questions. These studies were intended to enable analyses of Jeeves in its context of use, with results expected to reinforce those of our lab-based usability study. However, this was not the case, challenging the established view of the efficacy of lab studies in professional EUD contexts.

1.1   Related Work

Prior research has attempted to understand, and consequently bridge, this evaluation gap between the lab and the real world. Field methods such as contextual inquiry provide an understanding of usability "in use" and thereby external validity [25]; log data of user actions provides unobtrusive *in-situ* usage; longitudinal approaches such as the Experience Sampling Method (which Jeeves aims to facilitate, incidentally) can be employed to collect usability issues from users as they occur [12]. Such methods aid understanding of software usability outside the lab, but are seldom employed in EUD usability evaluation [23].

Irrespective of this preference for lab usability studies, continuous co-design with software end-users is a core component of an EUD approach. This is formalised by Fischer et al. through the *Seeding, Evolutionary Growth and Reseeding (SER) model*, which recognises the need for continuous re-evaluation and restructuring of tailorable systems [5]. The SER model supports Fischer's *meta-design* framework, advocating users as participating designers of software during use [6]. A pertinent example of meta-design in practice is described by Maceli, whose case study into the co-design of meme creation tools [13] showed how developers and end-users naturally engage in meta-design to improve their tools in the absence of formal research processes.

In short, we as meta-designers, must respond to in-use evaluation if our EUD tools are to be successfully employed. How, then, do lab usability studies help or hinder our identification of in-use issues? The remainder of this introduction provides an overview of Jeeves to afford context for our own lab and field studies.

Jeeves and Its Context of Use. Jeeves is an EUD tool intended for non-programmer researchers to create smartphone apps that collect data from participants as they go about their everyday lives, based on the aforementioned Experience Sampling Method (ESM) [12]. Jeeves employs a blocks-based programming paradigm through which researchers define different time and context-based triggers upon which to execute actions (primarily sending surveys, but also sending prompts or capturing contextual information such as location). Recent additions to the library of Jeeves blocks include participant "attribute" blocks, akin to programmatic variables, conditional statement blocks, and context-sensitive triggers. These extensions were derived from a review of literature detailing the potential benefits of modern smartphone ESM, and were positively received by interviewed psychology researchers [20]. However, the researchers who were interviewed did not actually use Jeeves.

Other novel ESM creation tools exist both in research and the commercial domain, many of which are listed by van Berkel et al. in their review of mobile ESM [3]. However, there is a notable lack of research into challenges of introducing ESM creation tools into practice. One exception is the work of Batalas and Markopoulos [2], who provide a detailed discussion of results related to real-world use of their *TEMPEST* platform. We seek to build upon this work by focusing on the contrasting results of different evaluation methods.

2 Lab-Based Usability Study

This paper focuses on a real-world contrast with the third lab-based usability study undertaken with Jeeves. (We refer the reader to [21] and [22] for details of prior studies.) This study was intended to focus on issues encountered in completion of complex tasks with the newly implemented extensions. Participants were 10 students at our university, recruited via advertisement in weekly student memos, and through circulating emails to students in the school of psychology. In total, six participants studied psychology, two studied medicine, and two studied humanities, with a mix of undergraduate and postgraduate students. Three psychology students reported experience with MATLAB, but no other programming experience was stated.

Prior to running this study, a 10 min tutorial video was shown to guide participants through the necessary information they would need to complete the study tasks, by demonstrating an example app specification being built. This also served as a useful reference for when participants were unsure how to proceed. Participants were instructed to think aloud as they completed their tasks, in order to understand *why* specific issues were encountered, but also to explicate participants' mental models of triggers, conditions and attributes.

2.1 Tasks

Nielsen's guidelines on designing study tasks were followed closely, by ensuring that participants were not primed with the trigger-action terminology of

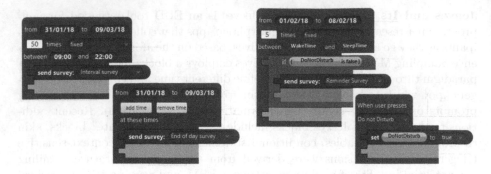

Fig. 1. Two of the 'faulty' triggers in the   **Fig. 2.** An example 'Do Not Disturb'
Task 3 specification   specification in Task 4

Jeeves [16]. The tasks were intended to address updated functions of Jeeves that
were perceived as useful for researchers to create personalised ESM study specifications [20] - primarily the use of "attribute" blocks to represent variables,
as well as conditional statements. Note that the hypothetical app end-users are
referred to in study tasks as *patients* rather than *participants*, to distinguish them
from the participants in this study. For the sake of space, we do not quote the
tasks verbatim. Instead, we describe the features each was intended to evaluate.

Task 1 - Attribute Usage: Participants were asked to design a specification
that would acquire patients' waking and sleeping times, and trigger a survey at
random times during the patients' waking hours. This task assessed whether the
sequence of creating attributes, assigning values to them, and then using these
attributes in the blocks specification, was understandable by participants.

Task 2 - Survey Button Creation: Participants were asked to design a specification allowing a patient to enter data upon pressing a button (i.e., event-
contingent experience sampling [12]). Further, they were asked to utilise actions
that would capture sensor data, including Bluetooth and GPS.

Task 3 - Patient Compliance Reaction: Participants were asked to load
a study specification that had been populated with simulated data of poorly
compliant patients. The compliance issue was due to a fault in the specification
causing a trigger to send surveys 50 times a day. Further, one survey was not
sent at all because its trigger did not have a time, both of which are shown in
Fig. 1. This task primarily assessed the readability of the blocks notation.

Task 4 - Do Not Disturb: Finally, participants were asked to implement a "Do
Not Disturb" button that would stop patients receiving prompts, an example
solution of which is shown in Fig. 2. This was a comparatively difficult task that
assessed setting attributes through actions, and adding conditional statements
into triggers. A similar application was demonstrated in the tutorial video, which
participants could adapt to the task's requirements.

2.2   Usability Issues Analysis

The study provided insights into how participants would tackle the more advanced features of Jeeves, with an aim to address problems that could lead to researchers' frustration and consequent abandonment of the EUD tool. Think-aloud monologues and post-study interviews were transcribed, and analysed in parallel with screen-capture recordings of their task completion.

While the blocks-based programming paradigm was found to be intuitive and liked by participants, who provided positive feedback on the visual metaphor, they also experienced confusion and frustrations that sometimes led to fundamental design breakdowns. The following issues were encountered most frequently or severely, and illustrate the primary concerns we had regarding the usability of Jeeves for a realistic deployment.

Issue 1 - Hidden Dependencies

Creating and assigning attributes in Task 1 raised issues with most participants, who were confused by the sequence of creating an attribute, creating a survey, assigning the attribute to the survey, and then sending the survey. Participants frequently attempted shortcuts by dragging and dropping attribute blocks into incorrect places in a misunderstanding of each step's purpose. It also gave rise to barriers where participants were oblivious to the fact that they had missed one of these steps. These instances of what Green and Petre define as *"hidden dependencies"*, suggest that a shorter sequence of actions might be necessary, or dependencies communicated more explicitly to users [7]. As attributes are created in one section of Jeeves, and applied in another, this caused confusion and provoked suggestions of alternative solutions from participants:

"Like in this window, you [define an attribute] in this window, in the survey design. But in the end you are using it [on the blocks canvas] so, I mean it transfers but for me it was confusing that you did it here" (P8).

Issue 2 - Too Much Abstraction

Issues were caused by unsuitable levels of abstraction. Five participants struggled to find a trigger that would only fire once. While this simply involved customising a timed trigger to fire at a single time, this was unclear to participants, who hunted for a more specific "one-off" trigger type. Over-abstraction also resulted in participants experiencing a barrier when attempting unavailable customisation. For example, one participant wished to specify the desired Bluetooth data returned from the "Capture Data" action:

"Capture data from...will this do? I'm not sure whether this is enough. Do I have to do anything about this Bluetooth? Um...I'm not sure" (P4).

Conversely, one participant suggested the possibility of creating his own abstractions out of more specific components for ease-of-use:

"So I have my press commands and maybe [I could] group them...maybe you could pull them onto each other and make them into a group" (P6).

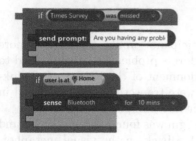
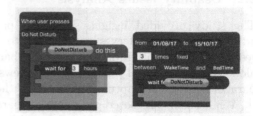

Fig. 3. If-conditions were misinterpreted as event-based triggers

Fig. 4. Two erroneous attempts at 'Do Not Disturb' functionality in Task 4

Issue 3 - Gulf of Evaluation

Task 3, where participants were asked to read a pre-created specification, gave rise to frequent evaluation barriers. Although participants could observe that patients were not completing surveys, six participants missed at least one of the faulty triggers shown in Fig. 1. This suggests a *"Gulf of Evaluation"*, defined by Norman as *"the amount of effort that the person must make to interpret the physical state of the device and to determine how well the expectations and intentions have been met"* [17, p. 39] As Jeeves does not currently provide feedback on the function of created specifications, some participants expressed doubt as to the correctness of their solutions to tasks, or were unaware of subtle mistakes that could cause faults in the apps they created. Some participants expressed a desire to test their apps, enabling trial-and-error learning:

"Can I run it and see like what I've placed and understand what's gonna happen? Like when you do a webpage you can see it straight away like what's happening that's what you do when you learn it online." (P9).

However, most participants were satisfied with their task completion and did not outwardly question their solutions, whether they were correct or not.

Issue 4 - Events and States

Task 4 cased the majority of issues for participants in attempting to combine event and state triggers. As found in prior work by Huang and Cacmak, participants had trouble separating triggers involving discrete, instantaneous events, and continuous, ongoing states [10], such that combining the trigger *event* with the "Do not Disturb" *state*, as shown in Fig. 2, introduced barriers for most participants. P2 initially assumed that an if-condition detached from a trigger would enable a change in the value of an attribute to be detected like a discrete event: *"I'm going to assume that this (if-condition) will be continuously running and that it doesn't need to be attached to a trigger object"* (P2) Although the if-condition block has an external connector to afford nesting within a trigger, the visual notation did not stop participants detaching it. Other examples of this error during task completion are shown in Fig. 3.

Issue 5 - Lack of Abstraction

In addition to barriers caused by over-abstraction, further barriers in Task 4 arose through *under*-abstraction. Five participants continuously searched for a "Do not Disturb" action, rather than implementing this functionality themselves. P5 explained this behaviour in her post-study interview:

"I realise a lot of the things that I wanted to do could be composed of the triggers and actions and conditions themselves but I guess for me, they'd be kind of like, simpler options? Or simpler components?" (P5).

As suggested by a participant in resolving Issue 2 (too much abstraction) further research could establish with researchers what useful fundamental blocks would be, so that commonly employed features could be constructed once and then reused as custom abstractions when necessary.

Issue 6 - Ambiguous Actions

Finally, the apparent ambiguity of the previously implemented "wait for" action was a notable source of error, causing barriers for many participants. This action was intended to pause execution of subsequent actions in a particular trigger. However, participants assumed that this action would pause notifications across the entire application, shown by one participant's faulty specification in Fig. 4, suggesting a misunderstanding of trigger concurrency. Further, three participants attempted to use a "Do Not Disturb" attribute with this action, in an attempt to wait until the attribute was false (Fig. 4, right).

2.3   Summary

Our observations, collated with direct (interview) and indirect (think-aloud) participant feedback, suggested that Jeeves could be applied with no prior programming experience, but that issues of *hidden dependencies, abstraction, evaluation,* and *ambiguity,* could lead to abandonment by researchers attempting more sophisticated behaviour. P5, a medicine postgraduate, explained that 'walk-up-and-use' functionality is not expected from highly useful software:

"a lot of programs you use in research you do need training, like SPSS... you have to use YouTube videos or you have to go on a course. It's not unusual for researchers to be used to having to do tutorials, classes, sessions..." (P5).

However, even if perceived usefulness overshadows ease-of-use in software, as suggested by Greenberg and Buxton [8], a follow-up quote from the same participant cemented the ongoing need to keep ease-of-use above a certain threshold:

"There is a frustration tolerance. You run the risk that people like me would get to this phase and go 'y'know what? I don't know how to do this. I'm just gonna email surveys through Qualtrics because I know what to do'." (P5).

3   Case Studies

Prior to updating Jeeves based on the lab study's feedback, the two case studies described in this section were conducted, with the intention of triangulating emergent "real" usability issues with participants' task-specific issues. The assumptions made about researchers' typical usage of Jeeves was a clear limitation of the study itself; while tasks were informed by publications in psychology journals that utilised ESM, the constraints of a lab study are not representative of practical application of an EUD tool in its intended context of use. It was therefore of interest to determine to what extent these usability issues would impact on researchers' use of Jeeves and if new usability issues would arise.

3.1   Case Study 1 - ESM During Sport Events

This study was conducted in collaboration with a psychology researcher at a local university and a researcher at a university in Germany, whom we refer to as Paul and Oliver in this paper. Both researchers had an interest in capturing experiences of fans during sporting events, but their knowledge of programming would not allow them to do this themselves, thus Paul saw how Jeeves could be used for this purpose. This section summarises events of interest within the case study, pertaining to study organisation, piloting and running the full study.

Study Preparation. In November, email correspondence began with Paul and Oliver in which requirements of a potential study were ascertained. It was decided that the goal was to conduct an ESM study with supporting fans of a basketball team at Oliver's university during a live game, prior to which a pilot study would be run with local students watching a live football game on television.

In early January, a Skype call was held, during which the researchers watched the video tutorial of Jeeves and used the screen-sharing function of Skype to collaboratively design a study specification.

During the call, collaborative completion of the study between Paul and Oliver was observed to be difficult. Oliver would dictate survey questions from the plan document while Paul created the survey in Jeeves, which was slow and cumbersome. Complications further arose when a means to obtain informed consent from participants had to be implemented into a survey. Initially, Paul copied the text from the PDF consent document, but it was then incorrectly formatted. It was suggested that providing participants with a URL link to the informed consent document would be simpler, which was agreed upon.

The lack of preview functionality for surveys resulted in difficulty, and an inability to duplicate similar questions also became an issue. Both Paul and Oliver made comparisons with *Qualtrics* - software they were both familiar with in their research, as illustrated in this dialogue:

> **Paul:** "Is there a way of previewing questions? I mean I guess it's kinda here, that'd be really useful. That's something *Qualtrics* does and it'd be quite useful. There's not a way of copying a question is there?"
>
> **Oliver:** "Paul, you also use *Qualtrics* right? I think it has very...smart features, especially what you said, copying questions, preview of questions, and also these randomisation things, orders, stuff like that."
>
> **Paul:** "Yeah there's a lot of good stuff in *Qualtrics*, it can't do everything we want it to do, but in terms of user features it might be worth..."
>
> **Oliver:** "Yeah I have to agree, but they sell this for a lot of money so..."

Following the Skype call, Paul suggested that a form of annotation would be desirable for communicating ideas to Oliver:

"...to add a comment, annotation...a note to yourself to say 'I've still got to do this' or 'remember to change that' or in a collaborative project, 'I'm not sure how this works' or 'what do you think of this?'...just to say 'Oliver this is for the half-time survey, just starting it for you, you finish it'."

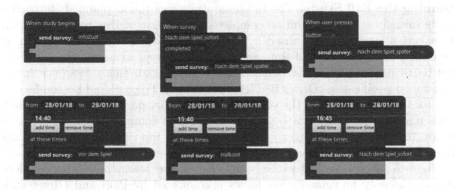

Fig. 5. The final specification for the study conducted at the basketball game

Conducting the Pilot Study. On January 13th, the pilot study was run. The first author was responsible for conducting this study, such that no issues were directly experienced by Paul and Oliver. While most participants faced no problems, there were exceptions not previously considered in lab evaluation.

For example, one participant had an incompatible device, running a lower version of Android than was necessary for the study. Another participant had privacy settings enabled on their device, so that they did not receive surveys at the same time as other participants. One participant turned up particularly late, and by the time they had installed the Jeeves Android app and initiated the study, they had missed the first trigger. The time for this trigger was adjusted through Jeeves so that it would be sent to their device, which meant that it was also sent to all other devices, causing confusion amongst participants.

Preparation for Full-Scale Study. A Skype call was set up to discuss the results of the pilot study and to plan for the full-scale study in Germany. Only the audio of this call was recorded, as no use of Jeeves took place.

Oliver was responsible for recreating the pilot study, with survey questions written in German, and trigger times adjusted to key phases of the basketball game. Given that the design was otherwise identical, Oliver commented that a feature to simply duplicate the pilot study specification would have been useful. At this stage, Oliver had a greater workload, involving the translation of the previous Jeeves pilot study into German, testing the new app (Paul did not own an Android smartphone and thus was unable to do so) as well as engaging in recruitment activities with the university sports team.

Given the various organisational activities involved, as well as the researchers' other commitments, development activities were put on hold. After the last update by Oliver on January 23rd, no further updates were made until January 27th - one day before the full study - when a bug was discovered in which participants who had registered were already being sent study surveys.

Running the Full Study. The full-scale study was run as planned; 40 participants initially signed up, and 30 completed every survey. Due to the variation of basketball match times caused by fouls and timeouts, Oliver was present at the match to adjust the half-time and full-time surveys as necessary, to ensure that participants would receive surveys at the appropriate times. However, in the final study specification, Oliver had left the "Button Trigger" and button he created for testing purposes in the version of the app that participants downloaded. Some participants found this button and ended up completing the post-match survey too early. (This trigger can be seen in the top-right of Fig. 5, showing that when the button is pressed, a post-match survey is sent.)

Figure 5 further indicates the simplicity of the researchers' specification. Indeed, the only implementation issues encountered by Paul and Oliver with Jeeves were instances of unavailable functionality (i.e., presentation of participants' informed consent forms) for which the authors either implemented the requested function, or the researchers found workarounds as required.

3.2   Case Study 2 - ESM in the Menstrual Cycle

This case study describes the progress of a collaboration with a second psychology researcher at a local university, and her postgraduate research student, whom we refer to as Deborah and Lucy. Deborah's area of research is in aggression, for which Jeeves was considered suitable for exposing contextual factors of aggressive behaviour, outside the constraints of the traditional laboratory experiment. Lucy's thesis project involved investigating the general variation of female aggression during the menstrual cycle.

Unlike the previous case study, where the first author was involved as a collaborator, the role taken here was as a passive observer. This precluded direct involvement with Deborah and Lucy, such that face-to-face meetings on the project were often not observed. However, insight was obtained through direct observation of their use of Jeeves, as well as frequent email feedback.

Study Preparation. In-person meetings were arranged in November to plan the preliminary tasks that would need to be undertaken prior to designing the study specification. Again, ethical documentation had to be submitted and approved, which delayed progress. A further meeting was held at the end of January to discuss the study's requirements, and the capabilities of Jeeves in fulfilling them. Deborah and Lucy watched the Jeeves tutorial video in order to understand the available features. Rather than beginning to implement the specification immediately after watching the video as before, a week passed during which Lucy planned her study design, before the next meeting.

While Deborah and Lucy's research question ultimately determined their study design, in this case the use of attributes was required in order to tailor the app to each participant's ovulation dates. Attribute creation appeared to be straightforward. Lucy created a survey question, created the date attribute, and then assigned the attribute to the question with no further issues, unlike the usability study participants, who appeared to struggle with this sequence:

"you can create a survey that would get all the attributes out for the times so...then we can create an 'if this date send this survey' so that when it gets to the correct date they will just get another trigger." (Lucy)

An issue of abstraction arose when the researchers wished to prompt a participant at a particular time if they had not completed their survey, but with no simple block that would allow them to do so, a clever workaround was employed, as shown in the blocks specification and adjacent dialogue in Fig. 7. In summary, the researchers had to add a question to their survey that would ask participants

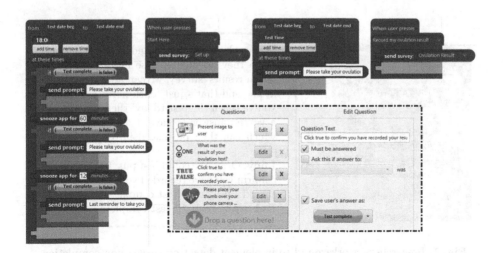

Fig. 6. Deborah and Lucy's pilot study specification, also showing part of their created survey (with an attribute designating confirmation of completion)

to confirm survey completion, thereby updating the "Test complete" attribute to stop reminder prompts being sent. (Researchers designed this workaround survey as shown in Fig. 6.)

Unlike the crippling issues experienced by lab evaluation participants in combining triggers with conditions and interpreting trigger concurrency, Deborah and Lucy experienced only minor issues, which were resolved quickly through discussion and referral to the tutorial video. After 45 min, the researchers had finished designing their study, and expressed satisfaction that they had independently implemented the specification in this short time.

Conducting the Pilot Study. Following the direct observation of study implementation, a series of circumstances arose that prevented the pilot study actually being initiated until one month later. The specification was not viewed by the researchers during this time (as indicated by the "last accessed" date and time feature of Jeeves). However, in the interim period, the researchers asked if functionality to capture participants' heart rate could be added. This resulted in a hasty integration of functionality from an unofficial online source, which it was not possible to rigorously test in the short time prior to study deployment.

The pilot study ran through March for 21 days, during which participants were required to report their ovulation result daily for 10 days of the study. Deborah and Lucy reported that the study had been a success, and were particularly pleased with the new heart rate functionality that worked without problems. However, other unforeseen issues arose, unrelated to their specification design:

"Participants were unsure about the permanent notification that said 'Jeeves running' on their phone...Two participants dropped out of the study saying that the app was 'annoying' them due to this" (Lucy)

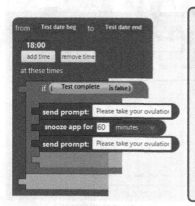

Deborah: If when we send the user input, when they do their 'please input your ovulation results' survey, we can add a question at the end that's just 'click here to confirm you've taken the test today' then you've got a yes/no answer to save it as an attribute, which can then be placed into that condition.
Lucy: Okay. We could just put 'Click true to confirm you have recorded your results'. Oh, should I drag this [test complete attribute]?
Deborah: Yeah, 'if test complete is false'

Fig. 7. Researchers' workaround to implement detecting survey non-completion

It was surprising that the small notification icon would cause such irritation as to lead to study drop-out. The icon appears irrespective of specification design, such that a preview feature would not have helped researchers correct this.

4 Discussion

Between our two pairs of psychology researchers, there were some notable differences in their application of Jeeves. The studies took place over different time periods, contrasted in complexity, and were designed and tested by researchers through different processes. Common to both, however, were usability issues and requirements that could not be anticipated from a lab evaluation. We frame our insights as considerations for the usability evaluation of *"public EUD"* tools - wherein one group of end-users develops software for a separate group [4].

4.1 Plan for Collaboration

In Paul and Oliver's case study, remote collaborative use of Jeeves emerged as a practice we had not considered. Previously, it was assumed that a single researcher would be responsible for EUD activities in a group collaboration, allowing single-user, task-based usability studies to retain some external validity. However, if the EUD task is a group effort, as it may often be, this introduces additional factors that cannot be explicated in such a lab study. Pipek and Kahler discuss how collaborative tailoring may take place in single-user applications, as *"shared context scenarios"* [19]. Indeed, our lab study probed Jeeves from a single-user perspective, but we discovered that collaborative use can occur regardless of an EUD tool's capacity to deal with it.

Mitigating the potential difficulty of evaluating an EUD tool in a real-world deployment, discount methods have been proposed that conceptualise group activities as *"mechanics of collaboration"* [18], which focus on basic actions such as communicating with group members, or keeping track of members' activity. We suggest that such methods be incorporated into preliminary evaluations of a new EUD tool where there is potential for shared use.

4.2 Evaluate Outcome Quality Objectively

In categorising measures of usability, Hornbæk distinguishes between *"outcome quality"* and *"perceived outcome"* as objective and subjective measures of usability respectively [9]. In designing the usability study, our measure of *outcome quality* was the accuracy of participants' final solution to a task. However, in the absence of an objective task-based measure, this became an issue for our case study researchers who were dissatisfied with the uncertainty of their *perceived outcome*:

"Whenever I do an online survey, I preview it and preview it and preview it multiple times, run through it, there are always errors...so I found that really frustrating that I couldn't actually see what it was that I'd coded." (Paul)

In EUD of ESM apps, Batalas discusses this tension between success from the perspective of the tool developer, and that of the researcher who uses the tool [2]. While the perceived outcome of a public/outward EUD tool can, to some extent, be measured through a preview function for researcher developers, the objective *outcome quality* is determined by the target group's response to the developed app. For example, in both our case studies, participants experienced issues that would not have been detected through an app preview. Thus, an ideal EUD tool should support the end-user developer in evaluating their own software with a target group, through a real-time feedback feature, for example.

4.3   Ensure Learnability and Retention

Irrespective of the assumptions of *what* researchers would do with Jeeves, further assumptions were made as to *how* and *when* their EUD activities would take place. While Paul and Oliver immediately began drafting a study specification after watching the tutorial video, Lucy took time to learn the functions of Jeeves prior to creating her specification. Thus, the **hidden dependencies** and **ambiguity** issues that hindered lab study participants were apparently surmountable through brief practice. This aligns with results of Mendoza and Novick, who show that prominent initial issues are often overcome through continued use [15].

However, "continued use" is unrealistic in some EUD contexts. As Tetteroo et al. observe, a successful EUD deployment is not necessarily that which is used daily [24]. In our case studies, the time involved in preparation and data analysis dwarfed that of the time actually spent using Jeeves. Further, even during the period of specification development, researchers' use of Jeeves was often spread several days apart. Indeed, depending on the nature of research, separate ESM studies could themselves be months apart.

We suggest that our lab study unearthed the *wrong type* of usability issues that only occur in a single usage session. This is certainly why we observed that, even in creating a complex study, Deborah and Lucy did not encounter the pertinent lab study issues. Where infrequent, sporadic usage patterns of EUD are likely to occur, more emphasis should instead be put on evaluating **learnability** and **retention** [9]. Again, reliance on a single-user, single-session evaluation method cannot provide a full picture of usability of an EUD tool over multiple and periodic instances of use. Retention, however, is relevant insofar as researchers choose to return, and the following two points capture how improving ease-of-use through simplification could lead to immediate abandonment.

4.4   Usefulness First; Ease-of-Use Later

Upon opening Jeeves with the intention of designing a new specification, researchers are faced with a choice - invest time in learning or re-learning this interface, or abandon it and return to familiar software? We assess how participants use Jeeves, but not why they might not attempt to do so when alternatives (such as *Qualtrics*, endorsed by Paul and Oliver) may be available.

Deborah expressed how functionality issues eventually overshadowed ease-of-use in achieving her statistical analysis:

"SPSS is very easy to pick up, but you reach a point very quickly where what you want to do is beyond the scope of what it really does and then you have to give up and move to R and start at the bottom of the learning curve again."

A key concern of our usability study was that many participants expressed feeling initially "overwhelmed". However, it appears that the danger of iterative lab studies is not only that we continue to refine a sub-optimal design, but also that we may sacrifice necessary functionality in pursuit of usability goals. A quote from Oliver acutely exemplifies this danger:

"For us, the research question is very important - that really determines which study design we have - and that determines which tool we use, and NOT vice versa. You don't do a study just because Jeeves exists."

4.5   Plan for Shifting Goals

We could try to determine a minimal but comprehensive feature set required by researchers, and subject these features to lab-based usability evaluations, but this also poses an issue. The ISO standard of usability describes it as *"The extent to which a product can be used by specified users to achieve **specified goals** with effectiveness, efficiency and satisfaction in a specified context of use."* [11].

The notion of "specified goals" can be easily applied to non-EUD software where the functionality of the software is constrained to writing a document or ordering a product online, for example. However, even in our attempts to introduce as much flexibility into Jeeves as possible, effectiveness cannot be easily measured by task completion when the tasks are at the liberty of users' imagination. A quote from Paul highlights a need for continuous innovation:

"As [Oliver] says, every study's different, and we're always dreaming up new and daft things and ways of asking things to participants...so there would always be a desire for more features. That will always happen."

Thus, usability is only relevant for as long as an EUD tool meets users' needs. With this consideration in mind, usability evaluation must be integrated into the SER process model, ensuring that not only the needs of users, but also the ease with which they can fulfil these needs, are accounted for.

5   Conclusion

By comparing a lab-based usability study and two case studies of an EUD tool in practice, we identified clear limitations to the insights that can be acquired through the former, when its use in practice is unconstrained and subject to unexpected changes. Perceived usability of Jeeves in practice was highly dependent on collaborative use, over multiple intermittent sessions, to develop software that meets the diverse and shifting requirements of both the researchers and their participants. Dispensing with the *individual* EUD view of single users developing for themselves, *public* EUD tools introduce a range of contextual variables that force different approaches to evaluating their usability.

By making this distinction of Jeeves as a public EUD tool, we do not suggest our findings are applicable to all EUD environments - many of which are intended for educational purposes, or for personal creations and customisations [1]. In such instances, the tasks that end-user developers desire to complete may be well-defined, developed software may be objectively assessed by its developer, and usage context may be predictable. Indeed, previous usability studies of Jeeves were critical in identifying major issues and bugs that detracted from user experience; such studies are still insightful if employed at key times.

Nevertheless, in just two field deployments of Jeeves, we identified new insights into *how* and *when* it is used that preclude evaluation in a lab setting. We conclude by reiterating that an EUD tool's usability, just like its usefulness, is inextricably linked to its context of use, and evaluations must go beyond the development paradigm and into this development context.

References

1. Barricelli, B.R., Cassano, F., Fogli, D., Piccinno, A.: End-user development, end-user programming and end-user software engineering: a systematic mapping study. J. Syst. Softw. **149**, 101–137 (2019)
2. Batalas, N.: EMA IDEs: a challenge for end user development. In: Díaz, P., Pipek, V., Ardito, C., Jensen, C., Aedo, I., Boden, A. (eds.) IS-EUD 2015. LNCS, vol. 9083, pp. 259–263. Springer, Cham (2015). https://doi.org/10.1007/978-3-319-18425-8_26
3. Berkel, N.V., Ferreira, D., Kostakos, V.: The experience sampling method on mobile devices. ACM Comput. Surv. (CSUR) **50**(6), 1–40 (2017)
4. Cabitza, F., Fogli, D., Piccinno, A.: "Each to his own": distinguishing activities, roles and artifacts in EUD practices. In: Caporarello, L., Di Martino, B., Martinez, M. (eds.) Smart Organizations and Smart Artifacts. LNISO, vol. 7, pp. 193–205. Springer, Cham (2014). https://doi.org/10.1007/978-3-319-07040-7_19
5. Fischer, G., Giaccardi, E., Ye, Y., Sutcliffe, A., Mehandjiev, N.: Meta-design: a manifesto for end-user development. Commun. ACM **47**(9), 33–37 (2004)
6. Fischer, G.: End-user development and meta-design: foundations for cultures of participation. In: Pipek, V., Rosson, M.B., de Ruyter, B., Wulf, V. (eds.) IS-EUD 2009. LNCS, vol. 5435, pp. 3–14. Springer, Heidelberg (2009). https://doi.org/10.1007/978-3-642-00427-8_1
7. Green, T.R.G., Petre, M.: Usability analysis of visual programming environments: a 'cognitive dimensions' framework. J. Vis. Lang. Comput. **7**(2), 131–174 (1996)
8. Greenberg, S., Buxton, B.: Usability evaluation considered harmful (some of the time). In: Proceedings of the SIGCHI Conference on Human Factors in Computing Systems, Florence, Italy, pp. 111–120 (2008)
9. Hornbæk, K.: Current practice in measuring usability: challenges to usability studies and research. Int. J. Hum.-Comput. Stud. **64**(2), 79–102 (2006)
10. Huang, J., Cakmak, M.: Supporting mental model accuracy in trigger-action programming. In: Proceedings of the ACM UbiComp 2015, pp. 215–225 (2015)
11. ISO: Ergonomics of human-system interaction - Part 11: Usability: Definitions and concepts (2018). https://www.iso.org/standard/63500.html. Accessed 18 Feb 2019

12. Larson, R., Csikszentmihalyi, M.: The experience sampling method. In: Csikszentmihalyi, M. (ed.) Flow and the Foundations of Positive Psychology, pp. 21–34. Springer, Dordrecht (2014). https://doi.org/10.1007/978-94-017-9088-8_2
13. Maceli, M.: Co-design in the wild: a case study on meme creation tools. In: Proceedings of the 14th Participatory Design Conference, pp. 161–170. ACM (2016)
14. Mehandjiev, N., Sutcliffe, A., Lee, D.: Organizational view of end-user development. In: Lieberman, H., Paternó, F., Wulf, V. (eds.) End User Development, pp. 371–399. Springer, Dordrecht (2006). https://doi.org/10.1007/1-4020-5386-X_17
15. Mendoza, V., Novick, D.G.: Usability over time. In: SIGDOC 2005, p. 151. ACM Press, New York (2005). https://doi.org/10.1145/1085313.1085348
16. Nielsen, J.: Usability Engineering. AP Professional, Boston (1993)
17. Norman, D.: The Design of Everyday Things: Revised and Expanded Edition. Basic Books, New York (2013)
18. Pinelle, D., Gutwin, C., Greenberg, S.: Task analysis for groupware usability evaluation: modeling shared-workspace tasks with the mechanics of collaboration. ACM Trans. Comput.-Hum. Interact. **10**(4), 281–311 (2003)
19. Pipek, V., Kahler, H.: Supporting collaborative tailoring. In: Lieberman, H., Paternó, F., Wulf, V. (eds.) End User Development, pp. 315–345. Springer, Dordrecht (2006). https://doi.org/10.1007/1-4020-5386-X_15
20. Rough, D., Quigley, A.: End-user development in social psychology research: factors for adoption. In: 2018 IEEE Symposium on VL/HCC, pp. 75–83, October 2018
21. Rough, D., Quigley, A.: Jeeves-a visual programming environment for mobile experience sampling. In: 2015 IEEE Symposium on VL/HCC, pp. 121–129. IEEE (2015)
22. Rough, D., Quigley, A.: Jeeves-an experience sampling study creation tool. BCS Health Informatics Scotland (HIS) (2017)
23. Tetteroo, D., Markopoulos, P.: A review of research methods in end user development. In: Díaz, P., Pipek, V., Ardito, C., Jensen, C., Aedo, I., Boden, A. (eds.) IS-EUD 2015. LNCS, vol. 9083, pp. 58–75. Springer, Cham (2015). https://doi.org/10.1007/978-3-319-18425-8_5
24. Tetteroo, D., Markopoulos, P.: EUD survival "in the wild": evaluation challenges for field deployments and how to address them. In: Paternò, F., Wulf, V. (eds.) New Perspectives in End-User Development, pp. 207–229. Springer, Cham (2017). https://doi.org/10.1007/978-3-319-60291-2_9
25. Wixon, D., Holtzblatt, K., Knox, S.: Contextual design: an emergent view of system design. In: Proceedings of the SIGCHI Conference on Human Factors in Computing Systems, pp. 329–336. Citeseer (1990)

My IoT Puzzle: Debugging IF-THEN Rules Through the Jigsaw Metaphor

Fulvio Corno, Luigi De Russis, and Alberto Monge Roffarello(✉)

Politecnico di Torino, Corso Duca degli Abruzzi, 24, 10129 Turin, Italy
{fulvio.corno,luigi.derussis,alberto.monge}@polito.it

Abstract. End users can nowadays define applications in the format of IF-THEN rules to personalize their IoT devices and online services. Along with the possibility to compose such applications, however, comes the need to debug them, e.g., to avoid unpredictable and dangerous behaviors. In this context, different questions are still unexplored: which visual languages are more appropriate for debugging IF-THEN rules? Which information do end users need to understand, identify, and correct errors? To answer these questions, we first conducted a literature analysis by reviewing previous works on end-user debugging, with the aim of extracting design guidelines. Then, we developed *My IoT Puzzle*, a tool to compose and debug IF-THEN rules based on the Jigsaw metaphor. *My IoT Puzzle* interactively assists users in the debugging process with different real-time feedback, and it allows the resolution of conflicts by providing textual and graphical explanations. An exploratory study with 6 participants preliminary confirms the effectiveness of our approach, showing that the usage of the Jigsaw metaphor, along with real-time feedback and explanations, helps users understand and fix conflicts among IF-THEN rules.

Keywords: End-user debugging · Internet of Things ·
Trigger-action programming · Visual languages

1 Introduction

The potential of the Internet of Things (IoT) is being increasingly recognized [7]: people daily interact with a growing number of Internet-enabled devices [13] in many different contexts, ranging from smart homes to smart cities. The IoT ecosystem is nowadays further enriched by online services such as messaging platforms and social networks [1]. By means of an Internet connection, users can therefore access a complex network of smart objects, either physical or virtual, able to interact and communicate with each other, with humans, and with the environment. Nowadays, end users can personalize such a complex network by programming the joint behavior of their IoT devices and online services. Several works in the literature demonstrate the effective applicability of End-User Development (EUD) techniques [23] for the creation of applications in various

© Springer Nature Switzerland AG 2019
A. Malizia et al. (Eds.): IS-EUD 2019, LNCS 11553, pp. 18–33, 2019.
https://doi.org/10.1007/978-3-030-24781-2_2

domains [11, 22], including the IoT [14, 36]. Particularly in this context, professional programmers cannot foresee all the possible situations end users may encounter when interacting with their IoT ecosystem. By placing the personalization of IoT devices and online services in the hands of end users, i.e., the subjects who are most familiar with the actual needs to be met, EUD is a viable way to make IoT applications comply with users' expectations [14]. Typically, users who want to personalize their IoT devices and online services can exploit the trigger-action programming approach, as implemented in popular visual programming platforms such as IFTTT[1] or Zapier[2]. Through trigger-action (IF-THEN) rules such as *"if the Nest camera in the kitchen detects a movement, then send me a Telegram message"*, users can connect a pair of devices or online services in such a way that, when an event (the *trigger*) is detected on one of them, an *action* is automatically executed on the second.

Along with the possibility to create such rules, however, comes the need to debug them. Despite apparent simplicity, in fact, trigger-action programming is often a complex task for non programmers [17], and errors in trigger-action rules can lead to unpredictable and dangerous behaviors such as a door that is unexpectedly unlocked. One of the most urgent challenges is, therefore, to provide users with tools to avoid possible conflicts [5] and assess the correctness [12] of the developed applications. Unfortunately, even if few recent works started to explore end-user debugging in the IoT [8, 26], open questions still remain. Which visual languages are more appropriate for debugging rules? Which information do end users need to understand, identify, and correct errors?

To answer these questions, we firstly conducted a literature analysis by reviewing previous works on end-user debugging in different contexts, with the aim of extracting design guidelines. Then, we used the extracted guidelines to implement *My IoT Puzzle*, a tool to compose and debug IF-THEN rules based on the Jigsaw metaphor. The tool interactively assists users in the composition process by representing triggers and actions as complementary puzzle pieces, and by providing real-time feedback to test *on-the-fly* the correctness of the rule under definition. Puzzle pieces, for example, deteriorate over time according to their usage (Fig. 2), while the tool is able to warn users in case of conflicts, namely infinite loops, inconsistencies, and redundancies (Fig. 3). Furthermore, the tool empowers end users in resolving problems through textual and graphical explanations. Following the Interrogative Debugging paradigm [18], for instance, the tool is able to answer questions such as *"why it is not working?"*, thus providing the user with a textual explanation of the detected problem (Fig. 4). An exploratory study with 6 participants preliminary confirms the effectiveness of our approach. During the study, each participant used *My IoT Puzzle* to compose a set of different IF-THEN rules that generated different conflicts. By collecting quantitative and qualitative measures, we observed that participants appreciated the intuitiveness of the adopted visual languages, including the Jigsaw metaphor.

---

[1] https://ifttt.com, last visited on February 26, 2019.
[2] https://zapier.com, last visited on February 26, 2019.

Furthermore, the provided feedback and explanations helped them understand, identify, and correct the conflicts they encountered.

2   Background

Following the explosion of the IoT, in the last 10 years several commercial platforms for end-user personalization such as IFTTT or Zapier were born. The aim of such platforms is to empower end users in customizing the behavior of IoT devices and online services through the trigger-action paradigm, typically. Despite the trigger-action programming expressiveness [2] and popularity [12], the definition of trigger-action rules can be difficult for non-programmers. Platforms like IFTTT have been criticized since they often expose too much functionality [17], and they adopt technology-dependent representation models that force users to have a deep knowledge of all the involved devices and online services [9,12]. As a result, users frequently misinterpret the behavior of IF-THEN rules [4], often deviating from their actual semantics, and are prone to introduce errors [16].

Therefore, one of the most urgent challenges in EUD solutions for personalizing IoT ecosystems is to provide users with tools to avoid possible conflicts [5] and assess the correctness [12] of the developed IF-THEN rules. In this context, work on end-user debugging is still in its early stage. While the majority of previous studies focus on mashup programming [6], spreadsheets [15], and novice developers [18], only a few recent works started addressing the problem of end-user debugging in the IoT. In EUDebug [8], in particular, the authors integrated an end-user debugging tool on top of IFTTT. EUDebug exploits a user interface modeled after IFTTT to warn users when they are defining any troublesome or potentially dangerous behavior. Through a formalism based on Petri Nets and Semantic Web ontologies, EUDebug is able to detect 3 types of problems among trigger-action rules: *loops*, *redundancies*, and *inconsistencies*. In *My IoT Puzzle*, we used the same approach for identifying and displaying problems between the composed rules. A similar tool for end-user debugging in this context is ITAD (Interactive Trigger-Action Debugging) [26]. In addition to warn users in case of rule conflicts, ITAD allows the simulation of trigger-action rules in fixed contexts.

In this work, we stem from both EUDebug and ITAD, i.e., the first two works that investigated how to detect conflicts and simulate IF-THEN rules, for taking a step forward: with *My IoT Puzzle*, our aim is to understand how we can make debug of trigger-action rules more *understandable* by end users.

3   Literature Analysis and Design Guidelines

To reach our goal, we firstly reviewed previous works on end-user debugging in different contexts, with the aim of extracting design guidelines (Table 1). The analysis was guided by the following research questions:

RQ1. Which information, e.g., feedback and explanations, do end users need to understand, identify, and correct errors in trigger-action rules?

RQ2. Which visual languages are more appropriate for debugging trigger-action rules?

3.1 End-User Debugging: How to Avoid and Correct Errors (RQ1)

Debugging is the process of finding the cause of an identified misbehavior and fixing or removing it. Different previous studies, e.g., [19,27], investigated how developers try to fix bugs, and discovered many slow, unproductive strategies. If it is challenging for programmers, the debugging process can become an insurmountable barrier for end users. In different contexts, ranging from spreadsheets [15] to mashup programming [6], studies have demonstrated that end users try to fix problems by following a "debugging into existence" approach [34], i.e., they continuously twist and fiddle their solutions until the failure "miraculously" goes away. Cao et al. [6], however, demonstrated that, if prompted with the right information, end users are also able to *design* applications and programs. In the context of mashup programming, for example, they proposed to add micro-evaluations of local portions of the mashup during the implementation phase, with the aim of reducing the effort of connecting the run-time output with the program's logic itself. We envision similar approaches also for our context, i.e., IF-THEN rules for personalizing IoT devices and online services. By providing real-time feedback during the composition of trigger-action rules, an EUD tool may empower users in frequently testing the correctness of their solutions (**GL1**), thus allowing them to update *on-the-fly* problematic rules (**GL2**), Table 1. This may increases the chances of fixing possible conflicts [6].

Previous studies on end-user debugging also highlight the benefits of providing users with textual and graphical explanations, to represent the run-time behaviors of the defined programs and their possible problems [24,25] (**GL3**). Indeed, Ko et al. [18] discovered that programmers' questions at the time of failure are typically one of two types: *"why did"* questions, which assume the occurrence of an unexpected run-time action, and *"why didn't"* questions, which assume the absence of an expected run-time action [18]. The same authors extended the Alice programming environment [38], a platform for creating interactive 3D virtual worlds, to support a "whyline" that allows users to receive answers concerning program outputs. Their work opened the way for a new paradigm, named *Interrogative Debugging*, that has been adopted in many different works on end-user debugging, ranging from tools to support more experienced developers [20] to interactive machine learning [21]. As preliminary suggested by Manca et al. [26], the Interrogative Debugging paradigm may effectively help end users debug their trigger-action rules (**GL4**). The event-driven nature of trigger-action rules, in particular, naturally leads to questions such as *"why this action have been executed?"* or *"why this event did not trigger?"*

3.2   Visual Languages for End-User Development (RQ2)

Besides the question of identifying which information end users need for debugging trigger-action rules, another important question is which visual languages are more appropriate in this context. Despite visual programming languages strive to simplify the intricate process of programming, in fact, they need to be tailored towards the domains in which they will be used [31]. The most common visual languages adopted in End-User Development tools can be categorized into 3 main categories: (a) form-filling, (b) block programming, and (c) data-flow.

Form-filling visual languages, also known as wizard-based languages, are extensively used in commercial platforms such as IFTTT and Zapier [12]. Also EUDebug [8] and ITAD [26], i.e., the first two works that explore end-user debugging in the context of trigger-action rules, exploit wizard-based interfaces. To compose applications with the form-filling approach, be they rules or other types of programs, the user makes use of menus and fields to be completed. Tools that exploit form-filling visual languages, in particular, guide the user through a pre-defined, bounded procedure, by reducing the user interaction in completing a series of forms step-by-step. Despite form-filling approaches have been proved to be intuitive and easy to use for simple use cases, their closed form can be perceived as restrictive [29, 30].

Another popular approach in End-User Development is block programming. A popular example of the approach can be seen in Scratch [32], a block-based visual programming language targeted primarily at children. With block programming, users can connect blocks of different sizes and shapes by dragging and dropping them on a work area. Differently from form-filling approaches, tools based on block programming are less restrictive, and stimulate the user creativity. One of the most appreciated ways of representing blocks, in particular, is the Jigsaw metaphor. Here, blocks are represented as puzzle pieces that can be combined on the go, thus decreasing the learning curve and motivating users to explore the underlying tool. An application example is Puzzle, a visual environment for opportunistically creating mobile applications in mobile phones [11]. We envision that block programming approaches based on the Jigsaw metaphor could be easily adapted to the composition of IF-THEN rules for IoT personalization (**GL5**).

Finally, the last category of visual languages commonly adopted in EUD is data-flow. Differently from the previous approaches, which were useful for simple use case such as the composition of a single rule, the process-oriented nature of data-flow programming languages makes them one of the best choice to represent complex use cases [3]. Process-oriented notations have been employed to provide increased expressiveness while still retaining easy-to-comprehend visualizations [10, 33]. The expressiveness of such notations, however, is often coupled with complex user interfaces [3]. This makes them difficult to be used at composition time, but useful to visualize complex information such as triggers, actions, and their relationships. For this reason, we envision that a data-flow visual language could be adopted for representing the behavior of multiple trigger-action rules (**GL6**), with the aim of helping users understand and identify unwanted run-time behaviors.

4   My IoT Puzzle: Design and Implementation

We integrated the extracted guidelines (Table 1) in *My IoT Puzzle*, our tool for composing and debugging IF-THEN rules. Under the hood, the tool exploits the EUDebug server [8], thus allowing the composition and the debug of IFTTT rules. Thanks to the RESTful API exposed by the server, the tool is able to detect the following problems among trigger-action rules:

Table 1. The design guidelines extracted by reviewing previous works on end-user debugging in different contexts.

Guideline	Description
GL1	A debugging tool for IF-THEN rules should empower users in frequently testing their solutions, e.g., by providing real-time feedback about possible run-time problems the rules may generate
GL2	During the debugging of trigger-action rules it is important to provide users with tools for updating *on-the-fly* their solutions, e.g., to remove possible errors during the rule composition process
GL3	In case of problems, a debugging tool for IF-THEN rules should provide users with textual and graphical explanations about the run-time behavior of the defined applications
GL4	The Interrogative Debugging paradigm, with which users can ask questions like *"why something happens?"*, can be easily adapted to the event-driven nature of trigger-action rules
GL5	Block programming based on the Jigsaw metaphor is understandable and easily adaptable to the composition of trigger-action rules
GL6	The data-flow visual language is suitable for representing complex information such as the run-time behavior of a set of trigger-action rules

- **Loops** arise when multiple rules are continuously activated without reaching a stable state. An example of a loop is:
  - *if* I post a photo on Facebook, *then* save the photo on my iOS library;
  - *if* I add a new photo on my iOS library, *then* post the photo on Instagram;
  - *if* I post a photo on Instagram, *then* post the photo on Facebook.
- **Redundancies** arise when rules that are activated at the same time have replicated functionality. An example of a set of rules that produce a redundancy is:
  - *if* I play a new song on my Amazon Alexa, *then* post a tweet on Twitter;
  - *if* I play a new song on my Amazon Alexa, *then* save the track on Spotify;
  - *if* I save a track on Spotify, *then* post a tweet on Twitter.

Here, the three rules are executed at the same time because the first two rules share the same trigger, while the second rule implicitly activates the third rule. They produce two redundant actions, i.e., the first and the third rule post the same content on Twitter.

- **Inconsistencies** arise when rules that are activated at the same time try to execute contradictory actions. An example of a set of rules that produces an inconsistency is:
  - *if* my Android GPS detects that I exit the home area, *then* lock the SmartThings entrance door;
  - *if* my Android GPS detects that I exit the home area, *then* set the Nest thermostat to Away mode;
  - *if* the SmartThings entrance door is locked, *then* set the Nest thermostat to Manual mode.

  Here, the three rules are executed at the same time because the first two rules share the same trigger, while the first rule implicitly activates the third rule. They produce two inconsistent actions, since they set 2 contradictory modes on the Nest thermostat, i.e., Away and Manual.

The user interface of *My IoT Puzzle* has been implemented with the Angular framework[3], by exploiting the jQuery[4] and Bootstrap[5] libraries. The interface iteratively assists end users in composing and debugging IF-THEN in 3 main phases, i.e., *composition*, *problem detection*, and *problem resolution*.

Composition. Trigger-action rules are composed through a block programming approach based on the Jigsaw metaphor (**GL5**). To design the composition metaphor 3 researchers produced and evaluated different mockups.

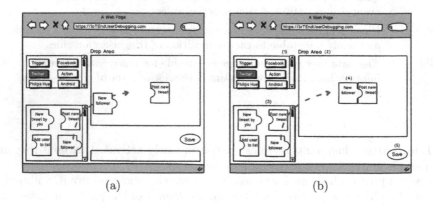

(a)   (b)

Fig. 1. Two mockups produced to design the composition metaphor.

Figure 1 shows an example of the produced mockups: to avoid complex solutions, we decided to use 2 types of puzzle pieces, only, one for triggers and one for actions. Triggers and actions are therefore represented as complementary puzzle pieces that can be dragged and dropped in a Drop Area.

---

[3] https://angular.io/, last visited on February 26, 2019.
[4] https://jquery.com/, last visited on February 26, 2019.
[5] https://getbootstrap.com/, last visited on February 26, 2019.

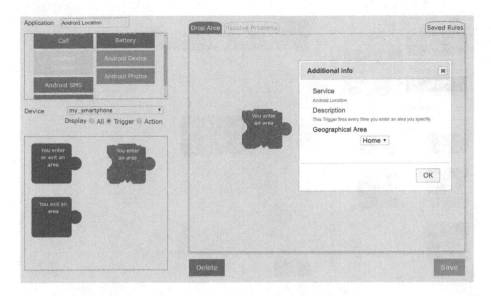

Fig. 2. Mary, the user of our example, starts to compose a new rule by dragging a new trigger on the Drop Area. The tool provides Mary with an initial feedback: the piece of puzzle is worn, since it has been already used in other rules.

Figure 2 shows an example of the *composition* phase. Mary selects a device (her *Android* smartphone) on which monitoring an event, and drops a specific trigger on the drop area (*"You enter an area"*). Then, she completes the trigger details by specifying the geographical area of her home. The tool uses initial feedback to preliminary allow the user assess her solution (**GL1**). Indeed, due to the complementary nature of the puzzle pieces, some wrong operations are prevented by construction: pieces of the same type, e.g., two trigger pieces, cannot be connected. Furthermore, as shown in Fig. 2, the dropped trigger piece is worn, since it has been already used in other rules. In *My IoT Puzzle*, in particular, puzzle pieces deteriorate over time according to their usage history. Using the same trigger in multiple rules, in fact, means that the involved rules will be executed at the same time, thus increasing the chances of introducing conflicts such as redundancies and inconsistencies.

Problem Detection. The *problem detection* phase starts every time that *My IoT Puzzle* detects loops, inconsistencies, or redundancies during the *composition* phase. Figure 3 shows the *problem detection* phase experienced by Mary. Having defined the trigger, she selects her kitchen *Philips Hue* lamp. She connects to the *"You enter an area"* trigger an action (*"Turn off lights"*) that is inconsistent with some previously saved rules. Therefore, the system warns Mary with a red feedback (**GL1**), and allows her to get more information on how to solve the issue.

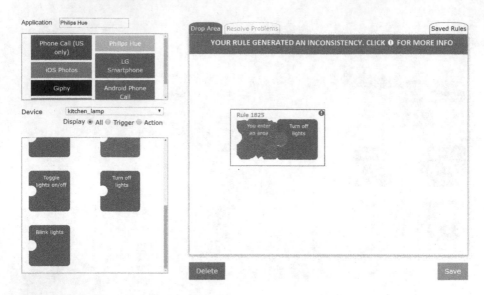

Fig. 3. Mary connects to the trigger an action that is inconsistent with some previously saved rules. The system warns Mary with a red feedback.

Problem Resolution. The *problem resolution* phase helps users understand and fix conflicts detected during the previous phases. Figure 4 shows the phase as experienced by Mary. She can see textual and graphical explanations of the detected inconsistency (**GL3**). For graphically explaining the problem, a data-flow visual language is used (**GL6**). Instead, the textual explanation follow the Interrogative Debugging paradigm (**GL4**), by explicitly describing *why* the problem is happening. Both the textual and graphical explanations, in particular, show that it already exists a saved rule that shares the same trigger, i.e., entering the home geographical area, but with an inconsistent action, i.e., turning on the kitchen *Philips Hue* lamp. Mary has the possibility of updating on-the-fly the problematic rule by changing the trigger, the action, and/or the related details (**GL2**).

5 Evaluation

We preliminary evaluated *My IoT Puzzle* through an exploratory study with 6 participants. Our aim was to assess whether the different features offered by *My IoT Puzzle*, ranging from the provided feedback to the graphical and textual explanations, helped participants correctly understand and fix potential conflicts in trigger-action rules.

Study Procedure. We recruited 6 university students (3 males and 3 females) with a mean age of 21.5 years (SD = 2.88) who had very limited or no experience in computer science and programming: on a Likert scale from 1 (No knowledge

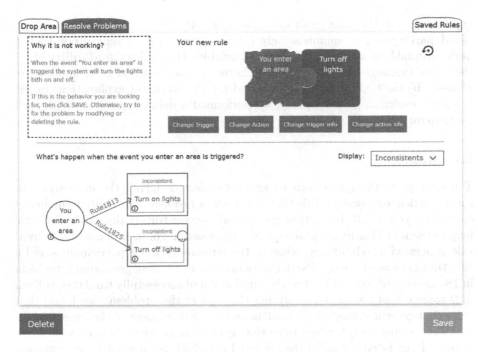

Fig. 4. By opening the Resolve Problems area, Mary can see textual and graphical explanation of the inconsistency, and she can resolve the problem by changing the rule.

at all) to 5 (Expert), participants declared their experience with programming (M = 1.16, SD − 0.40) and with the trigger-action approach (M = 1.00, SD = 0).

We brought each participant to our lab for a 45-minute session using *My IoT Puzzle*. At the beginning of the study, participants were introduced to trigger-action programming and the evaluated tool with an example of a rule composition. We then presented a task involving the composition of 12 rules (*composition* phase). Rules were presented one at a time on a sheet of paper in a counterbalanced order, and were artificially constructed to generate 2 inconsistencies, 2 redundancies, and 1 loop[6]. When *My IoT Puzzle* highlighted some problems (*problem detection* phase), participants were free to decide whether to save, update, or delete the problematic rule (*problem resolution* phase). All the sessions were video recorded for further analysis.

Measures. We quantitatively measured the number of problematic rules that were **saved**, **updated**, or **deleted**. Furthermore, after each highlighted problem, we asked participants to qualitatively provide an **explanation** for their choices. When they decided to update or delete a rule that generated a problem, for example, they had to demonstrate to understand the problem by retrospectively

---

[6] A detailed description of the rules used in the evaluation can be found in the Appendix.

explaining why the rule generated the issue. At the end of each session, we asked participants to quantitatively evaluate, on a Likert scale from 1 (Not understandable at all) to 5 (Very understandable), the **understandability** of (a) the visual languages and feedback used in the *composition* and *problem detection* phases, (b) the textual explanations, and (c) the graphical explanations in the *problem resolution* phase. Finally, we performed a debriefing session with each participant.

5.1 Results

Table 2 reports the quantitative measures collected during the evaluation. In total, participants saved a rule that generated a problem in a limited number of cases, i.e., 3 out of 30 (10%), thus preliminary demonstrating that *My IoT Puzzle* helped them in identifying problems in trigger-action rules. In 2 cases, the saved rule generated a redundancy, while in the remaining case a participant saved a rule that generated a loop. Participants deleted a rule that generated a problem in 18 cases out of 30 (60%), while they updated and successfully fixed the problem in 9 cases out of (30%). By analyzing the type of the problems, we found that rules that generated loops or redundancies were deleted most of the time (66.66% and 75%, respectively), while rules that generated an inconsistency were more frequently updated (58.33%) than deleted (41.67%). Such results are promising and suggest that feedback and explanations effectively assisted participants in understanding the highlighted problems. Both loops and redundancies, indeed, result in some functionality that are replicated, thus motivating the deletion. Inconsistencies, instead, are typically caused by a mistake over a set of rules with different and specific purposes, thus making the "update" choice the most appropriate.

Table 2. The number of times a rule that generated a problem was deleted, updated, or saved in the study.

	Rules	Deleted	Updated	Saved
Loop	6	4 (66.66%)	1 (16.67%)	1 (16.67%)
Redundancy	12	9 (75%)	1 (8.33%)	2 (16.67%)
Inconsistency	12	5 (41.67%)	7 (58.33%)	0 (0%)
Total	30	18 (60%)	9 (30%)	3 (10%)

We further investigated the results by analyzing the qualitative explanations given by the participants in case of a detected problem. We first tried to understand whether the participants who saved a problematic rule were aware of what would happened in the real world, or whether they simply made a mistake, thus unconsciously introducing a potential conflict at run-time. Both the users that saved a rule that generated a redundancy provided a sound explanation.

When 2 rules simultaneously turned on the same lamp with different colors, for example, P1 said *"I don't care about the color, the important thing is that the lamp is turned on."* On the contrary, P3 failed in providing an explanation for saving the rule that generated a loop. She said *"I don't know how to solve the problem. I would save the rule, and then I would try the involved rules in the real world, to see what happens."* For what concerns the problematic rules that were deleted, participants provided a sound explanation in 17 cases out of 18 (94.44%). Only in 1 case a participant discarded a rule without providing any explanation. Finally, participants made a reasonable change in all the rules that were updated, by successfully fixing the problem and by providing a sound explanation.

The promising results arising from the interaction between participants and *My IoT Puzzle* are confirmed by the answers they provided at the end of the study. Participants positively evaluated the understandability of the *composition* and *problem detection* phases (M = 4.50, SD = 0.54), and the understandability of the textual (M = 4.50, SD = 0.81) and graphical (M = 4.50, SD = 0.30) explanations in the *problem resolution* phase. Finally, users provided interesting suggestions to improve *My IoT Puzzle*. P1, for example, focused on the *composition* phase, by suggesting the possibility of composing multiple rules at the same time. P4 and P5, instead, focused on the *problem resolution* phase, and they asked to introduce recommendations and suggestions for updating problematic rules. P4, in particular, said that suggestions such as *"try to replace the trigger X with the trigger Y"* would allow non-expert users to better understand and fix the problem.

Discussion. Results are promising and demonstrate that *My IoT Puzzle* is helpful for correctly identifying and fixing potential problems in trigger-action rules. Results also confirm that the design guidelines presented in Sect. 3 are valuable. The provided information and the exploited visual languages effectively helped users understand, identify, and correct errors in trigger-action rules.

The Jigsaw metaphor, for example, was appreciated by the participants, and turned to be easy to use and understand: all the participants composed the proposed trigger-action rules without any problem. Also the feedback used in the *composition* phase turned to be useful for preliminary assessing the correctness of trigger-action rules. When using a worn piece of puzzle, for example, P3 said *"now I'm going to make a mistake, I need to stay focused."* Furthermore, if the typical reaction to an highlighted problem was a mix of surprise and uncertainty, the *problem resolution* phase progressively made participants aware of the detected conflict: in most of the cases, the provided feedback and explanations allowed them to successfully fix the problem, either by deleting or updating the rule that generated it. This confirms that the usage of different representations of the same information facilitates users in analyzing problems [35].

6   Conclusions and Future Works

Users are making use of End-User Development tools for trigger-action programming to personalize their IoT devices and online services. Which information do end users need to understand, identify, and correct errors in this context? Which visual languages are more appropriate for debugging trigger-action rules? In this paper, we investigated such questions by presenting *My IoT Puzzle*, a tool to compose and debug IF-THEN rules, based on the Jigsaw metaphor. The tool follows design guidelines extracted from a literature analysis. It interactively assists users in the composition process by representing triggers and actions as complementary puzzle pieces, and it allows end users to debug their rules through different real-time feedback, textual and graphical explanations. Results of an exploratory study with 6 participants preliminary suggest that the adopted visual languages are easy to understand. Furthermore, results show that users can successfully identify and fix conflicts between trigger-action rules with the help of textual and graphical explanations.

Acknowledgments. The authors wish to thanks Alessia Carosella for conducting the literature review and implementing the user interface of *My IoT Puzzle*.

Appendix: Rules Used in the Evaluation

The following trigger-action rules were used in the evaluation of *My IoT Puzzle*:

R1. *If* your Android smartphone detects that you enter the home area, *then* turn on the Philips Hue kitchen lamp.

R2. *If* your Android smartphone detects that you enter the home area, *then* turn off the Philips Hue kitchen lamp.

R3. *If* your Android smartphone detects that you enter the home area, *then* turn on a color loop on the Philips Hue kitchen lamp.

R4. *If* a new photo is added to the "ios" album on iOS Photo, *then* add the file on the "drpb" Dropbox folder.

R5. *If* a new photo is added to the "drpb" Dropbox folder, *then* upload the photo on Facebook.

R6. *If* there is a new photo post by you on Facebook, *then* add the photo to the "ios" album on iOS Photo.

R7. *If* your iPhone detects that you exit the work area, *then* lock the Smart-Things office door.

R8. *If* the SmartThings office door is locked, *then* arm the Homeboy office security camera.

R9. *If* the Homeboy office security camera is armed, *then* unlock the SmarThings office door.

R10. *If* a new song is played on Amazon Alexa, *then* post a tweet with the song name on Twitter.

R11. *If* a new song is played on Amazon Alexa, *then* save the track on Spotify.

R12. *If* a new track is saved track on Spotify, *then* post a tweet with the song name on Twitter.

The rules generate 2 inconsistencies, 2 redundancies, and 1 loop:

- R1 and R2 generate an **inconsistency**, because they share the same trigger while producing contradictory actions on the same device;
- R7 and R9 generate an **inconsistency**, because they produce contradictory actions on the same device and are activated nearly at the same time, since R7 activates R8, and R8 activates R9;
- R1 and R3 generate a **redundancy**, because they share the same trigger while producing two similar actions on the same device;
- R10 and R12 generate a **redundancy**, because they produce similar actions on the same online service and are activated nearly at the same time, since R10 and R11 share the same trigger and R11 activates R12.
- R4, R5, and R6 generate an infinite **loop**, because R4 activates R5, R5 activates R6, and R6 activates R4;

References

1. Akiki, P.A., Bandara, A.K., Yu, Y.: Visual simple transformations: empowering end-users to wire internet of things objects. ACM Trans. Comput.-Hum. Interact. **24**(2), 10:1–10:43 (2017)
2. Barricelli, B.R., Valtolina, S.: Designing for end-user development in the internet of things. In: Díaz, P., Pipek, V., Ardito, C., Jensen, C., Aedo, I., Boden, A. (eds.) IS-EUD 2015. LNCS, vol. 9083, pp. 9–24. Springer, Cham (2015). https://doi.org/10.1007/978-3-319-18425-8_2
3. Brich, J., Walch, M., Rietzler, M., Weber, M., Schaub, F.: Exploring end user programming needs in home automation. ACM Trans. Comput.-Hum. Interact. **24**(2), 11:1–11:35 (2017)
4. Brush, A.B., Lee, B., Mahajan, R., Agarwal, S., Saroiu, S., Dixon, C.: Home automation in the wild: challenges and opportunities. In: Proceedings of the SIGCHI Conference on Human Factors in Computing Systems, CHI 2011, pp. 2115–2124. ACM, New York (2011)
5. Caivano, D., Fogli, D., Lanzilotti, R., Piccinno, A., Cassano, F.: Supporting end users to control their smart home: design implications from a literature review and an empirical investigation. J. Syst. Softw. **144**, 295–313 (2018)
6. Cao, J., Rector, K., Park, T.H., Fleming, S.D., Burnett, M., Wiedenbeck, S.: A debugging perspective on end-user mashup programming. In: 2010 IEEE Symposium on Visual Languages and Human-Centric Computing, pp. 149–156, September 2010
7. Cerf, V., Senges, M.: Taking the internet to the next physical level. IEEE Comput. **49**(2), 80–86 (2016)
8. Corno, F., De Russis, L., Monge Roffarello, A.: Empowering end users in debugging trigger-action rules. In: Proceedings of the 2019 CHI Conference on Human Factors in Computing Systems, CHI 2019. ACM, New York (2019, in press)
9. Corno, F., De Russis, L., Monge Roffarello, A.: A high-level semantic approach to end-user development in the internet of things. Int. J. Hum.-Comput. Stud. **125**, 41–54 (2019)

10. Dahl, Y., Svendsen, R.-M.: End-user composition interfaces for smart environments: a preliminary study of usability factors. In: Marcus, A. (ed.) DUXU 2011. LNCS, vol. 6770, pp. 118–127. Springer, Heidelberg (2011). https://doi.org/10.1007/978-3-642-21708-1_14

11. Danado, J., Paternò, F.: Puzzle: a mobile application development environment using a jigsaw metaphor. J. Vis. Lang. Comput. **25**(4), 297–315 (2014)

12. Desolda, G., Ardito, C., Matera, M.: Empowering end users to customize their smart environments: model, composition paradigms, and domain-specific tools. ACM Trans. Comput.-Hum. Interact. **24**(2), 12:1–12:52 (2017)

13. Evans, D.: The internet of things: how the next evolution of the internet is changing everything. Technical report, Cisco Internet Business Solutions Group (2011)

14. Ghiani, G., Manca, M., Paternò, F., Santoro, C.: Personalization of context-dependent applications through trigger-action rules. ACM Trans. Comput.-Hum. Interact. **24**(2), 14:1–14:33 (2017)

15. Grigoreanu, V., Burnett, M., Wiedenbeck, S., Cao, J., Rector, K., Kwan, I.: End-user debugging strategies: a sensemaking perspective. ACM Trans. Comput.-Hum. Interact. **19**(1), 5:1–5:28 (2012)

16. Huang, J., Cakmak, M.: Supporting mental model accuracy in trigger-action programming. In: Proceedings of the 2015 ACM International Joint Conference on Pervasive and Ubiquitous Computing, UbiComp 2015, pp. 215–225. ACM, New York (2015)

17. Huang, T.H.K., Azaria, A., Bigham, J.P.: Instructablecrowd: creating if-then rules via conversations with the crowd. In: Proceedings of the 2016 CHI Conference Extended Abstracts on Human Factors in Computing Systems, CHI EA 2016, pp. 1555–1562. ACM, New York (2016)

18. Ko, A.J., Myers, B.A.: Designing the whyline: a debugging interface for asking questions about program behavior. In: Proceedings of the SIGCHI Conference on Human Factors in Computing Systems, CHI 2004, pp. 151–158. ACM, New York (2004)

19. Ko, A.J., Myers, B.A., Coblenz, M.J., Aung, H.H.: An exploratory study of how developers seek, relate, and collect relevant information during software maintenance tasks. IEEE Trans. Softw. Eng. **32**(12), 971–987 (2006)

20. Ko, A.J., Myers, B.A.: Finding causes of program output with the Java whyline. In: Proceedings of the SIGCHI Conference on Human Factors in Computing Systems, CHI 2009, pp. 1569–1578. ACM, New York (2009)

21. Kulesza, T., Burnett, M., Wong, W.K., Stumpf, S.: Principles of explanatory debugging to personalize interactive machine learning. In: Proceedings of the 20th International Conference on Intelligent User Interfaces, IUI 2015, pp. 126–137. ACM, New York (2015)

22. Lee, J., Garduño, L., Walker, E., Burleson, W.: A tangible programming tool for creation of context-aware applications. In: Proceedings of the 2013 ACM International Joint Conference on Pervasive and Ubiquitous Computing, UbiComp 2013, pp. 391–400. ACM, New York (2013)

23. Lieberman, H., Paternò, F., Klann, M., Wulf, V.: End user development. In: Lieberman, H., Paternó, F., Wulf, V. (eds.) End-User Development: An Emerging Paradigm, pp. 1–8. Springer, Dordrecht (2006). https://doi.org/10.1007/1-4020-5386-X_1

24. Lim, B.Y., Dey, A.K.: Toolkit to support intelligibility in context-aware applications. In: Proceedings of the 12th ACM International Conference on Ubiquitous Computing, UbiComp 2010, pp. 13–22. ACM, New York (2010)

25. Lim, B.Y., Dey, A.K., Avrahami, D.: Why and why not explanations improve the intelligibility of context-aware intelligent systems. In: Proceedings of the SIGCHI Conference on Human Factors in Computing Systems, CHI 2009, pp. 2119–2128. ACM, New York (2009)

26. Manca, M., Santoro, C., Corcella, L.: Supporting end-user debugging of trigger-action rules for IoT applications. Int. J. Hum. Comput. Stud. **123**, 56–69 (2019)

27. Myers, B.A., et al.: Making end user development more natural. In: Paternò, F., Wulf, V. (eds.) New Perspectives in End-User Development, pp. 1–22. Springer, Cham (2017). https://doi.org/10.1007/978-3-319-60291-2_1

28. Namoun, A., Daskalopoulou, A., Mehandjiev, N., Xun, Z.: Exploring mobile end user development: existing use and design factors. IEEE Trans. Softw. Eng. **42**(10), 960–976 (2016)

29. Reisinger, M., Schrammel, J., Fröhlich, P.: Visual end-user programming in smart homes: complexity and performance. In: 2017 IEEE Symposium on Visual Languages and Human-Centric Computing (VL/HCC), pp. 331–332, October 2017

30. Reisinger, M.R., Schrammel, J., Fröhlich, P.: Visual languages for smart spaces: end-user programming between data-flow and form-filling. In: 2017 IEEE Symposium on Visual Languages and Human-Centric Computing (VL/HCC), pp. 165–169, October 2017

31. Repenning, A., Sumner, T.: Agentsheets: a medium for creating domain-oriented visual languages. Computer **28**(3), 17–25 (1995)

32. Resnick, M., et al.: Scratch: programming for all. Commun. ACM **52**(11), 60–67 (2009)

33. Rietzler, M., Greim, J., Walch, M., Schaub, F., Wiedersheim, B., Weber, M.: home-BLOX: introducing process-driven home automation. In: Proceedings of the 2013 ACM Conference on Pervasive and Ubiquitous Computing Adjunct Publication, UbiComp 2013, pp. 801–808. ACM, New York (2013)

34. Rode, J., Rosson, M.B.: Programming at runtime: requirements and paradigms for nonprogrammer web application development. In: Proceedings of the 2003 IEEE Symposium on Human Centric Computing Languages and Environments, HCC 2003, pp. 23–30. IEEE Computer Society, Washington, DC (2003)

35. Subrahmaniyan, N., et al.: Explaining debugging strategies to end-user programmers. In: Proceedings of the IEEE Symposium on Visual Languages and Human-Centric Computing, VLHCC 2007, pp. 127–136. IEEE Computer Society, Washington, DC (2007)

36. Ur, B., et al.: Trigger-action programming in the wild: An analysis of 200,000 IFTTT recipes. In: Proceedings of the 34rd Annual ACM Conference on Human Factors in Computing Systems, CHI 2016, pp. 3227–3231. ACM, New York (2016)

37. Ur, B., McManus, E., Pak Yong Ho, M., Littman, M.L.: Practical trigger-action programming in the smart home. In: Proceedings of the SIGCHI Conference on Human Factors in Computing Systems, CHI 2014, pp. 803–812. ACM, New York (2014)

38. User Interface Group, U.: Alice: rapid prototyping for virtual reality. IEEE Comput. Graph. Appl. **15**(3), 8–11 (1995)

End-User Development of Voice User Interfaces Based on Web Content

Gonzalo Ripa[1], Manuel Torre[1], Sergio Firmenich[1,2(✉)], and Gustavo Rossi[1,2]

[1] LIFIA, Facultad de Informática, Universidad Nacional de La Plata, La Plata, Argentina
{sergio.firmenich, gustavo}@lifia.info.unlp.edu.ar
[2] CONICET, Buenos Aires, Argentina

Abstract. Voice Assistants, and particularly the latest gadgets called smart speakers, allow end users to interact with applications by means of voice commands. As usual, end users are able to install applications (also called skills) that are available in repositories and fulfill multiple purposes. In this work we present an end-user environment to define skills for voice assistants based on the extraction of Web content and their organization into different voice navigation patterns. We describe the approach, the end-user development environment, and finally we present some case studies based on Alexa and Amazon Echo.

Keywords: Voice assistant · End-user development · Web content

1 Introduction

The World Wide Web has become the main information source and service platform. In parallel, speech recognition algorithms and technologies around it have experienced strong advances in the last ten years, reaching a broad consumption by part of end users. Nowadays, we can see new kinds of gadgets that allow the access to content and functionalities already offered in the Web, but under another user interaction mode based on voice interaction. This is the case of voice assistants in the form of smart speakers such as Amazon Echo or Google Home. As any other smart device, these gadgets allow users to install applications (also called skills) that offer specific information services [1]. Some smart speakers' applications are related to the command of smart devices, or even a smart devices mashups by the use of platforms for IoT such as IFTTT [2] or Node-Red [3]. However, other kind of smart speaker applications are more focused on reading and interacting with information and services already published by existing Web applications, such as reading news from a news portal, or asking for a product's price from Amazon.com.

Suddenly, a process is ongoing regarding how Web applications owners move the access to their content and services to these voice-based user interaction devices. For instance, the booking site Expedia.com offers an Amazon Echo Skill that lets end users search prices for accommodation and flights. A similar process happened when smart phones emerged, and Web applications started to deliver native mobile applications for them. Nevertheless, different to this case where users are able to visit the Web site from

A. Malizia et al. (Eds.): IS-EUD 2019, LNCS 11553, pp. 34–50, 2019.
https://doi.org/10.1007/978-3-030-24781-2_3

the mobile Web browser, when a native application does not exist (in the case of smart speakers) there is not a generic way to access content and services not delivered by a native application or skill.

Web applications play a very relevant role in the users' daily life; we use them for reading news, to consume different services, for working, and even for interacting with smart devices in the Web of Things. In spite of the progress on Model Driven Engineering [4] and Multi-Modal User Interfaces [5], a large majority of Web sites are not developed with these technologies and specifications, therefore delivering device-specific applications (e.g. for providing voice access) is usually expensive.

This paper aims to fill the existing gap between the available smart speakers' applications and the preferred online Web services and contents that users consume on a daily basis by browsing the Web. We propose an end-user development environment by which end users may create their own extensions for voice assistants based on the abstraction and extraction of Web content and services that they are accustomed to use.

The paper is organized as follows. Section 2 presents a background on different aspects related to this approach. Section 3 introduces our approach and presents the rationale underlying our End-User Development environment, which is described in Sect. 4. Section 5 explains how the case studies used such as examples through the paper were developed for Amazon Echo. Finally, we give some conclusion and future works on Sect. 6.

2 Background and Related Works

This section presents a necessary background in different concepts and technologies related to our approach, before introducing it in Sect. 3. In this section, we also discuss about different works related to our intents.

2.1 Voice User Interfaces

Conversational agents and Virtual Assistants are not a new concept. Already on 1960, Licklider established the interest of "talking with computers" as one dimension to contemplate in human-computer interaction [6]. At that moment, speech production was more easily doable by electronic systems, but speech recognition had severe problems. Speech recognition algorithms evolved fast in the last decades, and we could appreciate research works for conversational agents (also known as conversational interfaces) almost twenty years ago [7, 8]. Nowadays, VUIs (Voice User Interface) are deployed among diverse kind of devices and interaction, such as smart phones, smart speakers, etc.

Although VUI started to be broadly used with their inclusion in smart phones (for instance, Siri in iPhone[1]) the emergence of gadgets such as Google Home or Amazon Echo are changing their daily use and pervasiveness. These smart speakers allow users to start some conversational interaction with a voice command expressed in natural

---

[1] Siri, https://www.apple.com/es/siri/, last accessed 3/14/2019.

language, such as *"Alexa, tell me the news"*, in the case of Alexa service from Amazon. Smart speakers are delivered with a set of base capabilities, for instance regarding the time and the weather, or other question-answer VUI that consumes vendors' services, play music, read news, etc.; new capabilities (also known as "skills") may be installed from repositories. In this way, other possible user tasks such as home automation, travel plan, online shopping, alternative information access, etc., may be added by installing third-party skills.

Currently, and just for analyzing one case, the Alexa Skill repository is organized in categories and offers more than 50.000 skills[2], almost doubling the number of skills available at the end of 2017 [9].

Table 1 lists the most relevant categories, the number of skills per category, an example of skill per category, and some samples of commands for this sample skill.

Table 1. Table captions should be placed above the tables.

Skill category	Amount of Skills	Skill example	Skill sample commands
Business & Finance	over 1.000	Marketplace	*"Alexa, what's my Flash Briefing?",* *"Alexa, what's in the news?"*
Communication	over 1.000	Mastermind	*"Alexa, Ask Mastermind to text < someone > ",* *"Alexa, ask Mastermind to ring my phone"*
Education & Reference	over 8.000	Couriosity	No direct commands, this skill offer aleatory content that end user may skip.
Games & Trivia	over 10.000	Twitch	*"Alexa, ask Twitch for followed channels",* *"Alexa, ask Twitch to play Monstercat"*
Lifestyle	over 7.000	Sleeptracker	*"Alexa ask Sleeptracker how I slept last night"*
Movies & TV	619	MDb's What's On TV Briefing	*"Alexa, what's my Flash Briefing?"*
Music & Audio	over 6.000	Connect Control for Spotify	*"Alexa, ask Connect Control to play on device 2"*
News	over 4.000	The Washington Post	*"Alexa, ask Washington Post for headlines"*
Shopping	153	Opening Times	*"Alexa ask Opening Times for Tesco Redruth Extra"*
Smart Home	over 1.000	Smart Life	*"Alexa, set hallway light to 50 percent"*
Sports	over 1.000	PGA Tour	*"Alexa, ask PGA TOUR for the leaderboard."*
Travel & Transportation	808	Madrid Transport	*"Alexa, open Madrid Transport"* *"incoming buses at 70"*
Weather	663	Temperature Now	*"Alexa, Temperature Now"*

As the reader may note, the range of services offered by skills is very broad, and it is also remarkable that for some categories there are more than 4.000 ones (e.g. News). However, this is not surprising if we consider that for a same purpose we have a great

---

[2] Alexa skill repository: https://www.amazon.com/alexa-skills/b?ie=UTF8&node=13727921011, accessed February 20th 2019.

variety of Web sources and services to achieve it. Consequently, it is straightforward to establish the possibility of creating new kind of skills using publicly available Web content and services (either in the form of Restful APIs or directly parsing and extracting the desired Web content).

Beyond this quantitative analysis, a recent study [10], shows that smart speakers users (the study was made with Google Home's users) use skills (in order of relevance, i.e., from most used to less used skills) related to Music, Information, Automation, Smalltalk, Alarm, Weather, Video, Time, Lists, Others. This lets us to do a more qualitative analysis related to the kind of skills users prefer. One more time, we can appreciate that for most of these categories there are several Web applications counterparts from where end users could read information or complete some business process using a device supporting normal Web browsing. Although some skills for automation of IoT devices could not satisfy this condition, it is clear that a very broad range of skills could be, or even are, based on existing Web contents and functionalities.

The possibility of creating personalized voice commands is also relevant and has already been studied in the context of multi-model user interfaces [11]. However, although this personalization system offers some kind of flexibility, end users are not able to manage the complete specification of VUI by their own.

In this paper, we investigate how Web contents can be extracted, processed and used (as responses) by VUI applications, particularly for smart speakers. Our approach, involves a set of tools that let end users without programming skills to be the ones that can create these VUI specifications using preferred custom web content sources.

2.2 Managing Existing and Third-Party Web Content

The idea of information extraction we use in this approach is similar to some techniques for Web Scraping [12]. Web scraping is the process of non-structured (or with some weak structure) data extraction, usually emulating the Web browsing activity. It is usually used to automate data extraction in order to obtain more information by processing it.

A common end-user driven technique for information extraction is the annotation of Web content. Some Web sites already tag their contents allowing other software artifacts (for instance a Web Browser plugin) to process those annotations and improve interaction with that structured content. A well-known approach for giving some meaning to Web data is Microformats [13]. Some approaches leverage the underlying meaning given by Microformats, detecting those objects present on the Web page and allowing users to interact with them in new ways. According to [14], only 5,64% among more than 40 million Web sites provide some kind of structured data (Microformats, Microdata, RDFa, etc.). This reality raises the importance of empowering users to add semantic structure when it is not available.

Several approaches let users adding structure to existing contents to ease the management of relevant information objects. For instance, Atomate it! [15] offers a reactive platform that could be set to the collected objects by means of rule definitions. Then the user can be informed when something interesting (such as a new movie, or record) is added, edited or removed.

Some End-User Development approaches arose to empower users to solve their particular needs by themselves. For instance, MashMaker [16] allows extracting widgets with their properties, and later inserting these widgets in other Web pages n order to modify the application. Another work proposes the structuring and extraction of client-side data models to create personal Web sites that run purely on client-side, i.e. the end user's Web browser [17]. SearchAPI allows end users without programming skills to create search APIs by visually selecting the UI parts of Web applications search engines. In this way, the domain objects that an application offers can be searched by emulating the user interaction [18]. Similar approaches have arisen under the technique called Web augmentation, and it still a promising technology for end-user development [22]. However, to the best of our knowledge there are not end-user development approaches for developing entire VUI specifications by reusing existing Web content.

3   VUI Specification by End Users and Based on Web Contents

In this section, we present our approach to define VUI by parsing Web content. First we present our approach in a glance, and Sect. 3.2 explains in details different underlying aspects.

3.1   The Approach in a Nutshell

The base of our end-user development approach for VUI is three-fold:

1. A mechanism for allowing users to select and define Web content blocks. For this purpose, we use Web content annotation and definition by means of visual tools and simple configuration. In the remaining of this paper, we call them content blocks.
2. A way to specify how these content blocks should be used in a VUI and how this VUI must behave. We found that flowcharts are a suitable to model VUI behavior structure; nodes represent a specific content block and connections represent how these contents must be organized and read.
3. An interpreter that processes a VUI specification, and obtain the Web pages' DOM dynamically, then provides them and finally give the response to the user with the extracted text content.

Our main idea is that end users can design flowcharts using the content blocks they previously created. The process starts by defining content block, which they can be used later in the flow editor to compose the VUI, to finally use these specifications from a native application on the voice-enabled smart device. Figure 1 depicts an overview of our idea, where the VUI specification (based on a flowchart) includes the content block A (from the Web Page A), and two other content blocks from Web Page B, one content block named B (that corresponds to a collection of related Web contents) and other named C. Imagine that the user wants to create a VUI for news based on the The New York Times' Web site. This user wants to include some elements from the site's home (Blocks 1, 2, 3, 4 and 5 from the image 2.a). These content blocks would be extracted individually, such as the elements A and C in the generic mockup example from Fig. 1.

However, this user also wants all the news for a specific news section from The New York Times (such as the highlighted one in the right image in Fig. 2); our approach allows defining a set of siblings elements to compose a content block, which would behave as the B elements in Fig. 1.

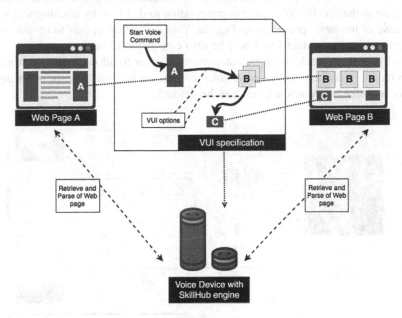

Fig. 1. Our VUI interpreter processes VUI specifications that are flows defining how parts of Web pages must be read in front of voice interaction.

3.2 Rationale: From Web User Interfaces to Voice Interfaces

In this section we present the four dimensions that defines our EUD environment for VUI.

Definition of Content Blocks

We foresee two ways to define content blocks. One of them is based on the individual selection of each useful part, such as Fig. 2a shows. In this case, the user must select the UI element (a DOM element) to create it's corresponding content block. The other way is to contemplate a set of UI elements as a whole content block that includes a collection of elements, such as Fig. 2b depicts.

Usually, Web applications expose in their UI a representation of domain objects such as news, products, articles, etc. This means that on the Web client-side a user could recreate a simple domain model based on the attributes presented in the UI. For instance, for the news presented in Fig. 2a, the attributes tittle, summary, date and author could be obtained from the UI. The same happens if we look for products in Amazon, whose UI presents name of the product, price, description, etc. The annotation process by which a content block is defined may consider this semantic specification, or be simpler and more direct and just consider the whole DOM element as a content block. In this last case, by parsing the target DOM element it is possible to decompose it to detect different parts relevant to the VUI (anchors, text, etc.) automatically.

Another important aspect is whether the content block is navigable or not. It is very common in a Web site to present excerpts of information for a given item and offering to navigate to the specific Web page corresponding to that item by clicking a link; this is the case of the news presented in Fig. 2a. This navigation option to obtain further information about a content block will be also considered in our approach.

Finally, content blocks must be categorized in order to allow flexibility when the VUI behavior is defined. In this way, voice commands such as "ask for *main news*", "ask for *weather information*", etc., can be defined.

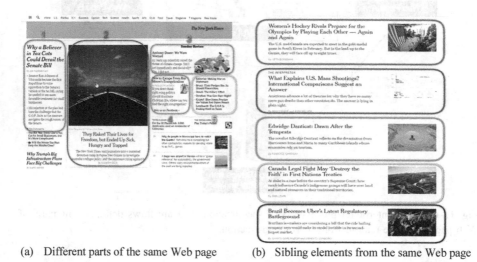

(a)   Different parts of the same Web page   (b)   Sibling elements from the same Web page

Fig. 2. Web content blocks: (a) unique items selection (b) sibling items selection.

A sample skill could be designed for using the content blocks from Fig. 2b, which is based on a set of siblings element sharing a topic. This skill could read the user the "Topics news" when he pronounces these work as a voice command. The skill may respond y reading the title of the first news, and ask to the end user if he wants to listen more about it or just to continue with the following:

- **User's Command voice:** "Topic news"
- **Amazon Echo:** "women's hockey rivals prepare for the olympics by playing each other again and again, *do you want to listen more about this news?*" (this answer first tell the first news from the topic, and then ask to the user if he wants to listen more).
- **User's Command voice:** "yes".
- **Amazon Echo:** "BOSTON — Three days after the United States women's hockey team lost to Canada, 5-1, in an exhibition game here on Oct. 25, USA Hockey unexpectedly added Cayla Barnes, an 18-year-old freshman at Boston College, to its roster. *Do you want to continue listening more about this news?*"

(a) News' Web page   (b) Search results in a news portal

Fig. 3. Web content blocks: (a) items details (b) search result items.

Access to Content Blocks

The Web is based on the concept of navigation among resources accessible by a universal resource location (URL). With this in mind, a specific Web site content can be retrieved if the URL is known. When facing a dynamic URL that changes in relation to published content or user session, navigation is another strategy to reach the Web content, given the Web site's home. However, when there are large sets of data in a Web site, search engines become essential to reach relevant information items. With this in mind, our approach considers three ways to access Web content:

- Direct Access: given an URL (which can be static or based on an API-based URL that allows to change some parameters values), it is possible to retrieve the Web page. This method is useful for getting the current state of a Web site that offers frequently updated information such as news, weather, etc. Figure 2, either (a) or (b), could be accessed in this manner.
- Navigation: when the desired content cannot be access by a predefined URL, navigating through the links that come with the Web page retrieved is possible. Navigation is also important for retrieving more information for a content block. For instance, reading the details for a main news may imply to follow the link that allows end users to navigate from the Web site's home to the specific news' web page, whose URL could hardly be known beforehand. Imagine that the user wants to know more about the news represented by the Element 3, in Fig. 2a. Then, a Web page similar to the presented in Fig. 3a would be retrieved, where this news is presented. In cases like this, navigation is used to reach the target content block.

- Search: in cases where the VUI requires querying a Web application for specific information, the automated use of search engines could be used. For instance, if only elements related to a specific domain are required (for instance, news related to "Venezuela", as Fig. 3b shows), then to emulate how the user would search it on the Web application could be useful. This method for Web content access is also relevant in the case of e-commerce, accommodation and flights Web sites, etc.

Despite how the target Web page that contains the desired content is retrieved, once it is obtained it is necessary to parse it and extract the content block. For this goal, each content block has a template extractor, which is defined by end users using visual selection and annotation tools. These annotations belong to the VUI definition and (among other aspects) contains the XPath expressions to extract a specific information element given a retrieved Web page.

Order in Which the Same Voice Command Reads Several Content Blocks

As we mentioned, this approach proposes using flow diagrams to arrange how content blocks are disposed in the VUI, because to respond a voice command, a sequence of content blocks will be read as a response. Once the content blocks are defined, it is important to define an order in which they will be read and under which voice inter-actions. For example, for the content blocks in Fig. 2.a, the voice command could be "Read today's news" and the order in which the news must be read may be (Block1, Block2, Block3, Block4, Block5), in which each block number corresponds to the numbers in Fig. 2.a, or any other the end user defines.

Configuration of the Vui's Behavior

As we said, in our approach a flow diagram defines the main structure of VUI responses. Besides the established order, different aspects of the VUI behavior must be defined:

1. How to read a content block: when the user says a command, the VUI will respond using one or a set of content blocks. However, which parts or properties to read for each of these content blocks may be different in distinct use scenarios. For instance, the user may be interested on reading just the main title or the complete content block for a news, or in a generic way, a specific collection of the semantic properties defined for that content block. Furthermore, if the block contains a navigable element, then it would be possible to offer deeper information that could be extracted by retrieving the Web page defined in the content block's link, etc.

2. How to continue to the next content block: beyond how to read a specific content block, when it is finished, there are different possibilities to continue with other related ones. This is part of the definition of the VUI behavior, in which the end user must be able to define among different options: read following block without asking, read following block without asking but pronouncing a predefining text, ask to the user if s/he want to continue, etc.

With these two aspects, we aim to give support to behavior variability for the proposed VUI. However, since it can be tedious and error prone to define each of these aspects for each element in the VUI flow (contemplating both nodes and arrows), we propose to use as a default option some VUI patterns. A pattern template defines the transversal behavior to manage content blocks (1) and the transitions among them (2).

However, to allow end users to customize their VUI and better support variability, they may change the pattern-based behavior for both a particular content block and for a transition to another content block. So far in our approach, a VUI pattern requires JavaScript programming skills to be defined, basically these are state machines for define the conversational behavior.

4 SkillMaker: A Web Browser-Based Environment for VUI Specification

In this section, we present SkillMaker, our EUD environment, through an example. We first present the tool for defining extraction templates for content blocks, and later the editor of VUI based on flow diagrams using these content blocks. The whole environment is deployed as a Web browser extension (in particular as a Google Chrome plug-in).

4.1 Contents Blocks Definition

We use content annotation as the method to define a content block [19]. The process starts when the user decides to define a content block for the current Web site, which is done by clicking the main button of the SkillMaker Web extension– point (1) in Fig. 4. The result of this is that the DOM elements are highlighted when the pointer is over them. When the user chooses a specific DOM element, he may drag and drop it – point (2) in Fig. 4 –into the extraction template definition box – point (3) in Fig. 4.

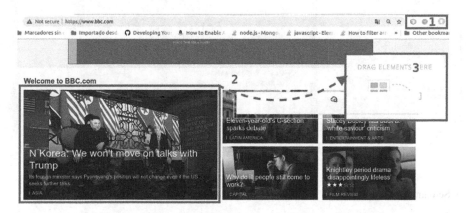

Fig. 4. Web content selection for defining a content block

Once a DOM element is selected, the annotation process starts by adding the semantic of the sub-DOM elements, such as Fig. 5 shows. A detailed view is shown in Fig. 6a, where the confirmation for the title property can be seen.

Fig. 5. Definition of a Web content block

The process continues (Fig. 6b) by asking the end user if related content (basically sibling elements) should be considered, in order to support content blocks such as the one in Fig. 2a. Figure 6b also shows that the tool detects navigation links for the selected DOM element automatically. In this way, the end user may consider this navigation (see "Can navigate?" checkbox in Fig. 6c). Figure 6c shows the edition form for other mandatory properties such as a category and a name.

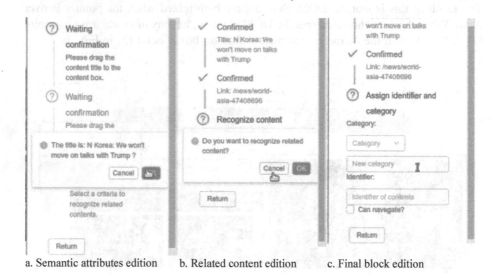

a. Semantic attributes edition   b. Related content edition   c. Final block edition

Fig. 6. Edition views of different steps of the block definition process

When the end user confirms the creation of this content block, the tool stores it and offers to open the flow editor, which is explained next. Otherwise, the user may continue with the creation of content blocks for the same Web page or any other.

4.2 VUI Definition and Deployment Through Examples

The flow editor, also deployed in the same Web extension, has access to the content blocks defined by the end user, which can be dragged and dropped into the diagram editor's canvas, as Fig. 7 shows. In this example, the content block selected is the one representing all siblings elements from Fig. 2b.

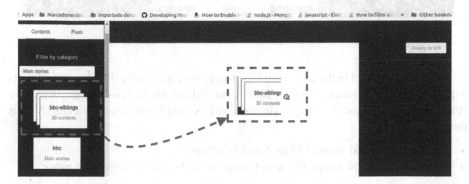

Fig. 7. Flow for read a set of sibling content blocks

After adding several more blocks into the canvas, and also some links among them, the flow looks like the one in Fig. 8. In these case, several content blocks representing the main news from different portals.

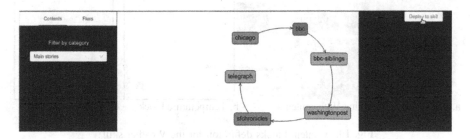

Fig. 8. A flow for reading the main news from each news portal

When the user clicks on the "Deploy to skill" button, the editor opens a modal window (Fig. 9) asking the user: (1) a name for the skill which will be used as a voice command to be answered with this flow, (2) the content reading pattern to use in the corresponding response. This last option relates to the Configuration of VUI behavior issue presented in previous section.

Fig. 9. Editing skill name and content reading pattern.

The skill designed in the flow from Fig. 8 uses the "Read only titles" pattern. In this example, 6 content blocks "main news" were defned for 6 news portals (Chicago, BBC, Washington Post, Telegraph, sfchronicles). A sample interaction with this VUI is the following:

- **User's Command voice:** "Main News headlines"
- **Amazon echo:** "N Korea We won't move on talks with Trump, *next news...*"

A second case study was based on existing and frequently used skills, such as those in the weather domain. This skill is defined to answer with the temperature and the humidity from Buenos Aires city, when the user says "Weather in Buenos Aires".

a. Web page highlighting Web contents   b. Temperature block   c. Humidity block

Fig. 10. Content blocks definition for the Weather skill

The skill was built using information from weather.com. Figure 10 shows the blocks definition process. Two content blocks are defined, one for temperature and a second one for humidity. Figure 11 shows the corresponding flow. Since the interesting content were detected as titles, we used the "Read only titles" pattern. A possible conversation excerpt is the following:

- **User's Command voice:** "Buenos Aires weather"
- **Amazon Echo:** "22, humidity 65%"

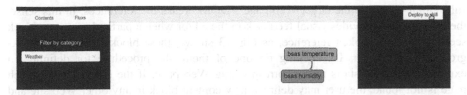

Fig. 11. VUI definition for the Weather skill

End-User Development Concerns

We mentioned before that variability is a key aspect in EUD environments; therefore, the general rules to read content blocks and the links used by the pattern may be replaced by manually editing how to read these elements. For the case of the content blocks, Fig. 12a shows the available options, which range from read everything, read only the titles property, and whether the VUI must ask the user before reading the content block or not.

Figure 12b shows the configuration for the links. In this case, the available options are to read a particular text before starting with the content block, read the block directly without asking, ask for reading the next content block (which has the same impact that set it up for the following block's configuration).

It is interesting to mention that these options came from the analysis of several examples that were useful to define the expressivity of the approach (further details are not included for the sake of space). However, new kinds of controls can be easily programmed.

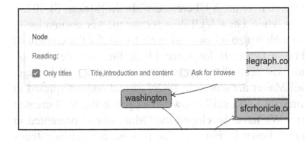

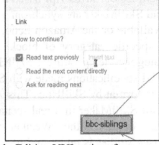

a. Editing VUI options for a Node

b. Editing VUI options for a Link

Fig. 12. Editing VUI options for replacing patterns rules

Our environment takes into account particularly the debugging concern described by Ko. [20] in the context of end-user software engineering approaches. This is because our approach is based on third-party Web content. The extraction template defined with our environment have references to DOM elements expressed in xPath. If a Web page changes its underlying DOM structure, these xPaths expressions may not work anymore. Although there are ways to make them more robust [21], it still is possible that a substantial change in the target Web page's DOM breaks the references. In this sense, the environment provides visual feedback in the editor when a particular content block seems to have a broken reference, as Fig. 13 shows; these blocks have a red background in the menu. By clicking on one of them, the procedure for defining an extraction template starts in the corresponding Web page. If the corresponding Web page is not found, the user may define a new content block in any other Web site and store it with the same name.

Fig. 13. Content block with missing or broken DOM references

5   Case Studies

Al the examples presented in the paper were used for defining case studies achieving real interaction. We have carried on these case studies using Amazon Echo, which is based on Alexa. For these case studies, we create SkillHub, an Amazon Echo skill that includes our Javascript-based interpreter for the VUI created with SkillMaker. SkillHub and SkillMaker are synchronized so when a new VUI flow is created, it is automatically available on the Amazon Echo. SkillHub also allows end users to ask for the content of a specific category of block. For instance, if for some block the user defines the category "temperature", SkillHub will read the current content from the Web page. VUI specifications made with SkillMaker are stored in JSON format and interpreted in this format by SkillHub. This Amazon Echo skill allows us to prove the VUI created with SkillMaker in a real scenario. We have developed the "Main news" presented in Fig. 8 and also the "Weather skill" shown in Fig. 11. The process for defining these cases studies is quick and trivial.

6   Conclusion and Future Works

VUI are being increasingly used to allow communication with smart devices. These devices usually allow end users to install third-party skills to support new behaviors. In this paper, we presented an end-user development approach to allow end users to create their own VUI-based skills for using their preferred Web sources for information and services. The creation of VUI based on Web content could be an interesting way for users to gain more control while interacting with devices.

We discussed the rationale and mechanics to transform Web content into VUI, which consists in extracting content blocks and arranging them in flow diagrams that will be interpreted for answering a voice command. We also showed our EUD environment, including the extraction template for content blocks and SkillMaker, our EUD tool to create VUI based on content blocks. The development time was very short; it just took some minutes for defining content blocks and the VUI for using them in SkillMaker. As a proof of concept we developed SkillHub, an Amazon Echo skill implementing our approach. We used SkillHub to interact with the voice commands defined using SkillMaker.

References

1. Zhang, N., Mi, X., Feng, X., Wang, X., Tian, Y., Qian, F.: Understanding and mitigating the security risks of voice-controlled third-party skills on amazon alexa and google home. arXiv preprint arXiv:1805.01525 (2018)
2. IFTTT and Amazon Alexa. https://ifttt.com/amazon_alexa. Accessed 13 Mar 2019
3. Rajalakshmi, A., Shahnasser, H.: Internet of Things using node-red and alexa. In: 2017 17th International Symposium on Communications and Information Technologies (ISCIT), pp. 1–4. IEEE, September 2017
4. Brambilla, M., Cabot, J., Wimmer, M.: Model-driven software engineering in practice. Synthesis Lect. Softw. Eng. 3(1), 1–207 (2017)
5. Elouali, N., Rouillard, J., Le Pallec, X., Tarby, J.C.: Multimodal interaction: a survey from model driven engineering and mobile perspectives. J. Multimodal User Interfaces 7(4), 351–370 (2013)
6. Licklider, J.C.R.: Man-computer symbiosis. IRE Trans. Hum. Factors Electron. 1, 4–11 (1960)
7. Cassell, J., et al.: Embodiment in conversational interfaces: rea. In: Proceedings of the SIGCHI Conference on Human Factors in Computing Systems, pp. 520–527. ACM, May 1999
8. Kadous, M.W., Sammut, C.: InCA: a mobile conversational agent. In: Zhang, C., W. Guesgen, H., Yeap, W.-K. (eds.) PRICAI 2004. LNCS (LNAI), vol. 3157, pp. 644–653. Springer, Heidelberg (2004). https://doi.org/10.1007/978-3-540-28633-2_68
9. White, R.W.: Skill discovery in virtual assistants. Commun. ACM 61(11), 106–113 (2018)
10. Bentley, F., Luvogt, C., Silverman, M., Wirasinghe, R., White, B., Lottrjdge, D.: Understanding the long-term use of smart speaker assistants. Proc. ACM Interact. Mob. Wearable Ubiquit. Technol. 2(3), 91 (2018)
11. Kurniawati, E., Celetto, L., Capovilla, N., George, S.: Personalized voice command systems in multi modal user interface. In: 2012 IEEE International Conference on Emerging Signal Processing Applications, pp. 45–47. IEEE, January 2012
12. Ferrara, E., De Meo, P., Fiumara, G., Baumgartner, R.: Web data extraction, applications and techniques: a survey. Knowl. Based Syst. 70, 301–323 (2014)
13. Khare, R., Çelik, T.: Microformats: a pragmatic path to the semantic web. In: Proceedings of the 15th International Conference on WWW, pp. 865–866. ACM, May 2006
14. Bizer, C., Eckert, K., Meusel, R., Mühleisen, H., Schuhmacher, M., Völker, J.: Deployment of RDFa, microdata, and microformats on the web – a quantitative analysis. In: Alani, H., et al. (eds.) ISWC 2013. LNCS, vol. 8219, pp. 17–32. Springer, Heidelberg (2013). https://doi.org/10.1007/978-3-642-41338-4_2

15. Van Kleek, M., Moore, B., Karger, D.R., André, P.: Atomate it! end-user context-sensitive automation using heterogeneous information sources on the web. In: Proceedings of the 19th International Conference on World Wide Web, pp. 951–960. ACM, April 2010
16. Ennals, R., Garofalakis, M.M.: Mashups for the masses (demo paper). In: Proceedings of the 2007 ACM SIGMOD International Conference on Management of Data (SIGMOD 2007) (2007)
17. Firmenich, S., Bosetti, G., Rossi, G., Winckler, M.: End-user software engineering for the personal web. In: 2017 IEEE/ACM 39th International Conference on Software Engineering Companion (ICSE-C), pp. 216–218. IEEE, May 2017
18. Bosetti, G., Firmenich, S., Fernandez, A., Winckler, M., Rossi, G.: From search engines to augmented search services: an end-user development approach. In: Cabot, J., De Virgilio, R., Torlone, R. (eds.) ICWE 2017. LNCS, vol. 10360, pp. 115–133. Springer, Cham (2017). https://doi.org/10.1007/978-3-319-60131-1_7
19. Firmenich, S., Bosetti, G., Rossi, G., Winckler, M., Barbieri, T.: Abstracting and structuring web contents for supporting personal web experiences. In: Bozzon, A., Cudre-Maroux, P., Pautasso, C. (eds.) ICWE 2016. LNCS, vol. 9671, pp. 77–95. Springer, Cham (2016). https://doi.org/10.1007/978-3-319-38791-8_5
20. Ko, A.J., et al.: The state of the art in end-user software engineering. ACM Comput. Surv. (CSUR) **43**(3), 21 (2011)
21. Aldalur, I., Diaz, O.: Addressing web locator fragility: a case for browser extensions. In: Proceedings of the ACM SIGCHI Symposium on Engineering Interactive Computing Systems, pp. 45–50. ACM, June 2017
22. Aldalur, I., Winckler, M., Díaz, O., Palanque, P.: Web augmentation as a promising technology for end user development. In: Paternò, F., Wulf, V. (eds.) New Perspectives in End-User Development, pp. 433–459. Springer, Cham (2017). https://doi.org/10.1007/978-3-319-60291-2_17

CAPIRCI: A Multi-modal System for Collaborative Robot Programming

Sara Beschi[1], Daniela Fogli[1(✉)], and Fabio Tampalini[1,2]

[1] Dipartimento di Ingegneria dell'Informazione,
Università degli Studi di Brescia, Brescia, Italy
s.beschi005@studenti.unibs.it,
daniela.fogli@unibs.it, tampalini@railab.com
[2] Railab S.r.l, Brescia, Italy

Abstract. This paper presents CAPIRCI (Chat And Program Industrial Robots through Convenient Interaction), a multi-modal web application supporting end users, with no expertise in computer science, to define and modify tasks to be executed by collaborative robots. The application provides two interaction modalities, the former based on a chat interface, the latter presenting a visual programming language inspired to block-based solutions but tailored to the domain at hand. In order to investigate how different kinds of users may accept and use CAPIRCI, a user study with 20 participants has been carried out. Participants were equally split in expert programmers and non-expert programmers; execution times do not show any significant differences between the two groups, while qualitative data collected through direct observation and interviews provide useful hints and suggestions for system refinement.

Keywords: Collaborative robot programming · Industrial robotics interfaces · Domain experts · Natural language interfaces · Component-based development

1 Introduction

Industry 4.0 European programs and related international initiatives in US, China, Japan and South Korea are promoting the computerization of manufacturing to create more efficient and scalable production flows, as well as fully customized products and services [34]. This scenario is transforming the industrial work environments and operators' daily activities by creating not only new opportunities but also several challenges [32]. Indeed, industries are more and more seeking workers with background in Information and Communication Technology (ICT) and particularly software programming [28]; furthermore, the demography is changing and many operators, even though expert in their work domain, risk to be set aside, due to the digital divide. Even though some research studies forecasting the workforce of the future observe how machines will probably replace humans in several jobs [12, 29], there is also the awareness that new types of interaction between operators and machines should be designed, giving rise to new job opportunities for supporting the different types of Operator 4.0 [33].

© Springer Nature Switzerland AG 2019
A. Malizia et al. (Eds.): IS-EUD 2019, LNCS 11553, pp. 51–66, 2019.
https://doi.org/10.1007/978-3-030-24781-2_4

One of the most important enabling technologies promoted by Industry 4.0 programs is represented by *collaborative robots*, namely industrial robots that share the workspace with human workers and help them in performing repetitive and non-ergonomic tasks [32, 35]. Collaborative robots are thus designed to work in direct cooperation with operators by means of safe and intuitive interaction technologies. Small and medium sized companies are increasingly introducing collaborative robots in their factories considering them more affordable, compact and easy-to-use with respect to traditional industrial robots [38]. In fact, collaborative robots contribute to create the conditions for increasing production flexibility; at the same time, they require to be quickly and easily operated by human workers, while guaranteeing a safe interaction.

Several interaction paradigms and tools have been proposed in the field of robot programming [26, 36]. Those focused on collaborative robots are mostly based on programming-by-demonstration and visual programming environments [38]. In programming-by-demonstration, the user must physically move the robot into the desired positions and record robot states or technology path, so that the same movements can subsequently be performed autonomously by the robot; in addition, if the robot is endowed by learning skills, a set of example movements under varying conditions can be shown by the operator, and then the robot becomes able to infer a generalized task model and reproduce the learned task on the basis of the current situation [38]. Visual programming environments, on the other hand, incorporate icons, diagrams, puzzle blocks, and other graphic representation that can be manipulated by the user to define sequences of instructions to be followed by the robot [40]. The conceptual model offered by these tools mainly derives from notations for software specification (e.g., flowchart diagrams [5]) or from experiences in computer programming education that proved successful with young learners, such as Scratch [31], Alice [17], or AgentCubes [20], and that propose block-based programming [18, 41]. However, most of these proposals require users to define tasks related to robot movement and manipulation by specifying positions and low-level operations. In addition, user studies carried out on some solutions underline the difficulties encountered by end users, not knowledgeable in computer programming, in the definition of such tasks.

The approach presented in this paper would like to overcome these limitations. In particular, we propose a new interaction paradigm for robot programming that arises from a twofold perspective: (i) first of all, we addressed the problem bottom-up, starting from the observation of the interaction with applications and devices that most people use every day (in particular, web sites and mobile apps for instant communication) and then iteratively developed a first intuitive interaction modality for robot task creation; (ii) at the same time, we aimed to combine this interaction modality with a visual language for robot programming that was at a higher conceptual level with respect to those proposed in literature. Inspired by literature on end-user development (EUD) [21, 27] and meta-design [8, 10] we thus worked on a domain-oriented design environment [2, 7], specifically studied for robot programming applications, but that could be easily extended and variously deployed by the problem owners. Therefore, we aimed to achieve different goals, such as providing users with a natural interaction to define simple tasks, but also allowing them to gradually learn new possibilities for complex task creation and thus favoring a migration path in their EUD skills. We aimed also to create a system that could be used in different situations, possibly in mobility or remotely, and thus suitable to mobile and small devices; this led us to create a rich internet application. Finally, we would like to design a solution that could be easily customized to the application domain, thus foreseeing the use of objects and actions related to the specific domain, with libraries of objects and actions defined by end users for different system instantiations.

In synthesis, a new approach to robot programming is here proposed, which combines natural language processing with component-based visual design to accommodate different users' attitudes and foster a "gentle slope of complexity" [22]. The approach led to develop a first prototype of a multi-modal system, called CAPIRCI[1] (*Chat And Program Industrial Robots through Convenient Interaction*); this system is aimed at supporting the easy creation of tasks for pick-and-place collaborative robots. The paper describes the functionality and implementation of CAPIRCI; a user test with 20 users has been also carried out to analyze and compare the system usability perceived by expert and non-expert programmers.

2   Related Work

The interest in human-robot interaction (HRI) is strictly related to the increased productivity and flexibility of industry production lines [36]. The review presented in [36] explores several challenges and issues concerning HRI including task planning and coordination, HRI evaluation and metrics, socio-related aspects, and intuitive robot programming. An interesting analysis is provided with reference to social aspects: it is observed how the current demographic trend is reflected to the workforce age, thus determining an increasing number of older people at work, with consequences on productivity and flexibility, due to long-term health problems, chronic diseases, misleading memory, limited learning capabilities, low motivations, etc. Given these problems, the challenge for the next years is to improve HRI and the allocation of tasks between humans and robots, also by considering ergonomics and human-related performance aspects [36]. Tsarouchi and colleagues [36] also underline some issues related to robot programming, which are examined in detail in the recent survey of Villani et al. [38] that specifically focuses on collaborative robots. In the following, we briefly consider related work discussing the main research trends in collaborative robotics and then we deepen the approaches proposed in the field of robot programming.

2.1   Collaborative Robots

In [38], the advantages brought to small and medium sized companies by collaborative robots are underlined and compared to traditional industrial robots; the latter lack in versatility and cannot be easily adapted to dynamic work environments or changes in production. Collaborative robots, instead, are suitable for small batches of production

---

[1] "Capirci" is an Italian word with a double meaning: "to understand each other" but also "I understand this".

and may leverage human flexibility and ability to adapt to unforeseen events. However, three main challenges are highlighted: (1) supporting *safe interaction*, because robots and human operators are not separated by fences and operate in a shared space; (2) providing operators with *intuitive user interfaces* to easily interact with robots and program their behavior; (3) achieving the previous goals through proper *design methods*. Safe interaction is addressed in several works, which discuss compliance to safety standards (e.g., [13, 16]) and collaborative modes that could be implemented in co-working scenarios (e.g., [14, 23, 39]); we do not consider this issue in the present paper since it is considered out of scope. Instead, we propose an interactive system and a design approach that aim to address the other two challenges.

As far as user interfaces for robot programming, the following sub-section is completely devoted to this topic.

2.2 Robot Programming

The traditional classification of robot programming approaches distinguishes between *on-line programming* and *off-line programming* [38]. The former includes *lead-through programming*, usually through teach pendant for moving the robot and registering trajectories and endpoints, and *walk-through programming*, where the human operator directly moves the end-effector of the robot through the desired positions. *Programming by demonstration* is regarded as an extension of walk-through programming, because in this case the robot not only reproduces the motions, but also learns which movements it must perform under different conditions and is able to generalize them [1]. Off-line programming does not require to occupy the robot but can be carried out with an independent tool that possibly allows simulating tasks in the 3D model of the robot [24]. This approach, however, usually requires a great programming effort and to manage the lack of absolute accuracy of the robot arms; therefore, software engineers instead of operators in the shop floor are called on to perform the programming activity; furthermore, each robot manufacturer has its own robot programming tool.

Nowadays, a variety of novel approaches based on multi-modal interfaces and augmented/virtual reality are being proposed. They result to be well accepted by users without programming expertise, thanks to the intuitive and natural interaction they offer by means of voice commands, tangible manipulation, gesture recognition, eye tracking, and so on [36]. However, they are still limited in terms of the complexity of robot tasks that can be programmed with them [38]; furthermore, they are currently being experimented in research laboratories, whilst, there are few applications in industrial contexts [26]. For example, the deployment of systems for speech recognition and natural language processing in industrial environments suffers of many drawbacks, such as misrecognition due to the complexity of natural languages, operator pronounce or simply background noise. Therefore, existing industrial applications that exploit vocal commands are usually based on a limited lexicon and a combination with other types of interaction [32, 37]. Similarly, we propose an approach that exploits speech recognition (voice-based or text-based), but which combines it with a component-based EUD technique [4], in order to help users smoothly learn the programming activity.

Component-based interaction techniques are at the basis of recent tools for off-line robot programming that have been designed and evaluated with real users. For example, Weintrop et al. proposed CoBlox, a visual programming tool for ABB's Roberta, a single-armed industrial robot [40, 41]. CoBlox provides a customized block-based language built with the Blockly library, which allows the user to write a robot program by dragging and dropping in a canvas puzzle pieces representing types of instructions. Syntax errors are prevented thanks to the "physical" incompatibility of puzzle pieces representing incompatible instructions. CoBlox encompasses two main panes, on the left one the user may create the robot tasks with block-based programming, whist the right one visualizes a 3D robot that must be used to position the robot during program construction and register the different locations to set the parameters of the program instructions. Literature work has shown that the block-based approach is effective to teach computer programming to children and teenagers [11, 15]; the challenge of CoBlox is to prove the effectiveness of this metaphor also for workers of all ages and backgrounds, who are not knowledgeable in computer programming, to customize robot behavior. To this end, the authors carried out a user study to compare CoBox with two other, more traditional, interactive tools for robot programming, such as ABB's Flex Pendant and Universal Robots' Polyscope [40]. The results show that the block-based approach has great potential for robot programming since it is easy to use and to learn also for adult novices. However, in the experimental activity the focus was mainly on movement tasks, by requiring the users to specify the low-level operations to carry out simple pick and place tasks. We are more interested in providing users with an easy way of defining complex tasks, and we assume that object recognition and knowledge of locations are features already available in the system.

Another proposal, still based on the Blockly library, is Code3 [18, 19], a system which includes three components: (1) CustomLandmarks, to create a library of objects and scene elements; (2) CustomActions, to create a library of manipulation actions through kinesthetic programming by demonstration; and (3) CodeIt, to support users in the creation of robot tasks in a way similar to CoBlox. The three components make the system complete for the definition of collaborative robot tasks, but if we focus on the CodeIt interface we can notice that the user must select the correct block in a list of several block types that refer to typical computer-oriented programming languages, such as loops, lists, variables, functions, etc. This might be difficult to learn by the different types of workers that can be called on to program collaborative robots in current industries. This limitation is confirmed by the perceived usability of the system that the authors evaluated with ten users through the System Usability Scale (SUS) [6] questionnaire: the resulting average score was equal to 66.75, thus below the value 68.5, which is considered the threshold for declaring that a system is easy to use [3].

Other approaches to visual programming proposed in literature appear as less intuitive that those mentioned above. For example, the interactive system presented in [28] is still component-based but components represent programming constructs that should be combined to create a behavior tree; even though this system allows specifying complex tasks, the user must understand and remember the notation adopted for the different types of nodes; therefore, s/he cannot be the usual worker at the shop floor (as demonstrated by the fact that the user study reported in [28] was carried out with students in math, engineering and computer science). In [35], task programming is instead performed by interacting with two traditional GUI windows: one that allows the specification of a linear sequence of skills (compositions of sensing and manipulation primitives able to generate a change in the physical world, e.g. "pick object") that make up a task (no other control structures are supported); and another window that enables parameter setting when the user would like to add new skills. The system is complemented by an intuitive online teaching feature to add single skills.

To overcome the usability limitations of existing solutions and taking more into account the characteristics of factory workers, this paper proposes a system that leverages users' knowledge of the domain concepts and provides a higher level of abstraction in the programming activity. In addition, the integration with natural language recognition features is aimed at facilitating the learning process.

3   CAPIRCI: A Mixed Approach to Collaborative Robots

This section presents CAPIRCI, a multi-modal interactive system for off-line collaborative robot programming. The idea underlying our approach is providing the users with two different but integrated ways for defining robot tasks: the former, based on natural language processing, should be firstly used to address the programming problem, by obtaining the specification of a simple task in an easy way; the latter, based on a component-based visual language, can be used to refine the program and, if needed, to make it more articulated. However, different users, with different attitudes, background and expertise in software programming, may use CAPIRCI according to their own preferences: for example, skilled users may prefer interacting only with the graphic interface, whilst the less skilled ones may decide to gradually acquire knowledge of how to program the robot through both parts of the system.

The visual interface is not based on existing tools for block-based programming (like Blockly), but can be regarded as a domain-oriented design environment [2, 7], where users can shape digital artifacts that capitalize on domain concepts and operators' mental models. Proper features are also implemented to prevent users' errors and facilitate reuse of designed solutions. To this end, we followed a bottom-up design approach [25] by first considering the needs, culture and characteristics of the individuals involved in the interaction with collaborative robots and then trying to understand how to build a tool that could become widely applicable. CAPIRCI is intended to be used in a variety of different factories, with different workers and different robots, and thus different tasks (not only pick-and-place); indeed, the tool has been conceived to be parametric with respect to the domain, and different libraries of objects, actions, and robot language parsers might be used to instantiate the tool for a specific industrial context.

3.1   System Architecture and User Interface

CAPIRCI has been implemented as a web application through the Python Web Framework Django. In particular, the back-end functions, written in Python according to the Model-View-Template (MVT) pattern, implement the natural language parsing features (exploiting available Python libraries) and the robot commands; whilst, the front-end application, written in the traditional web languages (HTML, CSS and Javascript) allows the user to interact with the interfaces for robot task creation. The whole CAPIRCI architecture is shown in Fig. 1.

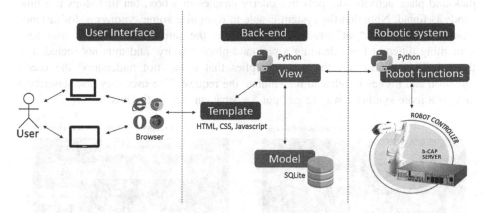

Fig. 1. CAPIRCI architecture and technologies.

Figure 2 is a screenshot of the home page of the application. Here, the user may access the available libraries, especially those containing robot tasks that could be executed or modified, and interact with one of the two cards to start the creation of a new task through the natural language interface or the graphic interface.

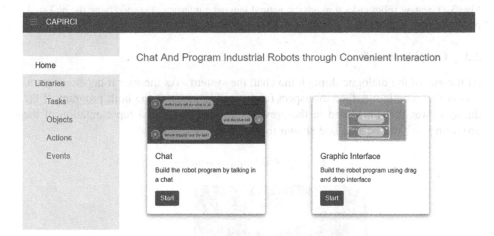

Fig. 2. CAPIRCI home page.

3.2 Natural Language Interface

The natural language interface can be used to easily specify a simple robot task. This interface presents itself as an instant messaging system, i.e. a chat, where the user can type messages to respond to system's requests or register them clicking on the microphone icon, similarly to widely used chat systems. Figure 3 shows a dialogue example related to the creation of tasks for a packaging line of a sweets factory. In particular, the user would like to create the task "candies in the box" by defining the pick-and-place activity that puts five cherry candies in a box, but that stops if a lime candy is found. Note that the system is able to recognize some synonyms, for instance "take", "pick" and "put" are all interpreted as the same action. If the user says something different from defining a pick-and-place activity, and thus not included in the CAPIRCI dictionary, the system replies that it has not understood the user's intention and invites him/her to reformulate the request. The user may also describe a task in a more synthetic way (e.g., "put 5 cherry candies in the box").

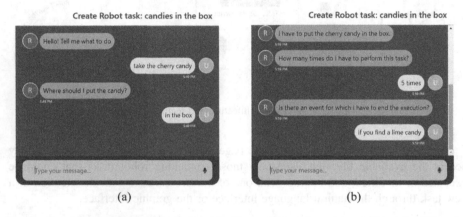

(a)   (b)

Fig. 3. Creating robot tasks through the natural language interface: (a) specifying the pick-and-place activity; (b) defining repetition and stopping condition.

3.3 Graphic Interface

At the end of the dialogue through the chat, the system asks the user if he/she wants to access the graphic interface to inspect (and possibly modify) the built program. If the dialogue was that illustrated in the previous section, the visual representation of the program results to be that one shown in Fig. 4.

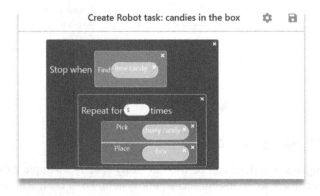

Fig. 4. The program created through the chat visualized in the graphic interface.

Here, the user can add or remove actions, change the objects to be manipulated, or even modify the control structures by changing their parameters or substituting them with other control structures. The system provides the user with explicative warning messages if some constraint concerning well-formed programs is violated.

The user can also directly access the graphic interface from the home page (see the right card in Fig. 2). In this case, the system shows a set of libraries on the left area of the screen and a canvas on the right part (Fig. 5). The latter is called "Project area" and suggests that the blocks available in the libraries must be dragged-and-dropped here to create a new program.

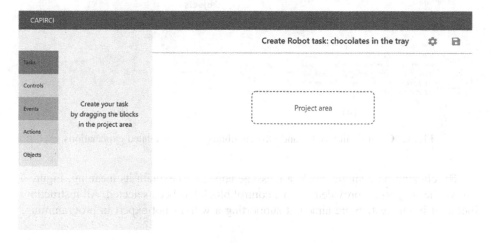

Fig. 5. The graphic interface before program creation.

The libraries in the left area contain different kinds of blocks, namely:

- *Tasks*, which contains blocks representing the previously created robot tasks (with both interaction modalities); in this way, the user can re-use a task and/or adapt it to obtain a different robot behavior;
- *Controls*, which includes the components for creating cycles and conditional behaviors;
- *Events*, where the user may find the conditions to be used in control blocks, such as the detection of an object, a signal from a sensor, etc.;
- *Actions*, which contains the different kinds of actions that the robot is able to perform (at the moment, *pick*, *place*, *shake* and *rotate*);
- *Objects*, which includes all the objects that can be manipulated in this particular instantiation of the system (for example, all the types of sweets that can be manipulated in the packaging line of the factory).

When a library is selected, its content is shown as a set of blocks and a message at the bottom provides some explanations of their meaning and how to use them. For example, Fig. 6 shows the Controls library (a) and the Objects library (b).

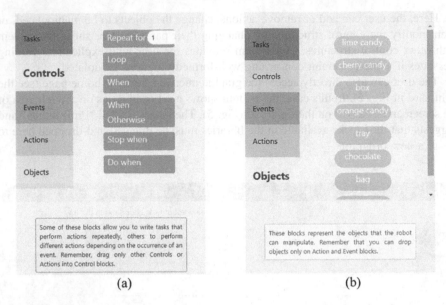

Fig. 6. Controls library (a) and Objects library (b) with related explanations.

By clicking on a single block, a message appears to explain its meaning. Figure 7 shows the suggestion provided when a control block has been selected. All instructions included in the system are aimed at supporting a worker not expert in programming.

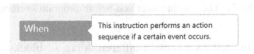

Fig. 7. A suggestion for the user about the meaning of a specific block.

To build a program the blocks must be composed according to a "put-in" logic. The outermost block controls internal ones. As shown in Fig. 8, when the user drags a block in a correct area, this area changes color (from light grey to white) and the user can release the block. If the user tries to release a block in a wrong area, such as an object block in an action area of a control block (see Fig. 9), or the area is already filled in, the system displays a warning message that suggests a solution.

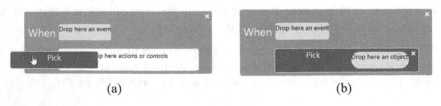

Fig. 8. (a) Putting a Pick action over a control area; (b) Dropping the Pick action.

Fig. 9. (a) Dragging and dropping an object in a wrong area; (b) A warning message suggests the solution.

4 User Evaluation

We conducted a user experiment of CAPIRCI with 20 users to investigate if the system is perceived as easy to use and to learn both by expert and non-expert programmers.

4.1 Methodology

Twenty participants sorted in two groups, according to their programming expertise, participated in the user study. Group 1 included 10 participants (1 female), all with at least a Bachelor degree in Computer Science; they usually perform programming activities for job or study and their age range in 23–52. The other 10 participants (4 females) were assigned to Group 2; they vary in terms of cultural background and profession, but all of them consider themselves as not expert in programming (8 out of 10 declared that they never programmed); their age range in 25–59.

After a brief training phase where an experimenter described the considered domain and showed how to create a simple program using the chat and how to edit it using the graphic interface, users were requested to carry out five tasks of increasing complexity. The first task should be performed with the chat and the second task with the graphic interface; the third task should be performed starting by using the chat and then the graphic interface should be used to modify the created program; the fourth task required to create a complex loop using the graphic interface; to carry out the fifth task the participants could choose the chat or graphic interface or both according to their preference. For each task, the execution time was collected. Qualitative data from direct observation, including difficulties encountered by participants and their comments were annotated as well. In addition, at the end of the experiment, an unstructured interview was conducted to better investigate the qualitative data and collect additional users' feedback.

Each participant was finally requested to fill in a questionnaire. The first 10 questions were the same of the SUS questionnaire [6] and allowed us to estimate the system usability. Four additional questions were then included in the questionnaire (still using the Likert scale from "strongly disagree" to "strongly agree") to gather users' opinions about the different interaction modalities offered by CAPIRCI.

4.2   Results

Table 1 reports the average execution time obtained for each user group. A t-test has been used to evaluate if the differences in these times are statistically significant. The null hypothesis is that there was no difference between the two groups. All obtained p-values are greater than the significance level 0.05, and therefore the null hypothesis cannot be rejected. This means that there is no relevant difference in execution time between expert and non-expert programmers.

Even though the difference is not significant, the execution time for Task 5 is lower for non-programmers than for programmers. Indeed, to complete it, the participants could freely choose between the chat and the graphic interface; interacting with the former is faster than interacting with the latter and 7 non-programmers out of 10 chose the chat, whilst 6 programmers out of 10 chose the graphic interface.

Table 1. Average execution time for each user group.

Average time	Task 1	Task 2	Task 3	Task 4	Task 5
Group 1	00:01:01	00:01:44	00:02:21	00:03:00	00:01:38
Group 2	00:01:06	00:01:47	00:02:55	00:03:07	00:01:28

As to the completion rate, all tasks except Task 4 were completed. For Task 4, 7 non-expert programmers did not understand that a loop was required, because the description simply told that the robot was near a conveyor carrying donuts and chocolates (the fact that the conveyor kept on arriving was left implicit); furthermore, the task required to define a different behavior depending on the arrival of a donut or a chocolate; this implied using a when statement, which caused some problems in a couple of users. Task 5, which was more articulated than Task 4 since beyond requiring to define a loop also included the management of an event to stop the program, was successfully completed by all users, thus showing that the system is easy to learn.

No significant usability problem emerged from the SUS questionnaire. The lowest SUS scores (assigned by a user belonging to Group 2) is equal to 50, whilst all other values are greater than 75. The mean values obtained for Group 1 and Group 2 are both very satisfactory (86.5 for Group 1 and 80.25 for Group 2, thus much greater than the threshold 68.5 [3]).

As to the additional four questions submitted to the users, we discovered that most of non-expert programmers (6 out of 10) preferred interacting with the chat, whilst the expert programmers were equally split in their preference for the chat and the graphic interface. Most of non-expert participants declared they felt very confident while using the chat because they were used to this type of system, where expert participants gave distributed scores. However, all participants agreed that the sentences created by the chat were clear and did not confuse them. The interaction modality provided by the graphic interface raised some critiques that emerged clearly also during the direct observation and in the final unstructured interview.

In particular, during the interview all users defined the chat easier and faster than the graphic interface: several participants told that they were fascinated by this programming modality and were willing to test it again. Someone pointed out that if one makes mistakes by programming with the chat, these can be solved using the graphic interface; in particular, some users declared they felt safer with it because the program can be changed at any time. This highlights that proposing a mixed approach was a successful choice.

Even though the chat has been considered a powerful tool, some users told that, at the beginning of the experiment, they were intimidated using it because they did not know what kinds of sentences the system recognizes. Furthermore, someone claimed that using the chat may increase the error probability. For this reason, one user suggested to add an auto-completion feature.

As far as the graphic interface, 4 participants have proposed to allow to copy and paste blocks already created directly in the project area, thus avoiding going back to look for them in the libraries. Two participants suggested to divide the *Objects* library in two sub-libraries, that one containing the objects the robot can manipulate (e.g., candies, chocolates, and donuts) and the other one with the places where the sweets can be put (e.g., bag, tray, and box). Unexpectedly, the drag-and-drop operation created some articulation problems and was difficult for some users. These ones tried to click on a block by expecting that it immediately appeared in the project area. One user would have preferred drop-down menus instead of drag-and-drop operations because he thought that these ones require more time and care. We suppose that with more practice these operations may become easier and provide a better user experience, but this would require an extended user study.

Given that this is our first prototype of CAPIRCI, we consider the results of the evaluation as very satisfactory. However, all the above observations will be taken into consideration for a future refinement of the interface.

5 Discussion and Conclusion

The paper has presented a novel mixed approach to collaborative robot programming. The idea of providing two interaction modalities, one based on some artificial intelligence functions for natural language processing, and one inspired to block-based programming, proved to be successful to support EUD activities and help non-expert programmers gradually learn how to create robot tasks. Indeed, the chat allows users to create simple tasks in an intuitive manner, and shows that users get quickly used to the limited scope of the language (as known in literature [30]); furthermore, the graphic interface can be used to refine tasks or create more complex ones, also through re-use of those previously defined.

Collaborative robots can be regarded as socio-technical systems, which thus require new frameworks for conceiving their control and management. One of this framework is meta-design [8, 9], which aims to provide the owner of problems with suitable social and technical means for participating in shaping the technology at use time. The case of collaborative robots is gaining momentum, but the approach to their programming is usually regarded as a matter of instructing human workers to learn programming language constructs. We tried to reverse the process and, by taking a meta-design perspective, we designed a domain-oriented environment [2, 7], capitalizing on usual interaction modalities, tools, activities and concepts belonging to the end users' daily world. Thus, the chat was designed to foster users' engagement and overcome learning barriers of robot programming; the graphic interface aimed to complete the system by supporting the definition of complex tasks through the combination of high-level blocks that recall domain-specific concepts.

CAPIRCI is only a first prototype of a long-term project about collaborative robots. We would like in the future to demonstrate the scalability and generalizability of the approach by making the tool easily customizable to different domains and different collaborative robots. As to future work, a comparison with the most recent tools for robot programming (especially Code3 [18] and CoBlox [40]) will be necessary to investigate whether the proposed mixed approach is better accepted by non-expert programmers than the single block-based visual language, also considering the complexity of tasks being created.

Our tool should also be extended in different ways: in particular 3D models of collaborative robots could be integrated in the system to support low-level operation specification and to allow robot simulation before deployment of robot programs on the shop floor. The chat may be improved by integrating more 'intelligent' functionalities that provide suggestions for task definition; this interaction modality also requires that a suitable 'undo' feature is designed and implemented.

Acknowledgments. The authors wish to thank all the participants in the user evaluation for their willingness and their valuable feedback.

References

1. Argall, B.D., Chernova, S., Veloso, M., Browning, B.: A survey of robot learning from demonstration. Robot. Auton. Syst. **57**(5), 469–483 (2009)
2. Arias, E.G., Eden, H., Fischer, G.: The Envisionment and Discovery Collaboratory (EDC): Explorations in Human-Centered Informatics, vol. 8. Morgan & Claypool Publishers LLC (2015)
3. Bangor, A., Kortum, P.T., Miller, J.T.: An empirical evaluation of the system usability scale. Int. J. Hum. Comput. Interact. **24**, 574–594 (2008)
4. Barricelli, B.R., Cassano, F., Fogli, D., Piccinno, A.: End-user development, end-user programming and end-user software engineering: a systematic mapping study. J. Syst. Softw. **149**, 101–137 (2019)
5. Bischoff, R., Kazi, A., Seyfarth, M.: The MORPHA style guide for icon-based programming. In: Proceedings 11th IEEE International Workshop on Robot and Human Interactive Communication, Berlin, Germany, pp. 482–487 (2002)
6. Brooke, J., Jordan, P.W., Weerdmeester, B., Thomas, A., McLelland, I.L.: SUS: a quick and dirty usability scale. In: Jordan, P.W., Thomas, B., Weerdmeester, B.A., McClelland, A.L. (eds.) Usability Evaluation in Industry. Taylor and Francis (1996)
7. Costabile, M.F., Fogli, D., Lanzilotti, R., Mussio, P., Piccinno, A.: Supporting work practice through end-user development environments. J. Organ. End User Comput. **18**(4), 43–65 (2006)

8. Fischer, G., Fogli, D., Piccinno, A.: Revisiting and broadening the meta-design framework for end-user development. In: Paternò, F., Wulf, V. (eds.) New Perspectives in End-User Development, pp. 61–97. Springer, Cham (2017). https://doi.org/10.1007/978-3-319-60291-2_4
9. Fischer, G., Herrmann, T.: Socio-technical systems: a meta-design perspective. Int. J. Sociotechnol. Knowl. Dev. (IJSKD) **3**(1), 1–33 (2011)
10. Fischer, G., Nakakoji, K., Ye, Y.: Metadesign: guidelines for supporting domain experts in software development. IEEE Softw. **26**(5), 37–44 (2009)
11. Franklin, D., et al.: Using upper-elementary student performance to understand conceptual sequencing in a blocks-based curriculum. In: Proceedings of the 2017 ACM SIGCSE Technical Symposium on Computer Science Education (SIGCSE 2017), pp. 231–236. ACM, New York (2017)
12. Frey, C.B., Osborne, M.: The future of employment: how susceptible are jobs to computerisation. https://www.oxfordmartin.ox.ac.uk/publications/view/1314. Accessed 24 Jan 2019
13. Fryman, J., Matthias, B.: Safety of industrial robots: from conventional to collaborative applications. In: Proceedings of the seventh German conference ROBOTIK, pp. 1–5 (2012)
14. Fujii, M., Murakami, H., Sonehara, M.: Study on application of a human-robot collaborative system using hand-guiding in a production line. IHI Eng. Rev. **49**(1), 24–29 (2016)
15. Grover, S., Pea, R., Cooper, S.: Designing for deeper learning in a blended computer science course for middle school students. Comput. Sci. Educ. **25**(2), 199–237 (2015)
16. Harper, C., Virk, G.: Towards the development of international safety standards for human robot interaction. Int. J. Soc. Robot. **2**, 229 (2010)
17. Herbert, C.W.: An Introduction to Programming Using Alice 2.2, 2nd edn. Course Technology Press, Boston, MA (2010)
18. Huang, J., Cakmak, M.: Code3: a system for end-to-end programming of mobile manipulator robots for novices and experts. In: Proceedings of the 2017 ACM/IEEE International Conference on Human-Robot Interaction (HRI 2017), pp. 453–462. ACM, New York (2017)
19. Huang, J., Lau, T., Cakmak, M.: Design and evaluation of a rapid programming system for service robots. In: Proceedings of the Eleventh ACM/IEEE International Conference on Human Robot Interaction (HRI 2016), pp. 295–302. IEEE Press, Piscataway (2016)
20. Ioannidou, A., Repenning, A., Webb, D.C.: AgentCubes: incremental 3D end-user development. J. Vis. Lang. Comput. **20**(4), 236–251 (2009)
21. Lieberman, H., Paternò, F., Klann, M., Wulf, V. (eds.): End User Development, pp. 1–8. Springer, Dordrecht (2006). https://doi.org/10.1007/1-4020-5386-X
22. Ludwig, T., Dax, J., Pipek, V., Wulf, V.: A practice-oriented paradigm for end-user development. In: Paternò, F., Wulf, V. (eds.) New Perspectives in End-User Development, pp. 23–41. Springer, Cham (2017). https://doi.org/10.1007/978-3-319-60291-2_2
23. Marvel, J.A., Norcross, R.: Implementing speed and separation monitoring in collaborative robot workcells. Robot. Comput. Integr. Manuf. **44**, 144–155 (2017)
24. Neto, P., Mendes, N.: Direct off-line robot programming via a common CAD package. Robot. Auton. Syst. **61**(8), 896–910 (2013)
25. Norman, D., Spencer, E.: Community-based, Human-centered design, 1 January 2019. https://jnd.org/community-based-human-centered-design/. Accessed 31 Jan 2019
26. Pan, Z., Polden, J., Larkin, N., Van Duin, S., Norrish, J.: Recent progress on programming methods for industrial robots. Robot. Comput. Integr. Manuf. **28**(2), 87–94 (2012)
27. Paterno, F., Wulf, V. (eds.): New Perspectives in End-User Development. Springer, Cham (2017). https://doi.org/10.1007/978-3-319-60291-2

28. Paxton, C., Jonathan, F., Hundt, A., Mutlu, B., Hager, G.D.: Evaluating methods for end-user creation of robot task plans. In: Proceedings 2018 IEEE/RSJ International Conference on Intelligent Robots and Systems (IROS), pp. 6086–6092. IEEE Press, USA (2018)
29. PwC. Workforce of the Future: The Competing Forces Shaping 2030. https://www.pwc.com/gx/en/services/people-organisation/publications/workforce-of-the-future.html. Accessed 24 Jan 2019
30. Ogden, W., Bernick, P.: Using natural language interfaces. In: M. Helander (ed.) Handbook of Human-Computer Interaction. Elsevier Science Publishers B.V., North-Holland (1996)
31. Resnick, M., et al.: Scratch: programming for all. Commun. ACM **52**(11), 60–67 (2009)
32. Rogowski, A.: Industrially oriented voice control system. Robot. Comput. Integr. Manuf. **28** (3), 303–315 (2012)
33. Romero, et al.: Towards an operator 4.0 typology: a human-centric perspective on the fourth industrial revolution technologies. In: Proceedings CIE46, Tianjin, China (2016)
34. Ruppert, T., Jasko, S., Holczinger, T., Abonyi, J.: Enabling technologies for operator 4.0: a survey. Appl. Sci. **8**(1650), 1–19 (2018)
35. Schou, C., Andersen, R.S., Chrysostomou, Bøgh, S., Madsen, O.: Skill-based instruction of collaborative robots in industrial settings. Robot. Comput. Integr. Manuf. **53**, 72–80 (2018)
36. Tsarouchi, P., Makris, S., Chryssolouris, G.: Human–robot interaction review and challenges on task planning and programming. Int. J. Comput. Integr. Manuf. **29**(8), 916–931 (2016)
37. van Delded, S., Umrysh, M., Rosario, C., Hess, G.: Pick-and-place application development using voice and visual commands. Ind. Robot. **39**(6), 592–600 (2012)
38. Villani, V., Pini, F., Leali, F., Secchi, C.: Survey on human-robot collaboration in industrial settings: safety, intuitive interfaces and applications. Mechatronics **55**, 248–266 (2018)
39. Vysocky, A., Novak, P.: Human–robot collaboration in industry. Mod. Mach. Sci. J., June, 903–906 (2016)
40. Weintrop, D., et al.: Evaluating CoBlox: a comparative study of robotics programming environments for adult novices. In: Proceedings of the 2018 CHI Conference on Human Factors in Computing Systems (CHI 2018), Paper 366, 12 pages. ACM, New York (2018)
41. Weintrop, D., Shepherd, D.C., Francis, P., Franklin, D.: Blockly goes to work: block-based programming for industrial robots. In: Proceedings of the 2017 IEEE Blocks and Beyond Workshop, pp. 29–36. IEEE Press, USA (2017)

Intervention and EUD

A Combination for Appropriating Automated Processes

Thomas Herrmann⑩, Christopher Lentzsch(✉)⑩,
and Martin Degeling⑩

Ruhr-University of Bochum, 44780 Bochum, Germany
{thomas.herrmann,christopher.lentzsch,
martin.degeling}@ruhr-uni-bochum.de

Abstract. Intervention is a new concept for human-computer interaction to help users to cope with the increasing complexity of automated processes in socio-technical settings. We relate the paradigms of End-User Development with it and show the differences, commonalities and emergent areas through a theoretical analysis of a smart home setting. Implications for the design of intervention user interfaces are derived and the interplay of interventions with and their support of End-User Development is shown.

Keywords: End-user development · Human-computer interaction ·
Intervention · Socio-technical systems

1 Introduction

Many end-users are confronted with systems that offer largely automated processes. They are embedded into a socio-technical context and increasingly replace systems that require fine-grained interactive control. This affects not only industrial settings but also end-user domains like e-commerce, data exchange in social network systems, or smart home settings. For most end-users, these systems and the underlying processes are hard to understand and therefore it is difficult to maintain the experience of being in control. When the number of systems being used and the options to pre-configure their procedures is steadily increasing, End-User Development (EUD) becomes challenging. We argue that in a relevant number of cases, end-users do only realize their need for adapting an automated process after it has already started. Once in progress, users occasionally may want to modify steps of the automated process, stop one or all of them, or at least want to understand the scope and effect of available alternatives. These needs for increased influence are not completely covered by EUD but require a specific type of interaction that we describe as "intervention" after Schmidt and Herrmann [1].

An intervention is a type of interaction where an automated process is modified by carrying out a more fine-grained control over a technology-supported process or where the process is completely interrupted [1]. The scope and effect of this intervention is limited – after a specified amount of time, the original process is resumed. The intervention helps users to adapt a process to their needs or to explore alternatives. Schmidt and Herrmann [1] employ the example of parking fully automated vehicles to

© Springer Nature Switzerland AG 2019
A. Malizia et al. (Eds.): IS-EUD 2019, LNCS 11553, pp. 67–82, 2019.
https://doi.org/10.1007/978-3-030-24781-2_5

explain the necessity of such an interaction paradigm. If the user only leaves the car, it will park itself. If s/he wants to control the parking location, e.g. to avoid a certain area, s/he has to intervene. The objectives of intervention are similar to those of EUD but interventions are ad hoc and their effects are not sustained.

With the following analysis, we theoretically investigate the differences and commonalities between intervention and EUD. EUD supports users who do not have a background in programming to develop or modify their own applications. Regarding Lieberman et al. [2] "End-User Development can be defined as a set of methods, techniques, and tools that allow users of software systems, who are acting as non-professional software developers, at some point to create, modify or extend a software artefact" (p. 2). We draw from this that a broad scope of possibilities can be provided to empower users with more or less technical skills.

We share the perspective of Fischer [3] that EUD takes place in a socio-technical context. This is true for intervention as well [4]. The use of technological infrastructure is intertwined with a social dimension represented by communication and collaboration of human actors, their interests, practices, competences, various role taking etc. Consequently, EUD and interventions are not mainly conducted individually but together with others. They do not only influence technical infrastructure but also the behavior of others within social interactions.

Intervention is a phenomenon that mainly occurs in exceptional cases and it is difficult to make it the subject of systematic empirical field studies. Therefore, we start with a theoretical analysis based on literature and by considering smart homes as an exemplary field that provide a rich collection of interrelated automated processes that cannot be a subject of fine-grained control, but where intervention is needed from time to as well as adaptation. Thus, we consider infrastructure as a web of relations (cf. [5]) where we focus on the dynamics of those relations that are represented by ongoing processes. They are also a subject of "… the tension between local, customized, intimate and flexible use on the one hand, and the need for standards and continuity on the other" ([5], p. 112).

Smart homes are a typical example for such an infrastructure with the following characteristics [6–9]:

- Many different appliances and services are running in parallel;
- smart home applications are used by multiple household members;
- service providers from outside can be connected to smart home arrangements;
- the needs of using smart home functionalities are changing, depending on contextual influences and are hard to anticipate;
- we can assume various and rich practices of employing smart home features.

Apparently, smart homes are socio-technical settings that include collaboration and dealing with privacy issues [7, 8]. Furthermore, multiple end-user development tools for the smart home are available, but lack support for collaboration and rule management [10]. Smart homes are also used to help elderly people to extend the time they live in their own homes [8]. This example suggests that a wide range of smart home users need an easy to use interface – also covering the possibility of including the help of others – for influencing the technical functionalities.

The question to be answered with respect to the possibilities and scenarios of smart home usage is: How can the difference and the commonalities between EUD and intervention be understood with the goal to integrate both of them from a socio-technical perspective? Furthermore, we want to point out that this theoretical analysis influences practical considerations of employing technology, of dealing with privacy requirements, and of guiding technical design.

In what follows, we first describe different concepts found in the literature that are related to the concept of intervention. Subsequently, we outline the various applications and their interplay in the case of smart homes to clarify the paradigm of intervention in a socio-technical context. Based on this we outline the interplay between intervention and EUD. The following discussion derives practical, privacy-related, and design-oriented implications from the theoretical considerations.

2   Related Work and Concepts in the Context of Intervention

The most recent theoretical descriptions of intervention in the context of human-computer interaction is given by Schmidt and Herrmann [1]: "Intervention in human-computer interaction is an action by the user that takes place during the usage of an automated system and initiates a diversion from the predefined behavior. Intervening interaction allows the user to alter the behavior of a process that is regularly highly automated, and continuously proceeds according to a plan or to situational awareness without the need for any interaction. This ad hoc change through exceptional control takes place in accordance with emerging user needs or situations" (p. 42). Furthermore, an intervention interface has to be provided that allows for awareness to identify the need for interventions and supports activities by tools or communication media to execute an intervention [1].

An earlier version of intervention within the context of human-computer interaction was coined by Herrmann [11] who relates this concept to the non-anticipated modification of dialogue sequences: "[…] the user aims at an anticipated subgoal using a non-anticipated dialogue-sequence, or […] aims at a non-anticipated sub-goal by her/his own methods" (p. 290). This concept differentiated between "regular task performance" – as it has been anticipated by the designers of an interactive system – and "non-anticipated use". The intervention according to Herrmann [11], and Schmidt and Herrmann [1] is also characterized by the interrelation between modification and exploration: An intervention can also be conducted to answer what-if-question, such as "What will happen if the system is used in an alternative way that has been neglected by the designers?". While Herrmann [11] suggests that users just employ the regular features of an interactive system to carry out irregular actions, Schmidt and Herrmann [1] suggest investing research for the design of an intervention interface.

2.1   Intervention in the Context of Implicit Interaction

The phenomenon of intervention is closely related to such types of automated systems that do not repeat the same procedure all the time but adapt to situations and behaviors of users. Therefore, they continuously exploit the contextual development of their environment. This concept is described as implicit interaction [12]. Schmidt [12] defines it as: "[…] an action, performed by the user that is not primarily aimed to interact with a computerized system but which such a system understands as input" (p. 191). Apparently, implicit interaction relies on sensors that register the development of a system's context and take it as input instead of requiring a user's control. Thus, implicit interaction enables a flow of automated behavior that is closely linked to the users' intentions without requiring continuous and explicit interaction – we describe this with our words as "interaction-free usage". However, it is expected that the context interpretation is not continuously appropriate, therefore interventions into the flow of implicit interaction are necessary. Thus, interventions represent the opposite side of implicit interaction.

To give an example, Schmidt and Herrmann [1] refer to automatic parking of a car: The granularity of control decreases from self-controlled to highly assisted to completely automated parking of a car. In an autonomous car, the user exits the car, and the car autonomously finds a parking space, parks, and comes back in time to pick the person up. If the driver wants to avoid that the car will park itself at a certain spot or area, s/he has to intervene.

We suggest that this concept of implicit interaction can also be transferred to the socio-technical level: For example, deriving hints from a customer's purchasing behavior to guide other customers is a result of implicit interaction. And apparently, there is a lack of intervention possibilities to suppress such exploitation in certain cases, e.g. if users do not want that their behavior is understood as a recommendation to others.

2.2   Intervention into Privacy-Related Processes and Data

A different line of research describes "intervenability" in relation to privacy and data protection, rooted in theories from sociology. Intervenability is considered [13] as a requirement for data protection in designing socio-technical systems. In the data protection discourse, which is driven by legal requirements, "intervenability" refers to the rights of the individual to withdraw consent, object to the results of an automated decision or request the deletion of their data. To implement these rights in the socio-technical processes of organizations, Rost and Bock [13] suggest implementing a single point of contact to which data subjects can address their requests; as well as the need for data flows to allow interruptions without disrupting the overall process. On a higher level, the idea is to allow individuals to infuse contingency into the data and data processing so that possible conclusions drawn from data in the context of other data does not necessarily lead to deterministic or solicited results. In the socio-technical context, for example, it has been argued that tracking users on the web to create profiles has a significant privacy impact as these profiles can affect what services users can access and what price they pay. One successful way of intervening in these profiles, besides blocking the tracking, has been to intentionally obfuscate the data to influence the profile in a specific direction [14].

Privacy-related interventions have seen some intentional adoption by business, too. Facebook uses highly automated processes to determine what advertisements are shown to which users. After these processes have been heavily criticized for being privacy invasive, non-transparent and manipulative, the social network has introduced two levels of intervention. First, users that feel uncomfortable with a particular ad can select it to be hidden from them in the future. Second, those that get the impression that there is something generally wrong with how they are targeted with ads can review and change ("Why am I seeing this ad") the underlying profile Facebook has created about them. Obviously, both types of influence, one being more a spontaneous intervention and the other being more systematic like EUD, do not only serve the purpose of giving control back to users. Facebook also benefits from the feedback as it allows them to adapt their algorithms and to supply more accurately targeted ads in the future. Research has also shown that the transparency provided by the social network about the effects of users' interventions and modifications is often vague, misleading or incomplete [15].

2.3 Interventions and Workarounds in Relation to End-User Development

The definitions cited above describe intervention as interactions that have not been anticipated or allow behavior patterns of users that deviate from predefined flows. Another way to deal with these kinds of situations are workarounds. Workarounds are specific ways of acting that are carried out intentionally to perform a specific task although these ways are not expected or allowed. In some cases, it might be even illegal or seems just to be appropriate by an observer [16]. Workarounds can alter the system. They are unexpected, unplanned and usually not directed to explore the system. Interventions allow to alter the system temporarily but provide revert mechanisms, while attempting to change a system and related automated processes – or at least parts of them – and thus are an endeavor of appropriation (cf. [17]). Workarounds try to get along with tasks without influencing the system but getting around its constraints.

By contrast, EUD has similar intentions as workarounds (to modify the ways of task handling) but by changing the underlying system. Our understanding of EUD is based on the overview by Liebermann et al. [2]. We assume for the context of using automated systems and processes that users are not regularly interacting with the employed technology (but only when doing interventions) and therefore a very low threshold of entering into EUD is necessary. Those kinds of low thresholds are provided by offering a mode of configuring a system for example by setting parameters or by graphical means. We suggest that most needs for EUD-based modification become only apparent during usage and that conducting such a modification appears the more desirable the more the results of EUD are needed.

We share the view of those scholars [18, 19] that emphasize that EUD always takes place in a socio-technical context and does not only influence the technical infrastructure but also the social dimension. Intervention and EUD are part of socio-technical processes and modify them. Thus EUD – as well as intervention – can be a collaborative endeavor that is supported by CSCW-applications [20]. EUD might be delegated to "gardeners" (cf. [21]) that are more experienced with modifying a technical system than regular users. We suggest that these gardeners might also be helpful for interventions. Furthermore, the subjects of EUD and interventions are not only algorithms but also people who routinely run or participate in a socio-technical process.

3   The Case of Smart Homes – Overview and Examples of Interventions

With the term "smart home", we refer to an ensemble of applications and services that are based on a growing number of sensors, actors and automated processes that benefit the users. Smart homes offer a broad scope of such benefits in the areas of safety, energy management, and lifestyle support [6–9] such as:

- energy saving by shifting energy-intensive procedures like washing to hours with high and potentially cheap availability of energy
- improving the climate and air-condition of the home e.g. through reducing heating on sunny days or at night
- automatic lighting ranging from a simple motion controlled night-light to complex arrangements of hundreds of individually controllable RGB light bulbs
- increasing safety and the privacy of the home, e.g. by identifying potential intruders or notifying about open windows and doors
- allowing more independence for people with special needs like elderly or disabled people through monitoring of the inhabitants and signaling potential accidents or illnesses, or by supporting them in everyday live (ambient assisted living).

These processes and services rely on implicit interaction to ease and automate common procedures. The user's regular interaction or usage history with the appliances of the household is collected to find repeated patterns which an intelligent agent could automate [9, 22]. Furthermore, these processes can be interrelated, for example by technical means if a motion sensor or speech recognition support various of those processes or if they are dependent on each other. Another type of interrelation can be provided by service providers that react on security issues as well as in the case that somebody needs help. The various processes might also be logically connected for example if the alarm system states that people are at home, but the light controlling motion detectors do not register any movement this could be interpreted as an indicator that help is needed. Such logical connections can be configured in advance using Event-Condition-Action (ECA) rules, e.g. "At 10 pm [event] if any windows are open [condition] remind me to close them [action]", and are employed to support EUD in smart homes [10, 23].

3.1   Interventions to Stop or Change Processes

A simple example of intervention support is the "Party Button" of many central heating systems. When pressed it keeps the heating in the whole house on during the night instead of turning it down earlier in the evening. It is designed as an exception. The system's behavior is changed only for this night and the default configuration is resumed the next day. This behavior is hard to design using ECA rules or implicit interaction since it occurs only exceptional. The conditions are not fully known in advance and it is hard to derive from people's behavior how long they will be present or active.

Heating systems in smart homes enable more fine-grained control such as separate rooms or individual radiators than the central ones considered before. Therefore, the design of an intervention interface could aim on a more precise and versatile control. Only specific areas like the living room or kitchen can be targeted. This allows limiting the intervention to a specific *scope*. Targeting only the living room for an evening of video streaming or the kitchen for a dinner party.

Misinterpreting the changes made to a heating system usually do not lead to severe consequences. This is different, however, with smart home appliances that are focused on safety and security as in the domain of ambient assisted living. Fall detectors can be integrated into the floor or put under the carpet. If the monitored person falls, an alarm is triggered without the need for pressing a button or using the phone. The system might be turned off on rare occasions to avoid false alarms e.g. if the grandchildren visit and jump and roll on the floor. If the systems are not turned back on afterwards, the expected monitoring and protection are not in place and an emergency can remain unnoticed. An intervention must be designed as such that the safety-related behavior is resumed if certain conditions are met. Either conditions can be an elapsed timer or the start of a new day or as needed in the latter example that the person is alone again and monitoring needs to be resumed. Therefore, a sensible intervention would allow pausing the monitoring for as long as the person is under supervision but resume operation otherwise. Having a *resumption condition* is critical in safety-related systems and a typical aspect of intervention design.

3.2 Interventions in Shared Settings

Furthermore, interventions need to consider context and actors, and their understanding of the system and the automated processes. Consequences of the intervention need to be immediately visible. This visibility allows exploring the system and trying out what-if-scenarios. "How does my energy consumption change if the average temperature is raised by 2 °C for a certain time span?" Immediate means to revert such changes in the event of unintended consequences are needed e.g. if the intervention will close the window blinds in all rooms of the house to avoid additional heat from the sunlight, it should be clear whether other residents are affected who might need daylight. All in all, exploration of possible adaptation and what-if-scenarios can be an important reason to intervene with the data of the usage or interaction history. E.g. if the user wants to see how the system would adapt if he worked a full time job instead of half time. Such explorations are usually not intended to change the systems configuration and end-users need to be confident that they can revert their actions. Therefore, undo-mechanisms are required to support the end-users to return to a known and working state.

Most smart homes are shared spaces and needs can be different among its members. Intervention can cause conflicts. Lifting all window blinds at 8:00 am is the default behavior. If a teenager applies an intervention to keep all blinds down until 2:00 pm to sleep in this can cause conflicts. E.g. if the scope of the intervention is not limited to the teenager's room and all members are affected which rely on the open blinds to wake up early. Therefore, applied interventions must not only be visible but potentially negotiable between the affected actors.

Interventions can also serve as a means to share control temporary with visitors. For the duration of their visit, certain interventions are allowed for the visitor. Like deactivating appliance like virtual private assistants (VPAs) to allow for private conversations. Control the intensity of light and genre of music played in the bathroom as well as the sink's water temperature. However, any changes made by the visitor are generally non-permanent and can be reverted when s/he leaves.

3.3   Interventions Offer Fine-Grained Control

Interventions do not only allow ending, pausing and resuming automated behavior but also switch to fine-grained control. When food is spilled on the floor, an autonomous vacuum cleaner can be instructed manually to clean it up. Some devices also allow to be used in a non-anticipated way such as switching it to manual control for cleaning to use it to play with the cat. Afterward, the intervention is stopped and the device is switched back to automated control and proceeds with its predefined routines.

3.4   Interventions in Profiles

To adapt to the users' needs and automate repeated sequences of interaction, smart homes maintain a history of technology-driven processes or of interactions with them and may create a profile of its user. Those profiles can also be a subject of intervention targeting the data used for automation instead of the automated processes itself. E.g., individual utterances towards a VPA might be deleted because they seem inappropriate afterwards or the users want to obfuscate their habits. Another reason for modifying a profile may be that a visitor of a smart home has special needs, and his/her way of using the smart home causes lasting but unwanted changes in the profiles of inhabitants. For instance, through his/her interaction with the smart home the profile might change and eventually lead to an inappropriate adaptation of services etc. Offering the regular inhabitants an interface for intervening into the underlying data of such an adaptation supports them to maintain control of their automated processes.

3.5   Key Properties of Interventions

Considering the presented examples in the context of smart homes several key properties can be identified which not all have been considered before. The first is the *resumption condition*—when is the automated behavior continued and the intervention stopped. Second the *scope* of the intervention—what is affected by it: a specific area, a system, a certain step of or a whole process and what actions have to be overtaken by the user. Additionally, interventions allow the *exploration* of possible changes regarding the configuration and data and their consequences for the users with accessible means to revert or to keep the changes.

4   The Relation of EUD and Intervention

4.1   Differentiation Between Means and Effects

In the following, we clarify the various aspects of how an intervention can take place and what may be affected by the intervention. Furthermore, we explain how the difference between intervention (c.f. Table 1) and EUD-based configuration (c.f. Table 2) looks like. For this purpose, we use the example of automated alarms like the fall detector in the previous section. Other typical alarms in households can be caused by movements in and around the house during certain periods (e.g. at the backdoor during the night) or by heat detectors. Possible interventions are suppressing false alarms or postponing the activation of an alarm before the occupant leaves the house.

An alarm can be the starting point of a complex socio-technical process where social actors are involved as well as social interaction. For example, the alarm of the fall detector triggers a contract-based service taking care of the fallen person. This includes bringing the person to a doctor for a medical investigation in every case because of the service provider's liability. To stop such a procedure, an intervention of social actors (e.g. relatives) who can prove that they are legitimated is required to take over the responsibility. For Table 1, we assume a scenario where a false alarm is triggered e.g. by a sensor that registers that someone has fallen to the ground or by evaluating multiple sensor inputs that indicate that somebody is not able to follow his or her typical everyday routines.

Table 1. Different modes of intervention into a socio-technical system

Intervention into ...	... the technical system	... the socio-technical system (affecting social actors)
Intervention by ...		
... employing technical means	(a) After an alarm is set off, the supervised person can reset it by entering a 5-digit code within one minute. Such a reset is only possible one time per hour	(b) Instead of entering a code, the supervised person starts an audio-video connection to his room for half an hour. Thus, the service employee can see and hear whether everything is okay
... including the help of social actors (socio-technical)	(c) Like (a) but the originator of the false alarm asks a relative or a member of the household to enter the code. This procedure has to be completed within 5 to 10 min	(d) The alarm's originator informs a relative who tries to stop the initiated procedure by calling an employee of the service provider

The nature of the procedures being started after such an alarm is that it runs predominantly automatic and the social actors being involved are instructed to follow pre-specified routines. Interventions, as described above, are an exception. If interventions take place more often, this can be a reason for a modification that is initiated by an end-user. These modifications in contrast to interventions change the automated behavior permanently. In this scenario, the modification can aim either on avoiding future false alarms or on improving the way of dealing with them. The examples of Table 2 refer to the second option.

Table 2. Different modes of configuration of a socio-technical system

Configuration of ...	... the technical system	... the socio-technical system (affecting social actors)
Configuration by ...		
...employing technical means	(e) The person to whom an alarm relates determines that he or she can reset the alarm by using speech recognition: After an alarm, the systems asks whether a serious incident took place and by the calling of a predefined phrase the alarm can be stopped	(f) The person being supervised modifies her/his contract with the service provider: after an alarm, the audio-video connection is automatically started and transfers pictures for 10 min that have to be observed before somebody is sent out
... including the help of social actors (socio-technical)	(g) A relative is asked to modify the alarm triggering mechanism as described in (e) and a protocol is signed documenting consent to such modification	(h) A relative negotiates with the service provider to change the procedure as described in (f)

The examples of the right column go beyond the usual scope of EUD since the behavior of social actors is influenced instead of those of a technical system. However, this an indirect way of influencing the technology: if the users or their relatives and the service provider agree upon the modification of the procedures or the contract this implies a change of the technical system.

Obviously, the handling of alarms, interventions and the preparation of configuration is accompanied by continuous elicitation of data that includes a significant amount of personal identifiable information. For example, establishing an audio-video channel as mentioned above conveys a lot of data about personal behavior. In many cases, collecting such data along automated or routinized procedures can be helpful to improve the quality of services or the safety of people. However, it can also happen that these possibilities can violate people's privacy. To counteract, intervention interfaces are needed: People can interrupt the automatic establishing of audio-video connections.

4.2   Series of Interventions as a Preparation of EUD-Based (Re-) Configuration

From the example of the two tables above, we can generally conclude that a series of the same type of intervention can be an indicator that a reconfiguration of the socio-technical system is necessary or reasonable. Such a point can also be reached in many other cases, for example if the party button presented in the previous section is not only used occasionally but several times a week throughout the year. As soon as the intervention is no longer an exception, the system must adapt or must be adapted.

This interplay is outlined by Fig. 1: Based on an initial configuration of a socio-technical system, regular usage of or collaboration within a system can be interrupted by casual intervention. Repetitive interventions of the same type can initiate adaptation. When an adaptation is made, the former exceptional state has become the new normality and the former normal state the exception. In such a constellation, the intervention can be used to undo the EUD-based modification. Furthermore, the EUD-based modification can also address the parameters of the intervention. For instance, the time span of delaying the shutdown of the heating system in the case of the party-button could be changed or the time span within which an alarm could be revoked.

The socio-technical view has to include two options. On the one hand, a user can directly execute an adaptation as it is typically suggested by end-user development [2]. This could possibly be supported by the system itself by proposing certain adaptations. On the other hand, a reconfiguration can be delegated to an authorized person or organization. Under certain circumstances, the re-configuration can only take place after it has been negotiated and approved by the group of potentially affected stakeholders. Within socio-technical arrangements, the effects of configuration and re-configuration can also address various roles.

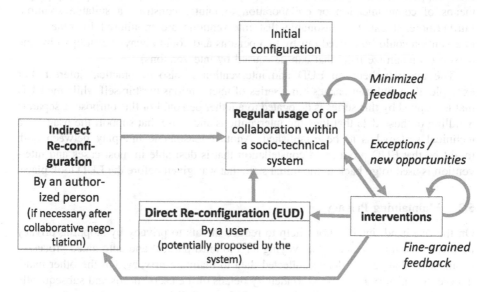

Fig. 1. The relationship between regular usage, intervention, and configuration (derived from Schmidt and Herrmann 2017)

5 Discussion

The theoretical comparison between intervention and EUD in a socio-technical context has also practical relevance. Furthermore, it is of special value to not only consider the functionality of a technical system but also the handling of privacy issues from the perspective of intervention and EUD. A key to realize the benefits of intervention is to explicitly design an intervention interface that can cover several automated and interrelated processes as it is the case with smart home applications.

5.1   Practical Relevance

Providing a well-designed intervention interface is a lightweight possibility to help users to adapt automatically initiated or running processes to ad hoc emerging needs. Even more important is the avoidance of risks: Without the possibilities of intervention, people tend to switch off the systems or avoid their usage. An example is the problem with Advanced Emergency Braking Systems (AEBS) that are used in trucks to avoid dangerous collisions. They are frequently switched off since they produce too many false-positive warnings [24, 25]. Intervention avoids these risks since it is its inherent condition that it is only possible within a limited scope, and that the regular process is resumed after a while or if the user remains inactive.

Employing the socio-technical perspective has practical relevance since intervention as well as EUD can be a collaborative matter. Possibly, a person A wants to intervene into an automated procedure that was specified by a user B by employing EUD-support. Thus, negotiation is necessary between the two parties requiring proper means of communication or collaboration to jointly construct a suitable solution. Furthermore, it can be reasonable that interventions are monitored by others; or, intervention could be carried out by two persons and could always be stopped by one person (to minimize risks that can be caused by interventions).

The interplay between EUD and intervention is also of practical interest. For example, if an end-user carries out a series of interventions her/himself while the EUD that is inspired by this series is delegated to another person. For this purpose, a separate handling of those data that logs the interventions and those that support the usage of a technical system has to be established. Another reasonable interplay between both might be that EUD produces a constellation that is desirable in most cases and intervention is used to go back to the initial state that was given before the EUD took place.

5.2   Maintaining Privacy

On the one hand, interventions help to reduce threats to privacy by stopping privacy invasive procedures (such as conveying data to third parties) and automated processes or allow to change and delete collected data to maintain privacy. On the other hand, intervention history is collected to identify details of the users' needs and subsequently areas of interest for end-user development. This possibility adds more data to the profile of the user. The decision not to share certain data at a certain point in time or to subsequently modify and delete certain interactions may provide more sensitive information than normal interaction data. However, the ability to explore what-if scenarios increases transparency and enables effective changes of the profile and introduces contingency.

Users can not only delete or change data in their profiles, but can also add data, such as random times when they might have used particular devices. Consequently, they can not only expand their profile and correct errors but also influence their profile in a particular direction. Service providers can hardly use these profiles for marketing purposes or for determining flexible insurance contributions because the profiles can partly be based on artificial data. It may be reasonable to automate such interventions because they may need to be applied regularly to achieve the desired results. These kinds of automated interventions can be a subject of EUD.

5.3   Implications for Design

The need for intervention interfaces has already been stated by Schmidt and Herrmann [1]. In the following, we draw implications for the design of such interfaces from our analysis and show how this interconnects with the requirements and potentials of EUD.

The recording of interventions that have taken place can help to identify the need for change and possible areas of interest for EUD. The integration of an intervention interface with EUD allows at least for three ways of utilizing the log file data of interventions: by the system itself to propose an adaptation, by the end-users themselves, or by their partners. The system has to be designed to differentiate between two types of data collected – what is needed for the services vs. what is needed to prepare EUD.

When users employ interventions to explore the system, they can be empowered to eventually start with EUD to replace the temporary effects being achieved by intervention with permanent changes. Based on the collected data of the applied interventions, areas or entry points for conducting EUD can be identified. EUD-support should display the actions and parameters of recent interventions so that they can serve as a starting point for further refinement by EUD.

With respect to shared applications in the smart home context, intervention interfaces could be designed in a way where others are notified or at least aware of an ongoing intervention. In some cases, others should or must have the opportunity to influence an intervention someone else initiated (intervention-into-intervention). Such conflicting interventions and possible needs demand to be negotiated. This can only be accomplished if both actors fully understand the interventions they want to employ and the consequences this will have. Interventions need to be perceived as a closed loop with a clear start and end point. Limiting the interventions with respect to a time span, the parameter scope or the frequency of its occurrence can support this perception.

Designing an intervention user interface is a complex challenge because many parameters and possible variants must be communicated ad hoc to the users without obstructing them. If the user has not fully understood the consequences of her/his actions or does not like the result, simple mechanisms are needed to return to the previous state.

Interventions can be the subject not only of software design before use but also of EUD during use. Allowing to combine several interventions into one or to define events and conditions for specific interventions to ease their repetition can be considered by EUD. Similarly, the parameters that characterize an intervention (like the delay time of party buttons) can be a subject of EUD. As interventions address emerging needs of the users, they cannot be fully specified in advance but must adapt to and be adaptable to the users' needs.

Consequently, an intervention interface has to include several parts:

- Awareness information that indicate a possible need for intervention,
- an easy way to start an intervention (but avoiding unintended starts),
- an immediate and continuing notification about the scope and implication of the intervention,
- possible undo of undesired implications,
- an offer for a transition from an intervention to EUD including a record of the scope and effects of the same type of interventions that took place.

6 Conclusion and Further Work

We relate the concept of EUD and intervention to ensembles of simultaneously used automated processes, as for example smart home technologies. For this realm, we have derived theoretical commonalities and differences that can help to guide the design of this kind of technologies and the organization of their usage.

Commonalities are:

- Both deal with non-anticipated needs and behavior (e.g. allow to use an autono-mous vacuum cleaner as a toy)
- They empower the end-users by helping them to be in control (e.g. by temporary overriding the energy saving defaults of a heating system)
- Both can be prepared by meta-design [26]
- They are embedded into socio-technical processes where various people or orga-nizations support or influence each other (e.g. in the case of alarms with its pre-specified routines).

Furthermore, intervention and EUD both influence different areas alike: The tech-nical functionality of a system (e.g. postponing the shutdown of the heating system by a party button), the content represented by data that is processed by functions, and that may be related to privacy concerns (e.g. hiding details of data collected by a smart meter through aggregating it), and the behavior of the people in the socio-technical system that interact with technology – either directly or through delegation – in the course of automated processes (e.g. by informing a service provider that an alarm was falsely activated). It has to be noted that every single instance of intervention or EUD may potentially affect all three of these areas at the same time. Beside spanning all these three areas, the end-user is not required to do EUD on her/his own, but can instruct others actors to do so. In addition, interventions can be launched on behalf of others.

The differences are:

- Intervention has only ephemeral effects on the way a system is used, while EUD aims to achieve a sustainable change of how somebody deals with an automated process
- The effects based on an intervention are only exceptionally desired while the effort being invested into EUD is the more efficient the more it aims at regularly occurring needs of users

- Intervention takes place ad hoc to cause immediate effects while EUD is oriented on future situations
- Possibilities to resume the regular mode and reverse the effects of interventions are necessary for intervention design, while EUD aims at changing of what is considered as regular.

Interplay between intervention and EUD:

- Intervention prepares EUD
- EUD helps to pre-specify the effects and limitations of interventions
- The intervention will revise the impact of the EUD if, exceptionally, it is not adequate.

The differences and commonalities shown and the derived design implications help to design interfaces for intervention and to prepare their socio-technical integration. In addition, they support the transition from intervention to EUD and provide end-users with lightweight means to adopt EUD. Vice versa, end-users could extend and adapt interventions through means of EUD.

Further research is needed to design intervention interfaces that cover an ensemble of intertwined automated processes, as in the case with smart homes, and evaluate them in a series of design cycles.

References

1. Schmidt, A., Herrmann, T.: Intervention user interfaces: a new interaction paradigm for automated systems. Interactions **24**, 40–45 (2017). https://doi.org/10.1145/3121357
2. Lieberman, H., Paternò, F., Klann, M., Wulf, V.: End-user development: an emerging paradigm. In: Lieberman, H., Paternò, F., Wulf, V. (eds.) End User Development, vol. 9, pp. 1–8. Springer, Dordrecht (2006). https://doi.org/10.1007/1-4020-5386-X_1
3. Fischer, G.: End-user development: from creating technologies to transforming cultures. In: Dittrich, Y., Burnett, M., Mørch, A., Redmiles, D. (eds.) IS-EUD 2013. LNCS, vol. 7897, pp. 217–222. Springer, Heidelberg (2013). https://doi.org/10.1007/978-3-642-38706-7_16
4. Herrmann, T., Schmidt, A., Degeling, M.: From interaction to intervention: an approach for keeping humans in control in the context of socio-technical systems. In: Proceedings of the 4th International Workshop on Socio-Technical Perspective in IS development (STPIS 2018) Co-located with 30th International Conference on Advanced Information Systems Engineering (CAiSE 2018), Tallinn, Estonia, 12 June 2018, pp. 101–110 (2018)
5. Star, S.L., Ruhleder, K.: Steps toward an ecology of infrastructure: design and access for large information spaces. Inf. Syst. Res. **7**, 111–134 (1996)
6. Alam, M.R., Reaz, M.B.I., Ali, M.A.M.: A review of smart homes—past, present, and future. IEEE Trans. Syst. Man Cybernet. Part C (Appl. Rev.) **42**, 1190–1203 (2012). https://doi.org/10.1109/tsmcc.2012.2189204
7. Balta-Ozkan, N., Davidson, R., Bicket, M., Whitmarsh, L.: Social barriers to the adoption of smart homes. Energy Policy **63**, 363–374 (2013). https://doi.org/10.1016/j.enpol.2013.08.043
8. Wilson, C., Hargreaves, T., Hauxwell-Baldwin, R.: Smart homes and their users: a systematic analysis and key challenges. Pers. Ubiquit. Comput. **19**, 463–476 (2015)

9. Cook, D.J., et al.: MavHome: an agent-based smart home. In: Proceedings of the First IEEE International Conference on Pervasive Computing and Communications (PerCom 2003), pp. 521–524. IEEE Computer Society, Fort Worth (2003)

10. Caivano, D., Fogli, D., Lanzilotti, R., Piccinno, A., Cassano, F.: Supporting end users to control their smart home: design implications from a literature review and an empirical investigation. J. Syst. Softw. **144**, 295–313 (2018)

11. Herrmann, T.: Support of intervening use. In: Ergonomics of Hybrid Automated Systems III, pp. 289–294. Elsevier (1992). https://www-imtm.iaw.ruhr-uni-bochum.de/sociotech-lit.php?file=Herr92-SoI.pdf

12. Schmidt, A.: Implicit human computer interaction through context. Pers. Technol. **4**, 191–199 (2000)

13. Rost, M., Bock, K.: Privacy by design and the new protection goals. European Privacy Seal (2011)

14. Degeling, M.: Online Profiling - Analyse und Intervention zum Schutz von Privatheit (2016). https://duepublico.uni-due.de/servlets/DocumentServlet?id=42157

15. Andreou, A., Venkatadri, G., Goga, O., Gummadi, K.P., Loiseau, P., Mislove, A.: Investigating ad transparency mechanisms in social media: a case study of Facebook's explanations. In: Proceedings 2018 Network and Distributed System Security Symposium. Internet Society, San Diego (2018). https://doi.org/10.14722/ndss.2018.23191

16. Alter, S.: Theory of workarounds. Commun. Assoc. Inf. Syst. **34**, 1041–1066 (2014). https://doi.org/10.17705/1cais.03455

17. Pipek, V.: From Tailoring to Appropriation Support: Negotiating Groupware Usage Faculty of Science (2005)

18. Barricelli, B.R., Cassano, F., Fogli, D., Piccinno, A.: End-user development, end-user programming and end-user software engineering: a systematic mapping study. J. Syst. Softw. **149**, 101–137 (2019). https://doi.org/10.1016/j.jss.2018.11.041

19. Fischer, G., Fogli, D., Piccinno, A.: Revisiting and broadening the meta-design framework for end-user development. In: Paternò, F., Wulf, V. (eds.) New Perspectives in End-User Development, pp. 61–97. Springer, Cham (2017). https://doi.org/10.1007/978-3-319-60291-2_4

20. Bødker, S., Lyle, P.: Community end-user development: patterns, platforms, possibilities and problems. IS-EUD 2017, p. 76 (2017)

21. Nardi, B.A.: A Small Matter of Programming: Perspectives on End User Computing. MIT Press, Cambridge (1993)

22. Heierman, E.O., Cook, D.J.: Improving home automation by discovering regularly occurring device usage patterns. In: Third IEEE International Conference on Data Mining, pp. 537–540. IEEE Computer Society, Melbourne (2003)

23. Ur, B., McManus, E., Pak Yong Ho, M., Littman, M.L.: Practical trigger-action programming in the smart home. In: Proceedings of the 32nd Annual ACM Conference on Human Factors in Computing Systems - CHI 2014, pp. 803–812. ACM Press, Toronto (2014)

24. Örtlund, R.: Evaluation of AEBS Real Life Performance - A Method for Using Limited Log Data Applied on Volvo Trucks (2017)

25. Inagaki, T.: Technological and legal considerations for the design of interactions between human driver and advanced driver assistance systems. In: Proceedings of NeTWork Workshop: Control and Accountability in Highly Automated Systems (2011)

26. Fischer, G., Herrmann, T.: Meta-design: transforming and enriching the design and use of socio-technical systems. In: Wulf, V., Schmidt, K., Randall, D. (eds.) Designing Socially Embedded Technologies in the Real-World. CSCW, pp. 79–109. Springer, London (2015). https://doi.org/10.1007/978-1-4471-6720-4_6

Facilitating the Development of IoT Applications in Smart City Platforms

Stefano Valtolina$^{(\boxtimes)}$, Fatmeh Hachem, Barbara Rita Barricelli,
Elefelious Getachew Belay, Sara Bonfitto, and Marco Mesiti

Dipartimento di Informatica, Università degli Studi di Milano, Milan, Italy
{valtolin, hachem, barricelli, belay,
mesiti}@di.unimi.com, bonfitto@studenti.di.unimi.com

Abstract. In smart city domain, several IoT platforms exist for supporting city managers and operators in controlling and managing events occurring in the city and making decisions to improve citizens' quality of life. In such systems, for the combination of heterogonous events operators have to manually face the interoperability barriers that arise when dealing with IoT devices belonging to cross-domain IoT platforms. This paper focuses on how to provide city operators with visual and easy-to-use strategies for developing IoT applications that need to access and integrate data originated by various devices spread through a city that communicate according to different communication protocols, event formats, structures and sometimes meaning. The purpose of these strategies is to reduce the time required for the development of IoT applications and the number of mistakes in the configuration of the IoT devices. In details, we propose a solution developed in Node-RED, a visual programming tool for wiring together sensors, actuators and services. Our contribution aims at presenting a solution specifically tailored for domain experts who need to develop different kinds of analysis on city data who are not computer experts, but experts in monitoring weather, traffic, or events that happen in the city. A usability analysis is finally reported in order to assess the design strategies that we have developed.

Keywords: IoT · Smart city · End-User Development · Node-RED

1 Introduction

A Smart City aims at improving the experience of the citizens through Information and Communication Technologies (ICT), while supporting social, business, and technological aspects of the city. To achieve that, the city provides public and private services that operate in an integrated and effective way. To make a city smarter, it is necessary to deal with a very large amount of data collected by interconnected devices that have to be grouped and processed to provide advanced services. These services leverage the difficulties in managing the connection with physical devices by exploiting IoT Brokers (like Mosquitto [1], FIWARE Orion [2], oneM2M [3]). By means of the publish-subscribe paradigm, these brokers act as a unified interface to the IoT devices, facilitating access to the middleware data. They make easier exposing sensor and actuator devices and allow applications to subscribe to the available channels for reading their

© Springer Nature Switzerland AG 2019
A. Malizia et al. (Eds.): IS-EUD 2019, LNCS 11553, pp. 83–99, 2019.
https://doi.org/10.1007/978-3-030-24781-2_6

observations. Systems like SmartSantander [4] are moving in this direction by exposing the devices to the cloud and facilitating the development of applications.

To deal with the massive data coming from these different IoT brokers on which the IoT devices are registered, city operators have to manually deal with the interoperability barriers that arise when they have to carry out analysis on integrated data for understanding what happens in the city. Indeed, the data produced by these platforms might adopt different formats (XML, JSON, CSV), and different schema and terminologies for representing the data; also the way data is transmitted differs on the basis of the protocol used (MQTT, AMQP, NGSI, OneM2M protocol). Therefore, the operators have to spend a lot of time configuring the IoT devices for reading observations from sensors and for cleaning and representing the information in a common format and meaning.

For supporting the city operators in the development of IoT applications, several visual programming environments have been proposed for the graphical design of workflows and dataflows as graphs of connected nodes representing tasks and datasources able to combine the streams of event flows generated by the IoT devices. Among the commercial systems, we mention Talend Studio [5], StreamBase Studio [6], Waylay.io [7], whereas in the open source arena, the most promising solutions are process engines such as Eclipse Kura (in conjunction with Apache Camel), Node-RED and Flogo. Most of these systems offer facilities for accessing and configuring IoT brokers and taking events generated by the controlled devices. However, the management of the interoperability barriers existing among them is completely delegated to the developers. An abstract approach, mediated by the use of a common Ontology, for accessing to the events generated by these devices is required that simplifies the development of IoT applications.

To deal with these problems the Snap4City [8] platform has been realized in the context of a pre-commercial procurement launched by the SELECT4CITY European project. The main goal of Snap4City is to put in the hands of city operators a flexible environment to quickly create a large range of smart city applications able to exploit heterogeneous IoT data and services. The current solution stems from real needs of smart cities like Antwerp, Helsinki, and Florence and aims at devising smart city services that combine public (open) and private data owned and managed by city operators addressing specific domains (e.g. transport, mobility, energy, health, tourist operators, culture and events).

In this paper we present a solution specifically tailored in the Snap4City platform for developing IoT applications based on Node-RED. Node-RED is a visual programming tool for quickly assembling data flows by wiring different kinds of building blocks that allow to handle IoT devices and different services for their management. In details, the Snap4City platform extends Node-RED with different building blocks that are specifically designed for city's data management. These building blocks rely on the use of the *IoT-Directory*, a service developed in Snap4City for dealing with devices, are able to access sensors and actuators in a uniform and semantically controlled manner independently of the IoT broker in charge of managing them.

In this paper, we describe how these extensions of Node-RED are able to facilitate city operators in the development of IoT applications. Our study aims at describing an End User Development (EUD) approach that can simplify the process of configuration of IoT brokers and make uniform the representation of the events generated by the different IoT brokers without forcing users to get bogged down in writing code.

To assess the effective utility of the developed framework, we have conducted a usability campaign with eighteen participants recruited among personnel and students of the University of Milano. The results of the user study have provided some indications related to the implementation of our solution. Specifically, our study has been focused on evaluating the effectiveness of the design of data flows in term of reducing the time required for the development of IoT applications and the number of mistakes in the configuration of the IoT devices.

The paper is structured as follows. Section 2 presents an overview of the interoperability issues that affect the smart city platforms and possible EUD strategies for empowering city operators in designing IoT applications. Then, Sect. 3 presents the Snap4City platform and the solution that we have developed for supporting city operators in designing flows for the acquisition of data from sensors and for sending commands and notifications to actuators. Section 4 discusses the usability campaign and the results obtained by enrolling eighteen users. Section 5 summarizes the main contribution of the paper.

2   City Operators Empowerment in Smart City Platform

2.1   Dealing with Interoperability in Smart City Contexts

Several platforms exist for supporting city managers in controlling events, managing what happens and making decisions to improve citizens' quality of life. An example is a project in Santander, Spain, that aims at supporting the development and deployment of Smart City applications [4] for processing a large variety of data, including traffic conditions, temperature, CO_2 emissions, humidity, and luminosity. Padova Smart City [9], Intelligent Cities (EPIC) project [10], ClouT [11] and OpenMTC [12], REPLICATE H2020, RESOLUTE H2020, Triangulum H2020, EIP [13] are other initiatives that provide smart city systems with a wide range of city services. In [14] and [15] authors present a survey of platforms that use both IoT and Cloud Computing as enabling technologies specifically suitable for the smart city scenarios and IoT such as Kaa, Bosch, FIWARE, CISCO, IBM and Carriots and few more.

In a smart city platform, the access to sensor events can be mediated by IoT brokers by mean of which IoT applications can subscribe to the real-time events produced by devices. IoT Brokers are mainly used for decoupling the event observations from their consumption. Specifically, a broker acts as a publish/subscribe system and in some cases (like Orion and OneM2M) they also offer APIs for querying the devices on behalf of applications, discovers resources, collects and aggregates data according to an internal model, notifies to applications if something happens to the devices.

Even if data are gathered through IoT brokers, these solutions do not solve the interoperability issue that happens when data are exchanged according to different communication protocols, event formats, structures and sometimes meaning. Interestingly, Gartner states in its Market Guide for IoT Integration [16] that "through 2018, half the cost of implementing IoT solutions will be spent on integration". Integration is thus a key for success of IoT but there is no "one-size-fits-all" solution.

Nowadays many efforts are devoted to design horizontal applications capable of integrating devices based on different protocols and belonging to different platforms. European projects (like OpenIoT, BIGIoT, Biotope, INTER-IoT, SymbIoTe) are moving in this direction and their idea is to offer facilities across all layers of the network stack in order to improve the interoperability among the different components involved in the management of sensors, actuators and network infrastructures. For example, XGSN [17] (extension of the GSN middleware [18]) proposes a middleware (at the base of the OpenIoT Project) that uses a Domain Ontology for mitigating the semantic interoperability issues arising when integrating heterogeneous physical and virtual sensors. These solutions capture elements of IoT applications through a standard semantic model, the W3C Semantic Sensor Networks (SSN) [19] that allows the abstraction/virtualization of sensors. This solution addresses the semantic interoperability between the data flows coming from distributed devices by specifying a uniform semantic model according to which significant events are represented and discovered.

In the proposed solution, we adopt a semantic model based on the Km4City Ontology [20] for aggregating data coming from distributed devices and we access these data through different IoT brokers. Km4city Ontology is used as semantic interoperability model in order to create a uniform layer abstracting from the physical details and mechanisms needed to access them through different IoT brokers. As IoT broker we take into account the ones that are typically used in smart city domains including FIWARE Orion Broker (NGSI protocol), Mosquitto (MQTT protocol) and RabbitMQ (AMQP protocol).

2.2 Visual Tools for Empowering City Operators

Our proposal stems in the frame of a European Project that aims at providing data coming from devices distributed in a city and made available through IoT brokers that rely on a common representation and meaning obtained by means of the Km4City Ontology. For dealing with these data and carrying out data analysis, we need an environment that can advocate the adoption of an End-User Development (EUD) approach [21] for supporting non-experts in computer science in designing services and dataflows [22–24]. EUD represents the ideal approach for empowering city operators and making them developers of IoT applications [25, 26] that are necessary for taking decision to solve problems related to the city. For example, suppose they need to design and develop IoT applications for monitoring the level of congestion of a street by regulating the duration of the semaphore lights and thus reducing the long queues in the principal streets. In the EUD approach this problem can be faced by providing a design environment where visual entities representing the devices are connected graphically to define the sequence of operations for checking the congestion of the streets and take decision on making longer the duration of the green light of a sequence of semaphores along the way or vice-versa to increase the duration of the red lights in other directions. Therefore, in such context, EUD activities need to support city operators for controlling and configuring more than one broker spread in different area of the city in order to combine and aggregate data coming from different devices.

This is a well-proven concept used in many data analysis/signal processing tools and allows non-programmers to define processes or algorithms. Commercial systems such as Talend Studio [5], StreamBase Studio [6], Waylay.io [7] offer graphical ETL (extract-transform-load) services for providing users with a workflow/dataflow editor for drawing graphs of connected nodes representing tasks and data-sources. In the open source arena, other solutions offer similar functionalities. The most outstanding examples are: Eclipse Kura [27] in conjunction with Apache Camel, Node-RED [28], and Flogo [29]. They leverage on communication protocols that are standards in IoT context of use, such as MQTT, FIWARE Orion, WebSockets or CoaP, but also other interfaces such as Twitter feeds or REST services. By exploiting these protocols and data sources, they are able to integrate and wire together hardware devices, APIs and online services to carry out data processing such as transformation, filtering, routing, aggregation, enrichment of data. These frameworks also share a development environment based on a visual flow editor to use without the need to write source code or create components using the SDKs and APIs.

Other visual strategies typically used in IoT field for modelling Event-Condition-Action rules can be described through the most famous systems that apply them: IFTTT[1], Atooma[2], and Yahoo's Pipes[3]. In [30–32] authors discuss how the first two design strategies support users without programming knowledge to define their context-dependent applications. Specifically [32] describes how these EUD strategies allow users to define sets of desired behaviors in response to specific events. This is made mainly through rules definition-wizards that rely on the sensors/devices states. Rules can be typically chosen among existing ones or can be tweaked through customization. Although this approach is well suited for putting in place a task automation layer across all sensors/devices in the IoT environment, it lacks in providing a full support for designing complete IoT applications able to combine huge numbers of heterogeneous city sensors and actuators published through distributed IoT brokers.

In general, environments based on visual flow editors, such as Kura, Node-RED, and Flogo, are more suitable to provide city operators with strategies for solving interoperability issues. These systems provide rich user interfaces able to support the full application lifecycle but in some cases specific conditions can be only created by adopting solutions based on programming languages paradigms (as for StreamSQL in StreamBase Studio or Java in Kura) or by personalizing existing templates having well-defined trigger policy (as in Waylay.io). Some frameworks are built for developers and integration specialists who are comfortable with writing code because it is quite complex to install and build an IoT integration service with this combination (e.g. Talend Studio, StreamBase Studio or Kura). Moreover, if we need to integrate not existing modules for accessing new IoT brokers we need to act on open source platforms. According to these considerations, Node-RED and Flogo are the most promising solutions.

---

[1] https://ifttt.com.

[2] http://www.atooma.com/.

[3] https://pipes.yahoo.com/pipes.

Node-RED focuses mainly on IoT edge integration on an IoT gateway; it is probably the most effective for rapid prototyping with a large portability and limited footprint. It is very easy to install and to create an IoT integration flow with just few clicks in a Web browser. It provides many preinstalled nodes based on *node.js* libraries that allow to perform different tasks, from interfacing to a light switch to accessing emails. It is possible to add new nodes by implement the related *node.js* library. As soon as these libraries are installed, new nodes appear in the Node-Red palette.

Flogo was built to realize very lightweight integration applications. Flogo is still a very young project under developer preview (released in October 2016 by TIBCO under BSD-style License). Briefly, Flogo is an ultralight Open Source Framework for IoT application and integration, which is based on *Go* language. Like Node-RED, it is a visual tool that is easy to install and get the hang of. The key difference with Node-RED is that it uses a less popular language and provides a smaller range of dashboard elements in the visual palette due to its youthfulness. Anyway, it is possible to deploy it on any device that supports *Go* binaries, and for this reason, it provides a very light-weight framework with great advantages in terms of cost, speed and agility.

In conclusion, comparing the current open-source solutions for graphically developing IoT applications, if you need an IoT gateway with powerful integration facilities and an easy-to-learn tool for designing IoT data-flows with a mature visual IDE, Node-RED appears to be a good solution.

Node-RED well supports the development of general dataflows allowing to connect and wire an extensive library of nodes already available and accessible through the integrated repository. Many of these nodes are provided by the Node-RED open source community and for designing IoT applications, some nodes exist that enable to get data from IoT devices by using common protocols such as MQTT, AMQP and NGSI.

Anyway, none of these systems provide support for the automatic configuration of IoT brokers and for facing the interoperability issues that arise when dealing with different IoT brokers thus demanding to the developers all these activities that can become quite long and complex when the number of devices that need to be handled is large. For this reason, in this paper we present an improvement of the visual IDE of Node-RED that is embedded in our Snap4City platform through the implementation of building blocks that can be used for graphically designing dataflows able to access data coming from a large number of sensors and actuators registered in the IoT directory and require to use different IoT brokers for their access.

3   City Operators Empowerment in Snap4City Platform

In order to provide city operators with a graphical environment for the specification of applications working with streams of IoT data and able to provide edge integration solutions we propose a solution based on the use of Node-RED platform integrated with the information about devices and their sensors/actuators contained in the IoT-Directory. The IoT-Directory [33] is a web application that through a common and uniform representation of IoT devices and their corresponding sensors and actuators (that are managed by different IoT brokers) can reduce the interoperability barriers that exist among them. This representation is based on the Km4city Ontology that allows to create a uniform layer abstracting from the physical details and mechanisms needed to access them through different IoT brokers.

Node-RED, as a basic feature, provides a set of building blocks that can be used for retrieving data from specific devices according to different protocols. Each block uses a configuration panel where to specify the address of the IoT broker for connecting to devices registered on it. For example, Fig. 1 shows a screenshot of Node-RED in which the user is configuring a sensor registered on FIWARE Orion broker [2]. In the configuration panel, the user has to specify the IP of the broker (service), its certificate, the name and ID of the device and other attributes.

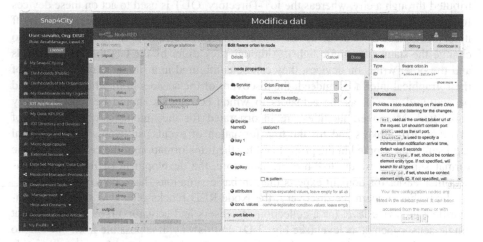

Fig. 1. A sensor registered on FIWARE Orion broker.

Once the block is manually configured and dragged and dropped on the Node-RED canvas, the user has to use specific function blocks for reading the sensor events and transforming them in a format that is suitable for their management with the events produced by other devices used in the context of the smart city. The implementation of the transformation function in the related blocks, must be carried out in JavaScript. This may be a huge obstacle for city operators who are not computer scientists but domain experts who have to act in real-life situations where it is crucial to implement timely and effective decision-making. Moreover, this activity of configuration and of writing transformation functions requires a lot of effort, especially when the number of devices to manage is very high and they belong to different IoT brokers.

To address these issues, in the context of this project, two building blocks (see Fig. 2) have been developed that interact with the IoT Directory for accessing in an unified view the devices registered in the IoT brokers and to offer the following features: (i) Discovery of devices and individual sensors/actuators; (ii) Automatic configuration of the related IoT brokers; (iii) data transformation from their external representation to the one adopted by Snap4City platform in case of sensors or vice versa from the internal representation to the one adopted by the broker in case of actuators.

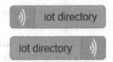

Fig. 2. The new nodes integrate into the Node-RED IDE

Both new building blocks, that we refer to as IoT-Directory_IN and IoT-Directory_OUT, have been designed for abstracting the whole set of available devices in a city. The IoT-Directory_IN is used for reading data coming from devices distributed through a city, whereas the IoT-Directory_OUT is used to act on these devices for example for changing a specific values of a sensor (e.g. its location or to switch off it) or the update a value of actuator (e.g. for regulating the lighting of a lamp or to change the status of a traffic light). Although they differ by the fact the first one reads and the other writes on devices, they can be configured in a similar way. By means of their graphical interfaces, indeed, the discovery of the sensors from which data should be acquired as well as the actuators to which commands should be sent is greatly simplified. Moreover, facilities are incorporated for the automatic configuration of involved IoT brokers and for the transformation of events' structures in the internal representation adopted in the project and for the transformation of the commands in the format supported by the IoT broker. Therefore, the development of IoT applications becomes easier for domain experts that, in basic situations, have no to write code.

For what concern the discovery, the Node-RED blocks offer two searching granularities: at device level (as a collection of sensors and actuators) (see Fig. 3-C) or at single sensors/actuators level (see Fig. 3-D). In this way, it is possible from one side to retrieve all the sensors/actuators that belong to a set of devices and from the other side to access to single sensors/actuators that belong to different devices but, for example, are located in the same area of the city. Independently from the granularity at which the search should be conducted, the IoT Directory presents two options to promote the search process. The first option is the search by location, where the user can choose to reduce the list of available entities into the ones that belong to a specific area only (see Fig. 3-B). The devices can be detected drawing a circle, a line or a geometrical shape on the map. The second option is the search by parameters, where the entities are filtered according to their properties (e.g. the entities that are of type "Ambient" and registered to the broker "FIWARE Orion"). Figure 4 shows the configuration panel that the user can use for specifying the parametric search. In this case, the use can retrieve data related to observed values (value-based search) coming from devices that meet the specified conditions. The conditions cover several parameters that a device can expose such as: the value type to retrieve (for example, temperature, humidity, ambient value), the kind of device (sensor or actuator), broker on which it is registered.

Once the operator has selected the entities she/he needs (for example, by flagging the values or the devices in the table at the bottom of Fig. 4) a flow for the acquisition of the values from sensors or for sending commands to actuators will be generated automatically. Depending on whether you use an IoT-Directory_IN or IoT-Directory_OUT node, the flow starts or ends with the brokers to which these entities are registered, includes the parsing of data received by the brokers in order to transform

Fig. 3. Configuration panel that user uses for searching and retrieving devices by using a map (B). The panel appears when the user clicks on an IoT Directory node (A). By using the tab "Device-based search" (C) the user can retrieve complete devices whereas by using the tab "Value-based search" (D) she/he can retrieve specific values from them.

the different and heterogeneous formats into a uniformed one according to the concepts exposed by the KM4City Ontology, and finally produces the output or the input that can be managed by entity or aggregated by their types.

The parsing is realized through a "transform" function block added to the flow, which is responsible for: (i) detecting the various formats and structures of the data received by the brokers, taking also into consideration the use of different protocols, (ii) reading the data according to its detected format and structure, in order to extract the required useful information out of it, (iii) reconstruct these data into a uniform structure of JSON format. Specifically, the first step in the parsing is to detect the format used (the supported formats are XML, JSON and CSV). Then the second step is to analyze the structure of the data to detect the required information, because even if two devices send data using the same format, their structures could be very different. We mainly care about the name of the sensor, the type of the data and its value. The final step is to reconstruct the identified data in a uniform way according to the Apache Avro format [34]. It is important to note that it is possible to receive data related to many sensors from a single device, while the requested ones are only few, then the "transform" block performs a filtering process too.

The flow created by few steps using IoT-Directory nodes would have been much more complicated to be generated manually. For example, the flow shown in Fig. 5, is created using IoT-Directory_IN by selecting the devices (a set of devices registered on FIWARE Orion broker) that exist in a specific area in Milano, and by enabling the option to aggregate the output of devices sharing the same type (aggregated according to a specified value: the temperature). Without IoT-Directory_IN, the operator has to enter manually the configuration of each broker related to each device, to parse and transform the data received by each one, and to detect the ones with a similar type in order to merge their output.

Fig. 4. Parametric search configuration panel user

As a result, by using these new nodes we provide city operators with a EUD strategy for accessing data having different types, with a uniformed format, which enable them to build the IoT application in an easy way. For example, they can design an application for warning the city manager when in the city the water consumption in greater than a specific level and the perceived temperature is very high or, they can design an application able to: (i) increase the lightning in the city when the fog levels detected in different streets is over a defined threshold, or (ii) to announce a warning if the wind speed is high and, the temperature and the pressure are low.

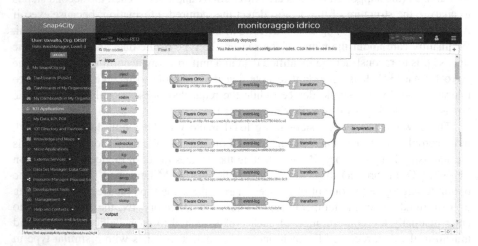

Fig. 5. The dataflow generated by using the IoT-Directory_IN node.

4 Evaluation of Usability

To evaluate the usability of the Node-RED extension developed in the Snap4City Platform, and to investigate how to improve it considering the perspective of domain experts, a user test has been carried out. We mainly focus on the capabilities and appearance of the application that can be able to provide a visual program interface. To this aim, we evaluated the application with the involvement of potential participants. The study consisted of two sessions: the first one was a brief introduction on how to create a Node-RED application and about the Snap4City Project fostered by the second session of the actual task performance of the usability test. In order to get a better understanding of the participants' opinion, we collected information about their profiles through an initial and a final questionnaire. The initial questionnaire was devoted at collecting demographic information about the participants, while the final one was composed of two different parts 1. SUS (System Usability Scale) [35]: A 10 items attitude Likert scale. 2. CUSQ (Computer Usability Satisfaction Questionnaire) [36]: A 19 items attitude Likert scale. A further unstructured interview with each participant concluded the user test sessions and allowed us to gather further information and suggestions on how to improve our Node-RED applications.

4.1 Participants

We were able to involve 18 participants (sixteen males and two females). Among these, 11 participants were in the age range between 25 and 34 years and the other 7 were in the range of 18 to 24. More specifically, participants were recruited among personnel and students of the University of Milano declared to have medium or high knowledge in computer programming. Participants' educational background also ranges from information technology diploma to post-graduate degree (2 diploma, 15 graduate and 1 postgraduate degree). All participants had quite ample computing and surfing experience in various computing platform. Their experience in data analysis of smart city ranges from "no experience" (16 participants) to "study/curiosity purpose" (2 participants). No participants, except one, had experience of creating a dataflow or workflow. No one also used Node-RED before the test.

The participants received a welcomed and general introduction about Node-RED and Snap4City Project. Before starting the test, the participants were asked to individually read the Participant Information Sheet and invited to pose any questions about the test objectives and modalities of conduction. Once the participants were satisfied with the answers, they were asked to read and sign the Informed Consent Form. Three tasks were assigned to the participants along with the task description to perform, and some of the resulting output is shown below. After performing the three tasks, the participants were asked to fill the post-test questionnaires.

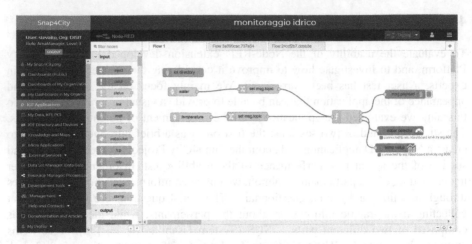

Fig. 6. Overview of the Node-RED application created for Task 1

4.2 Task Description and Protocol

We provided to the participants of our test three different tasks. Each task represents a real problem that city operators have to deal with in their daily activities. Below is a brief summary of each task description and the resulting interfaces (Figs. 5 and 6). Figure 6 shows the overall Node-RED application created for Task 1 using the IoT Directory node. In the canvas the operator can use the outputs of the dataflows generated by using the IoT Directory (in this case the temperature node as produced in Fig. 5, and the water node) for designing an IoT application devoted to monitor the water consumption in respect with the average temperature registered in a city (see Task 1 description below). Figure 7 also shows the resulting dashboard for Task 1, the dashboards appear when the user clicks on the dashboard nodes (the nodes in blues named "water detector" and "temp value") of the dataflow depicted in Fig. 6.

As we described in the previous section, once the user has dragged and dropped IoT Directory node in the canvas, there are various ways to select the devices as described in the following scenarios.

Task 1 Description - Suppose an employee of the municipality of Milano wishes to control the level of water consumption in the city. If the average consumption is greater than 100 cubic meters and the average outdoor temperature is above 27° then a warning has to be sent to the mayor office. The operator must also produce a graphical dashboard to display the water consumption and temperature. By using a map, the operator selects 10 sensors in Milano that monitor the consumption of water and 5 sensors used to control the temperature in the city. Each sensor updates the captured value every 30 min. In this task, we asked the user to test the "Value-based search" and "Parametric search" functionalities of our IoT Directory node to see its efficiency and effectiveness. The task also involves creating a dashboard using the Snap4City dashboard nodes (gauge chart and time trend) as shown in Fig. 7.

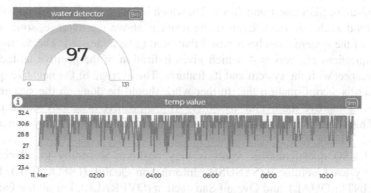

Fig. 7. Dashboards created for Task 1.

Task 2 Description - Suppose an employee of the municipality of Milano wishes to monitor the level of pollution for detecting possible critical issues that could cause asthma attacks or respiratory problems in the population. The operator selects sensors to check the values of PM10, nitrogen dioxide (NO_2) and ozone (O_3). The air quality index is calculated as the average value of the two worst pollution indicators. If this index is greater than 150 then a warning has to be sent to the mayor office. The operator must also produce a graphical dashboard for viewing the development of the air quality indicators.

Task 3 Description - Suppose an employee of the municipality of Milano wishes to monitor the Humidex index. This index takes into account air temperature and relative humidity and tries to calculate a single value that can describe the human discomfort in hot and humid days. The operator has to select meteorological stations of a specific area to check the temperature and humidity values. By applying a given formula[4] for calculating the Humidex index, the city operator has to send a message to the mayor office related to human discomfort.

All user tests have been performed with a think-aloud protocol and with the presence of an observer (direct observation).

4.3   Results

All participants completed successfully the user tests in a very short time, i.e. with an average time of 16 min for the first task and 13 min for each of the second and the third tasks, by creating correct data flows. It is evident that the IoT Directory node bolsters the task completion rate (100% completion rate) and reduces significantly the amount of time required to implement important tasks. Some problems that will enhance the usability of the applications have been highlighted during the test and have been confirmed by the unstructured interviews and the final questionnaires as described later in this section.

---

[4] $H = T + 0.5555 * (6.112 * 10^{(7.5*T/(237.7+T))} * UR/100) - 10)$ where T = temperature in Celsius, while UR = relative humidity.

The result of SUS questionnaires is 70, which is above 68, the result considered by SUS method as the average. Even if the result is above the average, some usability concerns of the system have been raised that need to be addressed. The average of the positive questions answers is 4, which gives indication of the positive attitude of the users in respect with the system and its features. The average of the negative questions is 2, which is a confirmation that further work should be done on the system and its interfaces to improve the overall usability. All the positive questions scored the same results. This suggests that the participants recognized the utility of the system and were not afraid of using it.

The CUSQ questionnaires result is very positive, according to all considered metrics: System Usefulness (SYSUSE), Information Quality (INFOQUAL), Interface Quality (INTERQUAL), and Overall Satisfaction (OVERALL). For all the factors, the results average is 4 (on a scale from 1 to 5 where 5 is "Strongly Agree"). All questions, except one, received a very good result: 4. This reflects perfectly the comments that were collected during the final unstructured interview (discussed below).

During the unstructured individual interviews that we took after each user test, some important suggestions for improving the system emerged. The main suggestions regard the need to provide users with more informative information messages that guide the design process of the dataflow. Other remarks focus on Node-RED interface itself rather than the functionalities of our IoT Directory node. For example, some users asked to arrange the list of the Node-RED nodes presented on the left palette of the canvas (where there are the types of nodes to be dragged on the flow) to give the possibility to use a button that redraws or expands all the sections in respect with their types.

With particular attention to IoT Directory node, most participants suggested no additional functionalities, however few of the participants suggested to add the possibility to carry out a multiple selection (such as select all and deselect all) of devices/values during the search and selection phase. In general, with respect to the use of Node-RED and the IoT Directory node all participants agreed in terms of their overall interaction and experience. Specifically, several participants reported that: *"IoT Directory node speeds up workflow development"*.

4.4   Validity

In terms of external validity or generalization of the results of a study to other participants, times, places and conditions, the threats of this study were selection of participants' and task complexity. The participants were intentionally recruited without experience of dataflow or workflow development, because our aim was to analyze the usability of our application from the point of view of inexperienced people. We are aware of the limitation to the generalizability of the results, since city operators might have a different level of computing experience. However, we can safely accept the results for workflow development because no special computing skill/experience is required. However, further studies are required including expert people. The complexity of the tasks is also determined considering the basic task of the city operators.

5 Conclusion

In this paper, we have discussed two Node-RED building blocks that have been integrated in the Snap4City platform with the aim of supporting city operators in designing effective dataflows. By using these nodes, our solution enables integration of devices disseminated in a city through a process carried out by domain experts who are expected to only have adequate knowledge of the context in which these devices are placed and of their meaning to make proper decisions. These building blocks facilitate wiring together all different kinds of devices, and allow city operators to carry out massive accesses to data sources instead of searching manually on all single brokers.

Finally, we evaluated the design strategy of our solution through a set of user tests in term of reducing the time required for the development of IoT applications and the number of mistakes in the configuration of the IoT devices. We tested the environment considering real scenarios where participants acting as city operators have to manage events, taking under control what happen and making decisions to improve citizens' quality of life. The positive outcome of our evaluation confirms that the use of EUD strategy in the development of our solution can improve the work of city operators.

Acknowledgments. The authors wish to thank the Select4Cities Consortium and all the participants in the user evaluation for supporting our work with useful feedbacks about the real needs of smart cities like Antwerp, Helsinki, and Florence.

References

1. Eclipse Mosquitto: An open source MQTT broker. https://mosquitto.org/. Accessed 14 Jan 2019
2. Fiware-Orion Context Broker. https://fiware-orion.readthedocs.io/en/master/index.html. Accessed 14 Jan 2019
3. OneM2M: Standards for M2M and the Internet of Things. http://www.onem2m.org/. Accessed 14 Jan 2019
4. Sanchez, L., et al.: Smart-Santander: IoT experimentation over a smart city testbed. Comput. Netw. **61**, 217–238 (2014). Special issue on Future Internet Testbeds Part I
5. Talend Studio. www.talend.com. Accessed 02 Feb 2019
6. StreamBase Studio. www.streambase.com. Accessed 02 Feb 2019
7. Waylay.io. www.waylay.io. Accessed 02 Feb 2019
8. Badii, C., et al.: Snap4City: a scalable IOT/IOE platform for developing smart city applications. In: 2nd IEEE International Conference on Smart City Innovations (SCI 2018), pp. 2109–2116. IEEE Press (2018). ISBN 9781538693803
9. Zanella, A., Bui, N., Castellani, A., Vangelista, L., Zorzi, M.: Internet of things for smart cities. Internet Things J. **1**(1), 22–32 (2014)
10. Ballon, P., Glidden, J., Kranas, P., Menychtas, A., Ruston, S., Van Der Graaf, S.: Is there a need for a cloud platform for European smart cities? In: eChallenges e-2011 Conference Proceedings. IIMC International Information Management Corporation (2011)
11. Tei, K., Gurgen, L.: ClouT: cloud of things for empowering the citizen clout in smart cities. In: 2014 IEEE World Forum on Internet of Things (WF-IoT), pp. 369–370. IEEE (2014)

12. Elmangoush, A., Coskun, H., Wahle, S., Magedanz, T.: Design aspects for a reference M2M communication Platform for Smart Cities. In: 2013 9th International Conference on Innovations in Information Technology (IIT), pp. 204–209 (2013)
13. Specification for Urban Platforms, EIP Project, version 2.2. European Innovation Partnership for Smart Cities & Communities (2016)
14. IoT Analytics: L List of 640+ Enterprise IoT Projects. https://iot-analytics.com/product/list-of-640-iot-projects/. Accessed 23 Oct 2018
15. Turck, M.: Internet of Things: Are We There Yet? (The 2016 IoT Landscape). http://mattturck.com/2016-iot-landscape/. Accessed 12 Dec 2018
16. Gartner: Market Guide for IoT Integration. ID: G00313179. https://www.gartner.com/doc/3352439/market-guide-iot-integration. Accessed 24 Oct 2017
17. Calbimonte, J.-P., Sarni, S., Eberle, J., Aberer, K.: XGSN: an opensource semantic sensing middleware for the web of things. In: International Workshop on Semantic Sensor Networks (2014)
18. Aberer, K., Hauswirth, M., Salehi, A.: A middleware for fast and flexible sensor network deployment. In: Proceedings of 32nd International Conference on Very Large Data Bases, pp. 1199–1202 (2006)
19. Compton, M., Barnaghi, P., Bermudez, L., et al.: The SSN ontology of the W3C semantic sensor network incubator group. J. Web Semantics **17**, 25–32 (2012)
20. Bellini, P., Benigni, M., Billero, R., Nesi, P., Rauch, N.: Km4City ontology building vs data harvesting and cleaning for smart-city services. J. Vis. Lang. Comput. **25**(6), 827–839 (2014)
21. Sutcliffe, A.: End-user development. Commun. ACM **47**(9), 31–32 (2004)
22. Petre, M., Blackwell, A.F.: Children as unwitting end-user programmers. In: Proceeding of the IEEE Symposium on Visual Languages and Human-Centric Computing (VL/HCC 2007), pp. 239–242 (2007)
23. Fischer, G., Giaccardi, E., Ye, Y., Sutcliffe, A., Mehandjiev, N.: Meta-design: a manifesto for end-user development. Commun. ACM **47**(9), 33–37 (2004)
24. Costabile, M.F., Mussio, P., Parasiliti Provenza, L., Piccinno, A.: End users as unwitting software developers. In: Proceedings of the 4th International Workshop on End-User Software Engineering, pp. 6–10. ACM, New York (2008)
25. Barricelli, B.R., Valtolina, S.: A visual language and interactive system for end-user development of internet of things ecosystems. J. Vis. Lang. Comput. **40**, 1–19 (2017)
26. Valtolina, S., Barricelli, B.R.: An end-user development framework to support quantified self in sport teams. In: Paternò, F., Wulf, V. (eds.) New Perspectives in End-User Development, pp. 413–432. Springer, Cham (2017). ISBN 9783319602905. https://doi.org/10.1007/978-3-319-60291-2_16
27. Eclipse Foundation. Kura Documentation. https://eclipse.github.io/kura/. Accessed 21 Jan 2019
28. Node-RED. Flow-based programming for the Internet of Things. https://nodered.org/docs/. Accessed 21 Jan 2019
29. Project Flogo: Docs and Tutorials for an Open Source ecosystem for event-driven apps. https://tibcosoftware.github.io/flogo/. Accessed 21 Jan 2019
30. Ghiani, G., Manca, M., Paternò, F., Santoro, C.: Personalization of context-dependent applications through trigger-action rules. ACM Trans. Comput. Hum. Interact. **24**(2), 33 pages (2017)
31. Desolda, G., Ardito, C., Matera, M.: Empowering end users to customize their smart environments: model, composition paradigms and domain-specific tools. ACM Trans. Comput. Hum. Interact. **24**(2), 52 pages (2017)

32. Caivano, D., Fogli, D., Lanzilotti, R., Piccinno, A., Cassano, F.: Supporting end users to control their smart home: design implications from a literature review and an empirical investigation. J. Syst. Softw. **144**(2018), 295–313 (2018)
33. Bonfitto, S., Hachem, F., Belay, E.G., Valtolina, S., Mesiti, M.: On the bulk ingestion of IoT devices from IoT brokers. In: IEEE International Congress on Internet of Things, Milan, Italy, 8–13 July 2019
34. Apache Avro. https://avro.apache.org/. Accessed 14 Jan 2019
35. Brooke, J.: SUS: a quick and dirty usability scale. In: Jordan, P.W., Thomas, B., Weerdmeester, B.A., McClelland, I.L. (eds.) Usability Evaluation in Industry. CRC Press, London (1996)
36. Lewis, J.R.: IBM computer usability satisfaction questionnaires: psychometric evaluation and instructions for use. Int. J. Hum. Comput. Interact. **7**(1), 57–78 (1995)

Analyzing Trigger-Action Programming for Personalization of Robot Behaviour in IoT Environments

Marco Manca, Fabio Paternò[✉], and Carmen Santoro

CNR-ISTI, HIIS Laboratory, Via Moruzzi 1, 56124 Pisa, Italy
{marco.manca, fabio.paterno, carmen.santoro}@isti.cnr.it

Abstract. The rising spread of humanoid robots in various settings of human life, and their increasing affordability, as well as the massive adoption of the Internet of Things (IoT) in various scenarios have made End User Development (EUD) for robotic and IoT applications an interesting research direction. In particular, in the EUD field, trigger-action rules have become popular for their simple structure, which enables users to create rules to implement their desired personalization. Such rules can be a precious source of information for various goals: understanding the aspects people are most interested in, the types of routines they would like to have, the kind of support/automation they would expect from the robot, and the environment in which the robot is immersed. However, since the number of rules that could be generated using such EUD tools could be significant, manual analysis of rules does not seem a viable solution. In this paper we discuss how a visual analytics tool supporting filtering, exploration and analysis of data generated by a EUD tool for programming humanoid robots immersed in IoT environments can be helpful for deriving relevant information associated with the personalization that users express through rules. The analysis can provide designers and developers of EUD tools and associated customizable applications with useful insights for improving the tools and the robotic applications themselves, and facilitate their adoption.

Keywords: EUD analytics · Personalization · IoT · Robots

1 Introduction

The massive adoption of the Internet of Things (IoT) in various scenarios ranging from smart home devices and smart cities to medical and healthcare applications, as well as the users' increasing need to personalise the application they use, have made end-user personalization of IoT environments the focus of several research contributions. The TOCHI special issue on EUD for IoT [11] provides a good introduction to this field. Some EUD tools are also becoming popular among users (see e.g. the IFTTT tool[1]), who are likely to rely on such rules on a daily basis. Recently, also general-

---

[1] https://ifttt.com/discover.

© Springer Nature Switzerland AG 2019
A. Malizia et al. (Eds.): IS-EUD 2019, LNCS 11553, pp. 100–114, 2019.
https://doi.org/10.1007/978-3-030-24781-2_7

purpose humanoid robots are becoming increasingly widespread in numerous settings since they can help users in many real-world tasks and their cost is becoming increasingly affordable. As such, a novel trend is emerging in the EUD area, focused on EUD solutions (e.g. with the support of personalization rule editors) that address customization of robot applications by users who are not professional developers in IoT settings.

Due to the pervasiveness and versatility of use of IoT/robot applications in numerous contexts, the interactions that *end users* carry out with EUD tools can represent a precious source of information e.g. for *developers* of EUD tools, to understand the personalization aspects which people are focusing on most, the types of routines they would like to put in place, the types of automations they would expect from robots and surrounding environments. However, since the amount of information that could be generated by such EUD tools could be significant [12, 20], manual analysis of the data produced as a consequence of end user interaction with EUD tools does not seem a viable approach to interpret such data and quickly make sense of user activities, interests, and preferred routines. To this regard, interactive visual analytics solutions can be useful to obtain valuable insights into large data sets generated by applications used in IoT settings. By providing EUD tool developers with visualization and analysis of relationships in the dataset (e.g. through interactive dashboards), new insights can be gained in an interactive manner, and they consequently should be able to make better decisions accordingly. Indeed, the provided visualizations are expected to make the dataset clearer by presenting information in intuitive and user-friendly ways, opening up the possibility to delve into data to unveil novel insights that can be translated into opportunities for improvement.

In this paper we present a contribution discussing how a visual analytics tool can be useful to support analysis, exploration and filtering of relevant data derived from the analysis of the interactions done by end users with a EUD tool aimed at personalizing the behaviour of a robot immersed in a IoT environment. While in this paper we consider a consumer (home) scenario for the evaluation, the presented approach could also be applied in other contexts of use (e.g. work settings). We propose a method aiming to derive higher-level information such as usage patterns followed by users while interacting with the tool, the types of rules that users were most interested in creating by using the tool, the most popular trigger and action types used, so as to facilitate the supported interactions and also the adoption of the EUD tool and the associated applications. The method also includes an interactive module that prompts users with relevant questions to gather feedback at the end of the tool use. In the paper we also discuss the feedback we gathered from a group of end users without knowledge in IoT programming who were asked to use an EUD trigger-action tool for creating various rules aimed at personalizing the behaviour of a robot immersed in a IoT environment.

More in detail, after introducing the context and the motivations of this work, in the next section we describe significant related work in relevant areas, then we describe the method we developed and the associated tool support for analysis of rules created by using a trigger-action rule editor. Afterwards, we report on a study we carried out to assess the potentialities of the presented method, discuss the results, then conclude with final remarks and viable directions for future work.

2 Related Work

2.1 Trigger-Action Programming

In recent years, interest in using trigger-action programming for IoT environments has considerably increased. Various studies have been carried out to investigate how to propose this type of solution and its benefits [3, 5, 6, 11], and several issues have been discussed. For example, whether the single trigger/single action solution proposed by IFTTT is the most effective one [19].

In parallel, another emerging trend is the rapid diffusion of robots, and the associated need to support even people without programming experience to modify their behaviour. Various EUD approaches have been pursued to make easy the development of robotics applications.

One technique is programming by demonstration [1], in which users do not have to explicitly program each detail of the robot behaviour, but they have just to demonstrate how to achieve the robotic task by providing examples through which the robot should learn the new expected behaviour. Another solution is the use of visual toolkits with more user-friendly interfaces that guarantee rapid interaction development without aiming to optimize the final resulting performance. In this area we can distinguish approaches that use iconic data flow representations of robot functionalities (such as Choregraphe [15]), and those that use block-based languages introduced by Scratch [16], which have also been applied in other domains. An example of a visual programming tool for user-friendly, rapid programming manipulators robots is in [10]. The system is designed to let non-roboticists and roboticists alike program end-to-end manipulation tasks. The authors present findings from an observational user study in which ten non-roboticist programmers were able to learn the system and program a robot to do manipulation tasks. Buchina et al. [2] propose a design of a Web-based programming interface that aims to support end-users with different backgrounds to program robots using natural language.

Still in the attempt of lowering the barriers to programming robots, and then make it more accessible and intuitive for novice programmers, Weintrop et al. [21] present a block-based interface (CoBlox) for programming a one-armed industrial robot. The results show that participants using the block-based interface successfully implemented programs faster with no loss in accuracy while reporting higher scores for usability, learnability, and overall satisfaction. However, they considered a rather limited scenario, with one-armed industrial robots, and the participants were asked to program a "pick and place" routine. In [8] an end user development solution based on trigger-action personalization rules able to support programming of robots immersed in IoT environments has been presented, showing the potential for using trigger-action programming to make Pepper robot[2] behaviour personalization possible even for people who are not professional software developers.

Thus, the trigger-action programming paradigm seems a promising approach to address in an integrated way the need of personalization. We can foresee its adoption

---

[2] https://www.softbankrobotics.com/emea/en/pepper.

and use by many users in different contexts. Indeed, for example 320,000 IFTTT rules involving 400 service providers have already been installed more than 20 million times [12]. This trend poses new issues and requires novel approaches to support developers of trigger-action based tools and IoT and robotic applications to analyse the actual use of their tools.

2.2   Visual Analytics of Rule-Based Behaviour

Visual analytics tools have been often used for analysing logs associated with user interactions with Web applications. Indeed, interaction logs provide detailed information about the sequence of steps which the users take in order to reach their goals and then provide useful information for revealing various pieces of relevant information, such as patterns followed by users while interacting with Web applications. As such, one typical use of the information contained in logs of user interactions is for usability studies. For instance, Harms and Grabowsky [9] proposed transforming the recorded user interaction in task trees that are then checked to identify usability issues. The goal of such contributions is to identify a method to record user interactions and then further analyse the logs in order to highlight usability problems. HistoryViewer [17] is a system that aims to support exploration of log data obtained from user interactions. A systematic mapping of web analytics and web usability has been reported in [14].

Regarding the visual analytics solutions existing in the IoT domain, a review of work on IoT and big data analytics is described in [18], particularly from the perspective of their utility in creating effective applications and services for several domains. In that review the authors examine the application of data analytics across IoT domains, provide a categorization of analytic approaches, and propose a layered taxonomy that defines and classifies analytics by their capabilities and application potential for research and application roadmaps.

An approach to repurposing Web analytics for the IoT is presented in [13], with the main objective of adding analytics to IoT deployments with minimal effort and cost. In that paper the authors highlight how, differently from the Web analytics domain where the overhead for incorporating analytics into a Web site is low, the IoT analytics sector is highly fragmented, more complex, with many developers that produce their own analytics dashboards often optimized for a specific application domain. Therefore, the authors highlight the benefits of leveraging existing analytics platforms and infrastructures in addressing barriers for a more widespread adoption of IoT-based analytics.

An initial attempt to provide a visual analytics tool for analysing rule-based personalization created by users has been presented in [4]. However, that tool has not been used for analysing personalization involving robots and IoT and it was only able to provide information associated with one single user per time. Therefore, it was not able to support comprehensive and summary analysis of data associated with several users, which is a key feature for more easily understanding latent trends in the datasets across various users.

3   Visual Analytics for EUD of Robotics and IoT

The main contribution of this paper is to describe a method aimed at providing suitable guidance in analysing information resulting from automated processing of datasets generated by users while interacting with an EUD tool based on trigger-action rules allowing users to specify personalisation of robot behaviour in IoT settings. The goal is to provide some means to facilitate analysis, interactive exploration and filtering of such data, so as to put users in a position to take more informed, data-driven decisions about how to improve the EUD tool and the associated applications. In parallel with this method we have also developed a prototype tool able to support the abovementioned visual analytics method.

Therefore, it is important to distinguish two levels (in terms of tools, users, tasks, etc.) involved in our approach. On the one hand, we have end users who create their personalisation rules by interacting with EUD tools. In our case, the EUD tool is called PersRobIoTE (Personalisation of Robots in IoT Environments), is based on the trigger-action paradigm, and it is aimed at supporting end users in personalising the behaviour of a robot immersed in an IoT environment. Figure 1 shows the user interface of the EUD tool when supporting the selection of relevant triggers associated with robot behaviour.

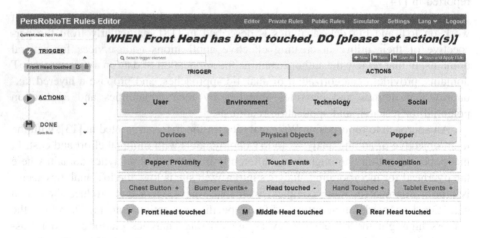

Fig. 1. The EUD tool supporting the specification of robot-related triggers

On the other hand, the data associated with the interactions of users with PersRobIoTE are expected to be analysed by e.g. developers of EUD tools or IoT application developers, to understand which kind of personalisation end users are more interested in. In order to support the latter case, the visual analytics aims to provide two types of representations:

- Interactive visualisation, filtering and exploration of time-oriented events occurred during the definition of trigger-action rules (*timelines*);

- Visual representations of meaningful indicators summarising and aggregating relevant data, so as to provide users with situational awareness and monitoring (*dashboards*).

The timelines provided offer a visualization of sequences of relevant events logged during users' activities in a time-dependent manner, also allowing the user to select the most suitable time resolution/granularity to be used for the analysis. The timelines may help developers to understand whether users encounter any issues in interacting with the personalization features offered by the editors, but they provide a limited analysis about the types of rules that users were most interested in, or about the most popular trigger and action. Figure 2 shows an example of timeline-based visualization of a user session where we can see that the user created three rules in less than half an hour.

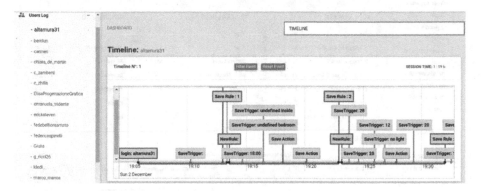

Fig. 2. An example timeline

Regarding the dashboards, two main types of dashboards have been designed. One is user-related and another one is a summary, providing an overview of the data associated with multiple users. Using the first type of dashboard, as soon as a user is selected (from the list of users who interacted with the rule editor), the dashboard shows an overview of the activities carried out by the considered user: the triggers and actions created in all the sessions (where, by "session" we mean the interval of time between a user's login and a user's logout from the system), the number of rules which had been modified by the user; the rules that have been created by users described in natural language, the context dimensions (users, environment, technology, …) involved in the rules saved, the most used triggers and actions grouped by categories, the time of each interactive session, and the number of rules that have been saved and not saved in all the sessions. Indeed, since both triggers and actions are categorised into hierarchies (e.g. the high-level elements of the trigger hierarchy are the context dimensions: "User", "Environment", "Technology", "Social", and each of such elements is further refined), for each trigger/action category/dimension there is a section which shows the number of times such categories/dimensions have been used in all the defined rules. The dashboard also provides indication of how long each user session lasted overall, and also how long it took to create and save every rule.

As for the summary dashboard, several pieces of information are provided (see an example in Fig. 3, top part of the tool):

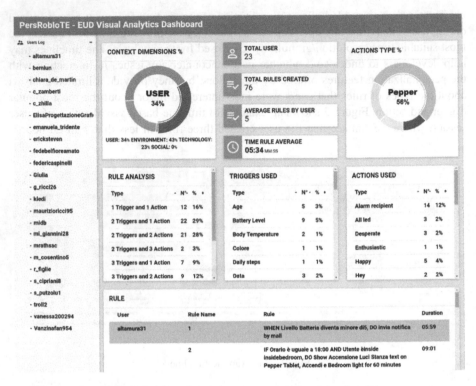

Fig. 3. The visual analytics tool showing summary information involving user groups

- a pie chart showing the percentages of context dimensions exploited in the rules created by all the users;
- another pie chart showing the various action types exploited in the rules created by all the users, divided in percentages according to their types;
- some descriptive statistical data about the number of users, the total number of rules created by such users, and then the average number of rules created by each, as well as the average time spent by each in creating one rule.

Another set of data is shown in the middle part of the tool, namely:

- the various rules created by users, shown in a way that highlights their structure (in terms of number of triggers and actions involved) and how many rules have been created according to that structure (this information has been provided both in terms of absolute numbers and in percentages)
- the triggers used in the rules (absolute values and percentages)
- the actions appearing in the created rules (absolute values and percentages)

In the bottom part of the panel, the tool shows the list of the various rules created by users described in natural language.

In addition, the tool has some further interactive capabilities allowing the user to obtain further details on demand about the information presented. For instance, as soon as a specific type of trigger (or, alternatively: a type of action) is selected in one of the dashboards shown in the middle part of the tool, in its bottom part the tool highlights the set of rules that involve that trigger (or that action), so as to better inform the user about the way they have been used concretely.

4   An Example Application

4.1   The Test Carried Out

A test was organized in order to assess the kind of information that the analysis tool can provide when used by a number of real users. In the test we involved a class of 26 university students (12 males, 14 females) in a master's degree programme on Digital Humanities at the local University. We asked them to use the PersRobIoTE tool for creating rules involving the personalization of a robot immersed in an IoT environment. Then, we analysed the type of outputs that the visual analytics solution offers accordingly, especially those associated with the information gathered on the rules created by such users.

In the test we wanted to understand possible aspects that can be improved in the use of the EUD tool, and also assess the kind of information that the visual analytics tool can accordingly provide. The test was organized in the following manner: introduction, familiarization, test execution, questionnaire. The students were first introduced to the main functionalities of the robot and the trigger-action rule editor, which enables the definition of rules involving both the Pepper robot and a number of smart IoT things. Next, users had to create some trigger-action rules having a pre-defined structure (using the PersRobIoTE tool), and then they had to answer a set of questions collecting their feedback on various aspects of the EUD tool. After 90 min (including introduction and familiarization), if they did not complete the exercise, they could finish it remotely afterwards.

The tool also included an interactive module prompting users with questions to gather relevant feedback at the end of the tool use. Thus, we informed students about this, asking them to provide honest feedback, saying that the test is an evaluation of the tool and not of their performance, and that any issue they could find would be useful to improve the tool. We asked their permission to log their interactions, and informed them that the gathered data would have been used for research purposes, and we would have avoided their identification.

The tasks they had to accomplish consisted in the creation of six rules. The requested rules vary in terms of complexity, types of trigger(s) and action. In particular, they were requested to specify rules structured in the following manner:

- Rule1 (1T, 1A): Simple trigger: Technology; Simple action: Alarm
- Rule2 (2T, 2A): Composite Trigger: Environment, User; Composite action; Pepper, Light

- Rule3 (2T, 1A): Composite Trigger: Environment, Environment; Single action: Pepper
- Rule4 (2T, 2A): Composite Trigger: Environment, Technology; Composite action: Light, Pepper
- Rule5 (2T, 2A): Composite Trigger: User, Technology; Composite action: Pepper, Reminder
- Rule6 (2T, 1A): Composite Trigger: Environment, User; Single action: Pepper

Thus, the tasks submitted to users were identified in such a way to cover the various possible contextual dimensions and actions. In addition, the requested rules varied in terms of structure, i.e. both simple triggers/actions or composite triggers/actions appeared in the rules (composite actions are combined through either Parallel or Sequence operators; while composite triggers can be combined through AND, OR, NOT Boolean operators)

At the end of the use of the EUD tool, they were prompted to provide answers that were interactively shown to them, and covering the following aspects: coverage of the hierarchies of triggers and actions, clarity of the logical organization in which triggers and actions are organized, clarity of the natural language text automatically generated to describe each rule, intuitiveness of the trigger-action approach, difficulties they found during the use of the tool, possible improvements to the tool.

4.2   Analysis of the Data Collected Through the Visual Analyzer

Using the visual analytics solution, it was possible to easily identify the most popular triggers and actions for which users wrote rules, as the tool is able to show various frequency/occurrence-related information associated with triggers and actions.

The rules created by users consisted of:

- 26 rules composed of 1 trigger and 1 action
- 52 rules composed of 2 triggers and 1 action
- 78 rules composed of 2 triggers and 2 actions

Therefore, regarding the rule structure, half the rules presented either a single trigger or a single action, whereas the remaining half consisted of 2 triggers and 2 actions.

According to the data gathered (and also as expected from the type of tasks assigned), users predominantly wrote rules for the "Environment" category (46%), "Time" being the most popular trigger type in that category, followed by "Motion". After the "Environment" category, the triggers most used belonged to the "Technology" and also "User" categories (both scored 27%).

As expected from the exercise, the most popular actions types regard Pepper (56% of rules), "Synthesize Text" being the most used Pepper-related action (followed, in equal amounts, by "Show Text" and "Play animation"). The most frequent actions, beyond the robot-related ones, were the ones associated with "Lights" category (22%). In addition, reminders were preferred by users to be shown on tablets, followed by voice, whereas Alarms were preferred to be sent by tablet and, as a second choice, by email.

Another useful analysis that can be done through the tool is the type of rule patterns that can be identified regarding the rule structure. In this case the pattern refers to the combination of specific trigger types with specific action types. In particular, we found out that the entities under the "Environment" dimension were mostly associated with actions belonging to the "Pepper" category, followed by the "Light" category.

The entities under the Technology dimension were mostly associated with actions belonging to the "Lights" and "Alarms" categories, in equal amounts. Finally, the entities under the "User" dimension were mostly associated with actions belonging to the "Pepper" category and then, to a minor extent, to the other action categories (i.e. "Lights", "Reminders", "Alarms").

It is worth pointing out that, while in this evaluation we asked students to create rules having specific structures and involving specific context types or action types, in more general cases (i.e. when users are free to create their own rules), this latter information could be key to understanding the actual personalisation preferences of users.

As for the operators for combining the triggers and the actions, the vast majority of people used the AND for combining triggers, and Sequential operator for combining actions. It is interesting to analyse the situations in which the OR operator was used to combine triggers, which can be attributed to Rule4/Task4, which requested that users combine Environment and Technology –based triggers. For instance, examples of composition of triggers involved in such rules were: "IF Living Room Light Level is low light OR LivingRoom Light Color is yellow", "IF Time is after 23:00 OR Bed Room Light Level is no light". This information can provide useful hints about triggers that were considered somewhat 'equivalent' by users (understanding when it is time to switch on some lights according either to the time, or to the light level of a room, or to the light level of a lamp).

Another set of information that the tool can provide is associated with time-related data. In particular, it is possible to know the time spent by each user to create each rule and also the average time spent in creating all the rules, as well as across the various sessions. In addition, the tool also provides the min, max, average time (and standard deviation) spent on creating rules, as calculated across all the considered users. In our case we obtained the following data: min 5 s., max: 35 min 5 s, average: 6 min 30 s, st. dev.: 6 min 1 s.

Since we have the time of day associated with the rules creation, the tool is also able to calculate when users prefer to create the rules, which in the study was between 3 pm and 6 pm.

4.3   User Feedback on the Rule Editor

The 26 users were overall able to create the requested rules in a correct manner, apart from some mistakes in distinguishing between events and conditions. In the end, the 156 expected rules were created by users. After using the tool, they had to answers to a number of questions. Overall, users expressed quite positive feedback on their experience with the EUD tool. In the following, we summarize the user feedback.

- *In the rule editor, did you find all the triggers and actions you were interested in? If not, what triggers or actions would be added in the hierarchies?*

Users said that overall the most used triggers and actions were available in the hierarchies. However, the majority of them suggested further options to add in the hierarchies and regarding e.g. additional household appliances like smart washing machines, coffee machines, as well as intelligent speakers (such as Google home or Alexa), air conditioning, oven, multi-room sound systems, as well as devices for opening/closing the home shutters. Two users asked for adding further home rooms. One user asked for the possibility to have "Alarms" or "Reminders" sent by either a smart band or a smartwatch wearable device, with also the possibility to include a vibro-tactile feedback. Two users suggested adding the possibility to have Pepper interacting with the surrounding environment (e.g. turn off the tv, move objects). One user asked for better controlling the lights (e.g. dimming them within a user-specified interval of time). One user highlighted the need to have a trigger for understanding whether there is motion in all the rooms of the house (e.g. something like "Motion in house"). Another user asked for having the possibility to control in a finer manner the radio or the TV (e.g. their channels). The "Weather" trigger was also identified as a useful addition to the tool in order to have the possibility to specify rules that depend on current weather conditions.

- *Do you think the terms used in hierarchies are sufficiently comprehensible? If not, what would you change?*

The terms used in the hierarchies were judged overall understandable, except for some specific ones. For instance, one user judged the term "Hue lamp" not easily understandable for those not accustomed to (Philips) Hue lights. One user suggested providing an example for each of the terms used in the hierarchies, to improve the clarity of the tool.

- *Was it easy for you to create a mental model of what you could do? If not, where did you have any problems?*

On the one hand, four users said that, in order to create a mental model of the tool, they needed first to explore the hierarchies, in order to get an overall picture of the possibilities supported by the tool. On the other hand, one of such users emphasised that the tool was very useful in guiding the user in the process of creating rules. Another user said that the sidebar helped him a lot in following the mental models needed to build the rules. One user suggested adding some examples of rules in order to further helping users to this regard.

- *Do you think the difference between events and conditions is correctly highlighted/ rendered by the instrument? If not, what would you change to improve it?*

The majority of users said that they did not find particular problems with understanding this difference. However, at the same time, they emphasised the need of further adding some hints for enabling especially people not familiar with such terms to more easily understand their different meanings. One user suggested rendering the difference between events and conditions by using some visual attributes of the associated text (e.g. using different colour or different font size or types, adding a legend). One user suggested adding this information also in the sidebar. Two users found this difference a bit difficult. However, one of them said that she, after having familiarised with the tool for a while, did not have problems anymore with such key concepts.

- *Do you have any suggestions to improve the usability/accessibility of the tool?*

One user said that further explanation and legends could be useful to better support user interactions. Another user suggested having a set of rules already available in the tool, in order to help especially novice users. Two users highlighted the need of renaming a rule without editing it from scratch. A couple of users suggested adding the possibility of having the complete hierarchy visualized at once (in the current version, apart from the top-level trigger/action entities, the other elements are refined and visualized on request, through an interactive selection). One user suggested to automatically move down the focus of the page when new elements of the hierarchy are expanded and are not visible, as in the current state explicit scrolling down is requested from the user.

- *Have you found any difficulty in expressing complex rules? If so, where?*

Building complex rules was found at a level of complexity comparable to rules composed of single triggers and single actions. Nobody complained about this aspect, one user explicitly mentioned the availability of the operators and of the rule structure in the sidebar as particularly helpful in following the specification of complex rules.

- *Did you find the feedback/error messages provided by the tool as sufficiently understandable and informative? Otherwise, in which situations?*

The majority of users said that they did not experience/notice any error message in their interactions. Regarding other feedback messages, the ones informing users of unsaved rules or concerning form fields not correctly filled in were highly appreciated by users and were found sufficiently informative.

5 Discussion

The method proposed, along with the associated tool, have shown to provide useful information in analysing the use of a EUD, trigger/action-based tool. In this case the analysis carried out enabled us to confirm that it was easy to create trigger-action rules in which even a combination of multiple triggers and multiple actions occurred, since test participants did not encounter relevant difficulties in fulfilling the tasks assigned, so producing a set of rules that were correct in their vast majority, while having just a short introduction to the approach. This to some extent motivates even more our work in proposing a method allowing people to analyse the interactions done with EUD tool, also in terms of rules produced, since it is easy to create rules, and therefore rule sets can grow very easily.

A possibility for exploiting the information that can be derived from analysing the triggers and the actions that are most used (or least used) by users could be, on the one hand, the possibility to populate the platform with examples of rules that are more frequently used by users, so as to quickly provide examples that are commonly considered as useful. On the other hand, the information associated with the types of triggers and actions that are not much used can be exploited to support users in discovering rules that involve triggers and/or actions they do not seem to be interested in, or alternatively they do not seem to be aware of.

Another useful information that can be gathered by the visual analytics solution is the kind of combinations that are most recurrent (or most preferred) by users for example in terms of complexity of the structure (e.g. 1 trigger and 1 action rather than 2 triggers and 2 actions), which can give useful insights about the typical structure in which users prefer to specify rules, and also the level of complexity according to which the rules are typically structured. Another interesting insight that such tools can provide is in the preferred combinations in terms of trigger types and action types.

In addition, the tool has some further interactive capabilities allowing users to obtain further details on demand about the information presented. For instance, as soon as a specific type of trigger (or, alternatively: a type of action) is selected in one of the dashboards shown in the middle part of the tool, the tool highlights in its bottom part the set of rules that involve that trigger (or that action), so as to better inform the user in which way they have been concretely used. Finally, it can also be useful to investigate when users feel more comfortable to specify their personalization rules.

This work can also provide contribution for strengthening the view of meta-design [22], one of the major frameworks for end-user development. Indeed, meta-design promotes the perspective of "designing the design process", in which creating the technical and social conditions for broad participation in design activities becomes as important as creating the artefact itself. The method and the tool presented in this paper are expected to improve the conditions for such collaborative design in which all the participant stakeholders incrementally acquire ownership of problems and actively contribute to their solutions. Indeed, thanks to the information provided by visual analytics tools effectively visualizing data associated with EUD tools, developers of EUD tools (aka *meta-designers*) should be able to better understand the problems of end users and then more suitably design EUD tools accordingly, so as to have end users more easily adopt EUD tools in the long term.

6   Conclusions and Future Work

In this paper we present a contribution aiming to propose the use of visual analytics to support analysis of the interactions carried out by users with trigger-action rule-based personalization tools. We have also presented the application of the proposed method to data generated by the use of the PersRobIoTE tool. However, the method proposed can be easily applied and extended to other tools with similar purposes.

Such method aims to derive higher-level information such as usage patterns followed by users while interacting with the tool, the types of rules that users were more interested in creating by using the tool, the most popular trigger and action types used, so as to facilitate the supported interactions and therefore in the end also make easy the adoption of the EUD tool and the associated applications.

We also present a first application to the data generated by a class of university students without any experience in IoT programming who were asked to use a EUD trigger-action tool for creating various rules aimed at personalizing the behaviour of a robot immersed in a IoT environment. This study offers useful material for understanding the kind of support offered by the presented visual analytics solution, and how it can be exploited and further extended.

Future work will be dedicated to adding further features to the visual analytics tool, in order to enable its users in more flexibly specifying the data they are more interested in, and it will be exploited for analysing the personalization rules created in the trials that will be carried out in an international AAL project. In addition, we also plan to carry out an evaluation of the visual analytics tool with developers and domain experts to better assess it through their feedback.

References

1. Alexandrova, S., Cakmak, M., Hsiao, K., Takayama, L.: Robot programming by demonstration with interactive action visualizations. In: Proceedings of the 2014 Robotics: Science and Systems Conference (2014). https://doi.org/10.15607/RSS.2014.X.048
2. Buchina, N., Kamel, S., Barakova, E.I.: Design and evaluation of an end-user friendly tool for robot programming. In: Proceedings of IEEE International Symposium on Robot and Human Interactive Communication (RO-MAN 2016), pp. 185–191. IEEE (2016). https://doi.org/10.1109/ROMAN.2016.7745109
3. Cabitza, F., Fogli, D., Lanzilotti, R., Piccinno, A.: Rule-based tools for the configuration of ambient intelligence systems: a comparative user study. Multimed. Tools Appl. **76**(4), 5221–5241 (2017)
4. Corcella, L., Manca, M., Paternò, F., Santoro, C.: A visual tool for analysing IoT trigger/action programming. In: Bogdan, C., Kuusinen, K., Lárusdóttir, M.K., Palanque, P., Winckler, M. (eds.) HCSE 2018. LNCS, vol. 11262, pp. 189–206. Springer, Cham (2019). https://doi.org/10.1007/978-3-030-05909-5_11
5. Desolda, G., Ardito, C., Matera, M.: Empowering end users to customize their smart environments: model, composition paradigms, and domain-specific tools. ACM Trans. Comput. Hum. Interact. (TOCHI) **24**(2), 12 (2017)
6. Ghiani, G., Manca, M., Paternò, F., Santoro, C.: Personalization of context-dependent applications through trigger-action rules. ACM Trans. Comput. Hum. Interact. **24**(2) (2017). Article No. 14
7. Glas, D., Satake, S., Kanda, T., Hagita, N.: An interaction design framework for social robots. In: Proceedings of the 2012 Robotics: Science and Systems Conference (2012). https://doi.org/10.15607/RSS.2011.VII.014
8. Leonardi, N., Manca, M., Paternò, F., Santoro, C.: Trigger-action programming for personalising humanoid robot behaviour. In: ACM Conference on Human Factors in Computing Systems (CHI 2019), Glasgow, Paper 445 (2019)
9. Harms, P., Grabowski, J.: Usage-based automatic detection of usability smells. In: Sauer, S., Bogdan, C., Forbrig, P., Bernhaupt, R., Winckler, M. (eds.) HCSE 2014. LNCS, vol. 8742, pp. 217–234. Springer, Heidelberg (2014). https://doi.org/10.1007/978-3-662-44811-3_13

10. Huang, J., Cakmak, M.: Code3: a system for end to-end programming of mobile manipulator robots for novices and experts. In: Proceedings of the 2017 ACM/IEEE International Conference on Human-Robot Interaction (HRI 2017), pp. 453–462. ACM, New York (2017). https://doi.org/10.1145/2909824.3020215

11. Markopoulos, P., Nichols, J., Paternò, F., Pipek, V.: End-user development for the Internet of Things. ACM Trans. Comput. Hum. Interact. (TOCHI) **24**(2) (2017)

12. Mi, X., Qian, F., Zhang, Y., Wang, X.F.: An empirical characterization of IFTTT: ecosystem, usage, and performance. In: IMC 2017, pp. 398–404 (2017)

13. Mikusz, M., Clinch, S., Jones, R., Harding, M., Winstanley, C., Davie, N.: Repurposing web analytics to support the IoT. IEEE Comput. **48**, 42–49 (2015)

14. Pellizon, L.H., Choma, J., da Silva, T.S., Guerra, E., Zaina, L.: Software analytics for web usability: a systematic mapping. In: Gervasi, O., et al. (eds.) ICCSA 2017. LNCS, vol. 10409, pp. 246–261. Springer, Cham (2017). https://doi.org/10.1007/978-3-319-62407-5_17

15. Pot, E., Monceaux, J., Gelin, R., Maisonnier, B.: Choregraphe: a graphical tool for humanoid robot programming. In: Proceedings of the 18th IEEE International Symposium on Robot and Human Interactive Communication (RO-MAN 2009), pp. 46–51. IEEE (2009). https://doi.org/10.1109/ROMAN.2009.5326209

16. Resnick, M., et al.: Scratch: programming for all. Commun. ACM **52**(11), 60–67 (2009). https://doi.org/10.1145/1592761.1592779

17. Segura, V.C.V.B., Barbosa, S.D.J.: HistoryViewer: instrumenting a visual analytics application to support revisiting a session of interactive data analysis. PACMHCI 1(EICS), 11:1–11:18 (2017)

18. Siow, E., Tiropanis, T., Hall, W.: Analytics for the Internet of Things: a survey. ACM Comput. Surv. **51**(4), 36 pages (2018). https://doi.org/10.1145/3204947. Article 74

19. Ur, B., McManus, E., Pak Yong Ho, M., Littman, M.L.: Practical trigger-action programming in the smart home. In: Proceedings of the SIGCHI Conference on Human Factors in Computing Systems (CHI 2014), pp. 803–812. ACM, New York (2014). https://doi.org/10.1145/2556288.2557420

20. Ur, B., et al.: Trigger-action programming in the wild: an analysis of 200, 000 IFTTT recipes. In: CHI 2016, pp. 3227–3231 (2016)

21. Weintrop, D., et al.: Evaluating CoBlox: a comparative study of robotics programming environments for adult novices. In: Proceedings of the 2018 CHI Conference on Human Factors in Computing Systems (CHI 2018), Paper 366, 12 pages. ACM, New York (2018). https://doi.org/10.1145/3173574.3173940

22. Fischer, G., Fogli, D., Piccinno, A.: Revisiting and broadening the meta-design framework for end-user development. In: Paternò, F., Wulf, V. (eds.) New Perspectives in End-User Development. Springer, Cham (2017). https://doi.org/10.1007/978-3-319-60291-2_4

Cuscus: An End User Programming Tool for Data Visualisation

Mariana Marasoiu[1]($\boxtimes$), Detlef Nauck[2], and Alan F. Blackwell[1]

[1] Department of Computer Science and Technology,
University of Cambridge, Cambridge, UK
{mariana.marasoiu,alan.blackwell}@cl.cam.ac.uk
[2] Applied Research, BT, Ipswich, UK
detlef.nauck@bt.com

Abstract. We present Cuscus, a tool for data visualisation that is informed by ethnographic fieldwork across different professional sectors. Cuscus allows end-users to create novel visualisations by defining visual properties in a spreadsheet. We also report on user studies in the contexts of data journalism and business analytics, and discuss further extensions to this new interaction paradigm.

Keywords: Data visualisation · Spreadsheets · Graphics editors

1 Introduction

Different kinds of visualisations are needed by many people who work with data, from science to journalism, personal lifelogging or running a business. Live data visualisation usually requires a programming language or library such as D3.js, whereas data visualisation for print is created using professional graphics software. However, many people who want or need to do data visualisation are not experts, but are familiar with widespread EUD tools for data analysis such as spreadsheets. We are particularly interested in situations where the visualisations available in business tools such as Microsoft Excel [5] or Tableau [8] are too constrained for the novel story that an analyst wants to tell, but the programming skills necessary to develop novel visualisations in a tool such as D3.js [15] are too complex to be accessible.

Informed by fieldwork and formative studies with professional data journalists, data scientists, and business analysts, we have developed a paradigm for constructing novel visualisations that is accessible to end-user programmers. The "sweet spot" from our formative studies is a range of visual design elements that are comparable to those available in a slide presentation application

Mariana is a Vice-Chancellor's Scholar and is supported by an EPSRC industrial CASE studentship co-sponsored by BT. She is also supported by a Qualcomm European Research Studentship in Technology.

A. Malizia et al. (Eds.): IS-EUD 2019, LNCS 11553, pp. 115–131, 2019.
https://doi.org/10.1007/978-3-030-24781-2_8

such as PowerPoint, but supporting links to data in spreadsheet form for live visualisation in an unlimited variety of graphical forms.

We present Cuscus, a tool for constructing data visualisations, aiming to offer the graphical flexibility of a drawing editor within the context of a spreadsheet. We represent the visualisation in both graphical form and spreadsheet format, considering shape properties as data columns, and each shape as a data row. The user can then specify properties of a shape through formulas referencing incoming data, whilst still being able to adjust properties that are not data-bound through direct manipulation. By allowing the user the fine-grained control of specifying each shape property through formulas, Cuscus supports the creation of novel visualisations accessible to end-user programmers.

2   Design Process

The design of the prototype is informed by ethnographic study of a visual analytics consultancy [27], followed by a collaboration with data journalists and data scientists [28]. This fieldwork was complemented by a Research through Design process consisting of sketching and building multiple design alternatives to explore the design space [19]. Some of these alternatives were presented to the experts under study, followed by further design iterations. We should note that the fieldwork was not intended to supply a set of requirements to be satisfied, but rather to develop an understanding of the current practice of professional data analysts across multiple domains. Our goal was to understand the potential for new kinds of visualisation practice and tools to support wider audiences via end-user programming.

We analysed our observations of data analytic work practices using both open coding [32] and a coding scheme from the Patterns of User Experience framework [12]. We highlight here the main design principles and strategies that we aimed to address through the design of Cuscus, briefly presenting first the observations that informed each of them. We also use these design strategies as a framing for evaluating our tool, which we will discuss later on when reporting on user studies and observations.

2.1   Open Coding Findings and Design Implications

The consultancy we studied used Tableau [8] as the primary tool in their visual analytics work. Tableau is a direct manipulation tool where users drag and drop data fields onto different panels located around the visualisation canvas (called 'shelves' and 'cards' due to their appearance). The user does not interact directly with the visualisation being created, but controls how selected data is visualised through shelves and cards that expose properties of the visualisation. In contrast, in vector graphics editors, used by data journalists and information designers, the user manipulates each shape directly.

Design Strategy: INCREASE DIRECTNESS OF INTERACTION. Allow the end-user to interact directly with the shapes and marks that form the visualisation.

Besides doing data analysis themselves, the consultancy team was also offering tutorials and teaching workshops on Tableau. Their clients were already using Microsoft Excel [5] for analysis, but wanted further support for exploration and presentation. In contrast, the journalists we collaborated with were using spreadsheets as their primary tool for data analysis. Cairo notes that this is typical for data journalism, where the widespread practice for preparing visualisations for publication is to create a chart in a spreadsheet application and then export it into a graphics editor such as Adobe Illustrator [1] where its appearance can be adjusted [17].

Design Strategy: USE TOOLS THAT END USERS ARE ALREADY FAMILIAR WITH. The design of Cuscus hybridises two widely used tools that stood out from our fieldwork as relevant for data visualisation: spreadsheets and graphical editors.

An important step in data analysis is 'wrangling' data into the right form for visualisation [24]. This was confirmed in our field studies. Tableau offers the ability to create derived data fields, a feature we observed being used heavily by our data analysts. Whereas input data in Tableau is read-only, spreadsheet tools encourage editing data in place, blurring the line between input data and wrangled data.

Design Strategy: SUPPORT THE PROCESS OF DATA ANALYSIS. The Cuscus interface has 3 spreadsheet panels, the first for importing datasets, the middle for manipulating the input data if needed, and the third corresponding to the visualisation.

2.2 Closed Coding Findings and Design Implications

The Patterns of User Experiences (PUX) framework was developed from the Cognitive Dimensions of Notations [21] and consists of a set of activities and a set of patterns of experiences, organised in 7 groups (experiences of visibility, structure, meaning, interaction, thinking, process and creativity). Each pattern of experience consists of a reference number (e.g. SE4) and a short description.

In Tableau, the analyst works with read-only data columns, and whilst this offers a concise view of the data, it is less helpful for debugging activities. For example, in one instance we noticed that the analysts needed to create a table showing the data computed by several calculations, in order to debug these calculations. This pattern of experience was similarly observed during the iterative design of Lyra [34], where users noted that it was difficult to observe the effect of a data transformation based only on the visualisation and the data schema.

Design Strategy: VE1: THE INFORMATION YOU NEED IS VISIBLE. We expose data values by using spreadsheets as the underlying paradigm of processing data.

Related to the importance of visibility, we noticed that it was difficult to observe the dependencies between different Tableau calculations, as well as between the data and the visualisation. This is partly caused by the user primarily interacting with the visualisation through shelves and cards rather than with the marks forming the visualisations.

Design Strategy: SE1: YOU CAN SEE RELATIONSHIPS BETWEEN PARTS. In Cuscus, visual elements are represented both graphically and in spreadsheet format, making the relationship between data and visuals explicit. We further emphasize this mapping by highlighting the corresponding spreadsheet row when a shape is selected and manipulated, and vice versa.

As mentioned previously, Cairo describes a typical process in data journalism for creating an information graphic: opening a dataset in Excel, creating a chart to visualise it, followed by importing the chart in Adobe Illustrator to highlight interesting patterns [17]. Other graphic designers also rely on manual visual encoding in order to maintain the flexibility afforded to them by graphics editors [9, 25]. However, these processes are error prone. The quantities need to be entered manually and, since the properties of the visuals are not bound to underlying data, when it changes the visualisation needs to be adjusted manually, or even completely redrawn.

Design Strategy: PE2: THE STEPS YOU TAKE MATCH YOUR GOALS. In Cuscus, the visualisations can be modified both through direct manipulation of the visuals, and by changing the formulas that generate them.

3   Brief Review of Tools for Visual Analysis

Using the categorization of a survey of InfoVis authoring tools published in the major HCI and InfoVis venues [20], we can differentiate between several types of tools for creating visualisations: visualisation spreadsheets, template editors, shelf configuration tools, textual programming, visual dataflow systems and visual builders. Of these, we briefly review the more relevant categories of end-user development centered tools.

Template editors have a predefined set of charts that are available for visualising data, and the user maps the data to be visualised to the data inputs of the templates. Existing spreadsheet tools like Microsoft Excel [5] follow this paradigm. Commercial tools that rely on templates include Infogram [4], RAW-Graphs [7] and Datawrapper [2]. Template editors are useful for visualising data quickly, as the user is able to create a chart with only a few button clicks. However, the kinds of visualisations that a user can create and the options for customisation are restricted to those pre-implemented by developers.

Shelf configuration tools do not offer a fixed menu of visualisation types, but instead offer a set of graphical elements and a way of mapping data to their properties. Mapping is done by dragging and dropping data columns (also known as attributes) onto 'shelves' - the data inputs of the visualisation. Whilst the set of charts that can be created is not limited explicitly (as it is for the template editors), the restriction is on the visual elements available and which properties can be set by data. Tableau [8] is an example widely used by data analysts.

In *visual builders*, the user starts by selecting which graphical mark to use in the visualisation, followed by mapping the desired data columns onto some properties of the graphical element. Some tools support the construction of visualisations at the level of basic shapes (e.g. Gold [30], Lyra [34], Data Illustrator [26]), or with some added chart abstractions, such as axes (e.g. iVisDesigner [31], iVoLVER [29]).

Using the above framework, Cuscus could be described as a *visual builder* tool. However, one of the main differences from both shelf configuration tools and visual builders is that these tools usually require the user to work with whole columns of data rather than individual data points, whereas Cuscus allows the users to work on a single shape at a time, and so at data *point* level rather than data *column* level. This stemmed partly from our decision to use spreadsheets as the data representation, which encouraged working on one cell at a time, partly from the pattern PE2: THE STEPS YOU TAKE MATCH YOUR GOALS and design strategy INCREASE DIRECTNESS OF INTERACTION, suggesting that every element of the visualisation be under the control of the user. This design choice echoes Huron and colleagues' work on constructive visualisations [22], where their tangible token-based setup encouraged a bottom-up visualisation construction approach: the user starts off visualising a small part of the data and iteratively develops the rest of the visualisation as they add more data.

A novel aspect of Cuscus is that the visualisation is exposed to the user in a similar representation as the data: a shape is a row in a spreadsheet. We expect that the user workflow in Cuscus consists of alternating between working in the graphics editor and working in the spreadsheet. This is related to work by Bigelow and colleagues on a bridge model [10] for combining edits between a generative visualisation toolkit (D3.js) and a drawing tool (Adobe Illustrator). However, in Cuscus we avoid the need for a bridge by embedding the spreadsheet and the drawing tool in the same application, with the same internal representation. Our strategy is also different from most tools that use a drawing-style interaction for creating visualisations, where the properties of the visualisation are presented in side panels, and data binding is done through drag and drop (e.g. Lyra [35]) or drop-down menus (e.g. Data Illustrator [26]).

4   Cuscus - A Spreadsheet-Graphics Hybrid for Visualisation

4.1   The Cuscus Interface

The Cuscus interface, as shown in Fig. 1, is split into two sections: the graphics editor in the top part, where the user can create and manipulate shapes and where the visualisations are created, and the spreadsheet editor in the bottom part containing several side by side groups of sheets for data manipulation and visual representation.

Spreadsheet Editor. Spreadsheets are initially organised in three panels for data input, wrangling and visualisation. We aimed to replicate the basic functionality of spreadsheet tools such as Google Sheets or Microsoft Excel. Our internal spreadsheet data structure is a dependency graph-based execution engine [18], on top of which we have added a spreadsheets-specific type system and a set of intrinsic operations and functions. The rightmost panel contains the spreadsheet representations of groups of shapes from the graphics editor.

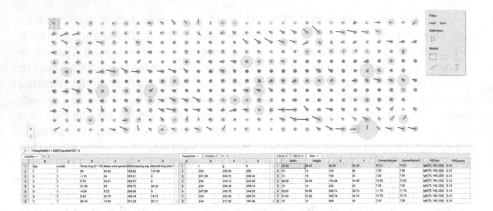

Fig. 1. The Cuscus prototype for data visualisations, designed as a hybrid between a spreadsheet editor and a graphics editor. It was used here to create a visualisation of the weather in Cambridge, UK in 2017. Each point represents a day of the year, with various graphical marks encoding temperature, wind speed and direction, and rainfall.

Graphics Editor. The graphics editor supports direct manipulation of various shapes, with an interaction style similar to Adobe Illustrator or Microsoft PowerPoint. Each shape has a set of handles for resizing and moving on the canvas. The graphics editor is represented as an infinite zoom and panning canvas, allowing the creation of multiple visualisations, side by side, or away from view. Controls in the bottom-left corner allow zoom to fit all graphics on the canvas. The right-hand panel includes buttons for creating new shapes, and to save and load the workspace. We support text and basic shapes, with further shapes easily added in future.

Implementation Details. Cuscus is primarily implemented in Dart [16] and HTML5, and uses the Javascript-based Ohm parser generator [36] to parse spreadsheet formulas. Visualisations are represented as SVG format embedded in HTML. New datasets can be loaded in a new sheet from CSV files, and the entire workspace can be exported and imported through JSON files.

4.2   Spreadsheet Representation of Graphic Elements

When the user draws a shape on the screen, a new sheet is created in the rightmost spreadsheet panel. Instead of the typical spreadsheet columns (A, B, ... AA, AB, ...), the columns of this sheet correspond to a set of properties that define the shape type (e.g. Width, Height, X, Y, FillColor, ...) as can be seen in Fig. 2A. Attributes mainly relate to SVG shape type, with some CSS style attributes (e.g. 'font-size' for the text graphic). The first row of the new sheet is already filled in with the values of the graphic drawn on the screen.

Formulas can be used in the cells of this sheet as they would usually be used in spreadsheets. For example, in Fig. 2A, the formula used for calculating the height of the second bar is $= AVERAGE(DataSheet!A2 : D2)$, where $DataSheet$ is a sheet not shown in the image containing some data, and $A2 : D2$ is a cell range reference in that sheet over which the $AVERAGE$ function is applied.

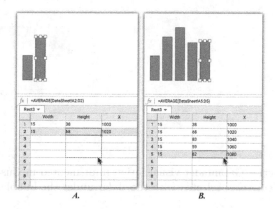

A.   B.

Fig. 2. Demonstration of the fill down feature for creating new shapes by copying down the row representing an existing shape and automatically adjusting the relative references in formulas, thus referencing subsequent data points in the data input sheet.

4.3   From Single Shapes to a Visualisation

"Fill down" (or more generally, "fill into adjacent cells") is a common feature in spreadsheet tools where the user selects one or more cells and drags the fill handle in the bottom-right corner of the selection to fill in adjacent cells. It is often used as a way to easily copy formulas across the spreadsheet. Since cell references are by default relative to the current cell, "fill down" adjusts the coordinates of the cell references in the formula to maintain the positional distance (e.g. the formula $= A1 + A2$ becomes $= A2 + A3$ when filled down one cell, and $= B1 + B2$ when filled right one cell).

Cuscus relies heavily on this spreadsheet feature for multiplying the shapes in the visualisation. Once the formulas for the first few shapes have been broadly defined, the user can "fill down" the last row defining a shape, thus creating copies of that shape that reference subsequent data points (see Fig. 2). This feature encourages users to start designing the visualisation by focusing on one or a small number of data points to start with, and adding more data in the visualisation later on.

4.4   Interactive Widgets

By representing visual structure in the same way as data, we get some interactivity for free, enabling construction of interactive widgets. Figure 3 shows a recreation of the Bubbles chart from Hans Rosling's Gapminder [3]. We created bubbles for every country and year, and use the opacity property of the bubbles to select which year to show. The slider widget is created by using a cell in the middle panel to read the X value of the slider shape and transform it into a year relative to the length of the time axis. A bubble is then visible if its year is the same as the year selected with the slider, and transparent otherwise.

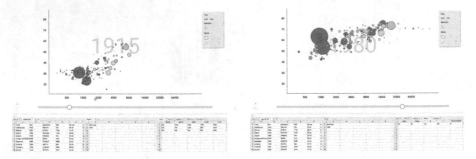

Fig. 3. The interactive Gapminder visualisation implemented in Cuscus, showing two snapshots of different years selected with the slider under the bubble chart.

4.5 Limitations

Not all potential shape properties are exposed in the UI, but more could be added in future. We plan to experiment with variants for some columns to simplify formula writing. For example, the X and Y properties for the Rectangle mark refer to the top-left corner of the rectangle, so formulas need to factor in the width/height of the rectangle if they wish it to be positioned relative to another corner. Alternative columns could offer the possibility of the formula value to compute the center of the rectangle (useful for e.g. scatter plots), or the bottom-centre (useful for column charts), with the user able to choose visual layouts.

Cuscus currently supports only Cartesian coordinates, meaning that polar coordinate visualisations such as pie charts cannot be created. Geographical projections can be achieved by end-users by finding the formulas for transforming lat-lon into x-y coordinates. Due to the infinite canvas, implementing other types of coordinate system would require introducing an abstraction for delimiting the area of the canvas that belongs a visualisation. There is also no abstraction for layout algorithms, but these could be implemented using the existing spreadsheet lookup and range functions.

5   Evaluation

5.1   Example Visualisations

One of the primary goals of Cuscus is to support the design and creation of visualisations that are difficult or even impossible to create in existing end-user tools for data analysis, such as Excel, Tableau or RAWGraphs, and would otherwise require programming.

To demonstrate the expressivity of Cuscus, we have used it to construct all of the visualisations in this paper, some being new visualisations (for example Figs. 1 and 6), and some being recreations of other visualisations (Figs. 3, 4, 5).

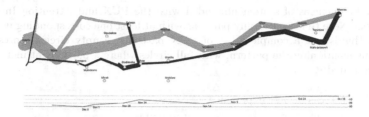

Fig. 4. A recreation of Minard's famous visualisation of Napoleon's Grand Army in the 1915 campaign towards Russia.

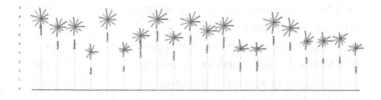

Fig. 5. A recreation of the OECD Better Life Index visualisation [6].

5.2   User Study with Data Journalists

To obtain access to a group of data journalists, we designed a study that could be administered during breaks at a trade conference (DataJConf 2018). A time restriction of 30 min led us to use a protocol based on the "champagne prototyping" technique [11], in which a small number of credible participants are interviewed by a researcher as to whether a tool under evaluation is self-explanatory, collecting qualitative data for coding within an analytical framework.

The research questions in this study were (1) whether our target audience would understand the representation of visual elements in spreadsheet form and the opportunities for interaction, and (2) whether the representation of the data analysis process in juxtaposed spreadsheets was useful. The study alternately presented functionality of the interface, then asked participants to give examples from their day to day work where that functionality would be useful.

Each interview was transcribed by the first author. The transcripts were coded according to the PUX and Attention Investment [13] frameworks. The results are summarised in Table 1.

Tool Status. At the time this study was run, basic functionality to create and manipulate shapes, spreadsheet formulae and fill down was in place. However data wrangling could only be done programmatically and there was no ability to load and save the workspace or to import csv files. There was no panning and zooming, and only rectangles and lines were available as graphic elements.

Participant Profile. The 5 participants were all conference attendees. Three were data journalists, one a graphic designer transitioning into data journalism and one a computer scientist. All had some experience with Excel, and all

Table 1. Frequencies of statements coded with the PUX and Attention Investment frameworks. Note that we list only patterns with at least one corresponding user statement, so this is not a complete list of PUX patterns. Empty circles represent one participant mentioning the pattern, with full circles where a participant mentions the pattern repeatedly.

Patterns of user experience	
VE1: The information you need is visible	○○
SE1: You can see relationships between parts	○○○
SE2: You can change your mind easily	○○○
SE4: You can compare or contrast different parts	○
ME3: Similar things look similar	○
ME6: The visual connotations are appropriate	●
IE1: Interaction opportunities are evident	○○○
IE3: Things stay where you put them	○
IE4: Accidental mistakes are unlikely	○
IE6: It is easy to refer to specific parts	○○
TE1: You don't need to think too hard	○●
TE5: You are drawn in to play around	○○
PE2: The steps you take match your goals	○○○○
PE4: You can be non-committal	○
PE5: Repetition can be automated	○○
PE6: The content can be preserved	○
Attention investment	
Investment risk: what may go wrong when using Cuscus	○
Investment cost: attentional effort of using Cuscus	○○●●
Investment payoff: effort to be saved if using Cuscus	○○●●
Alternative: basis of decision not to use Cuscus	○

mentioned using other tools for data analysis and visualisation (including R, Python, Tableau, PowerBI, DataWrapper, Infogram).

Results. For most aspects, all 5 participants were able to give examples from their experience where a tool like Cuscus would have helped. When unable to find an example from their own experience, they were able to suggest other situations or groups of people who would find it useful. Through the examples they gave, participants seemed to understand and find useful the dual representation of the visualisation in graphic and spreadsheet form, as well as the utility of having juxtaposed spreadsheets for separating input data from data wrangling and visualisation.

PUX Analysis. The 5 participants made a total of 30 statements regarding the design of Cuscus which could be coded using the Patterns of User Experience framework. We discuss here the patterns that appeared most frequently.

Pattern PE2: THE STEPS YOU TAKE MATCH YOUR GOALS was a design principle for Cuscus and was mentioned by 4 participants, all in a positive context. Most participants mentioned support for interaction, such as being able to directly interact with the shapes in the visualisation (*"having something which feels like an SVG editor inside of [Cuscus] hooked up to the data feels really nice"* (P4)).

Another key element of our design was the pattern SE1: YOU CAN SEE RELATIONSHIPS BETWEEN PARTS. Three participants had positive comments about the relationship between the spreadsheets and the visualisations and appreciated being able to see visuals responding to changes in the spreadsheets. However, two of these participants also mentioned that they felt like the process of creating a visualisation was *"a bit complex"* (P2), a trade-off for our design with pattern TE1: YOU DON'T NEED TO THINK TOO HARD.

One effect of treating shape types as primary objects with properties bound to data is that the pattern SE2: YOU CAN CHANGE YOUR MIND EASILY is not well supported. Some participants picked up on this: *"[...] here it feels like that's a large change, because it's a switch from that being like the bar shapes to the line shapes. So I guess it does seem like you would want to be confident going in when you start doing this"* (P4).

Attention Investment Analysis. All the factors of the Attention Investment framework were mentioned by the participants. *Investment cost* was mentioned in relation to needing to be comfortable with Excel (e.g. *"For me, I get what you're doing right away, but for somebody who's maybe somewhat less technologically savvy, I guess [...] would that be a bit too much?"* (P5)), and that the speed for creating a visualisation was an important factor in their work (e.g. *"For what I'm doing, I don't want to spend a lot of time in charts. I want something quick and easy because I'm looking at it in just the exploratory way, and I need to move on."* (P5)).

Investment payoff was usually discussed in terms of what you could do in Cuscus but not in other tools (e.g. "to put error bars [in Excel] is really time consuming." (P1)), and also that it supports editing the visualisation in a graphics editor-like interface, where the connection to data is maintained.

Discussion on *investment risks* were related to the SE2: YOU CAN CHANGE YOUR MIND EASILY pattern discussed above, whilst the *basis of decision not to use Cuscus* was related to the formatting of the visuals in a spreadsheet rather than a graphic palette.

5.3 User Study with Business Analysts

Since the evaluation with data journalists indicated potential interest in the novel approach, and the participants were able to understand how Cuscus works, we conducted a second study to elicit more in-depth feedback on the tool during use. As our target users are people with some spreadsheet experience looking to create novel visualisations, they can be found in various work contexts. For our second study we turned to the business context and we set up a study at an annual week-long workshop on data science at BT in Ipswich.

The primary goal of this second user study was to understand the experience of participants using Cuscus to create data visualisations, and how this might differ from tools they have used previously. We were also interested in collecting general usability feedback. In order to collect data that would answer these questions, we opted for an open-ended task with think-aloud protocol, followed by a usability questionnaire. Each study started with a short demonstration of the system, followed by asking the participant to create a visualisation using any of 4 datasets provided. Since we were not evaluating participants' creativity with the tool but wanted to encourage it, we had on the table printouts of novel visualisations and infographics published by professional visualisation designers, and the participants were informed that they could use them as sources of inspiration. After around 30 min, at a good break point in the construction of the visualisation, the participants were asked to stop and move onto filling in the usability questionnaire. The questionnaire was derived from the Cognitive Dimensions Questionnaire [14], using Patterns of User Experience as the underlying framework. The questionnaire lists the patterns of experience as statements that the participants were asked to agree or disagree with on a 5-point Likert scale, followed by a free text box for each statement asking them for an example of tool use for the given rating.

Tool Status. The tool was fully implemented as discussed above in Sect. 4.

Participant Profile. The 8 participants who signed up were all attendees at the workshop and volunteered their time during practical sessions. One participant was unable to continue after the initial demonstration, and we do not include their data. Four participants did not have time to complete the questionnaire, and were asked to finish it at home. One did not return the questionnaire, and we do not include their data. Five of the remaining six participants described themselves as using visualisations to analyse data frequently. The final participant reported some experience with Excel but does not do much analysis.

Results. All 6 participants who attempted to use Cuscus were able to create one visualisation in the 20–30 min they had with the tool. Figure 6 shows participant responses to the Likert scale questions. Most answers demonstrate agreement, but we discuss below patterns where the participants had varying opinions, as well as the patterns used to inform the design.

VE1: THE INFORMATION YOU NEED IS VISIBLE P2 mentioned lack of help, whilst another participant mentioned that *"Columns of information cannot fit in one screen"* and suggested that Cuscus should be best used on a large monitor (P6).

SE2: YOU CAN CHANGE YOUR MIND EASILY P1 noted that *"Changing of formulas would be required to change presentation"*, whilst others noted the need for undo.

SE3: THERE ARE ROUTES FROM A THING YOU KNOW TO SOMETHING YOU DON'T For some participants, the tool *"seemed intuitive"* (P3) and were able *"to implement a color mapping which didn't seem to be part of the intended functionality."*

Strongly disagree	Disagree	Unsure	Agree	Strongly agree	
					VE1: The information you need is visible
					VE2: The overall story is clear
					VE3: Important parts draw your attention
					VE4: The visual layout is concise
					VE5: You can see detail in context
					SE1: You can see relationships between parts
					SE2: You can change your mind easily
					SE3: There are routes from a thing you know to something you don't
					SE4: You can compare or contrast different parts
					ME1: It looks like what it describes
					ME2: The purpose of each part is clear
					ME3: Similar things look similar
					ME4: You can tell the difference between things
					ME5: You can add comments
					ME6: The visual connotations are appropriate
					IE1: Interaction opportunities are evident
					IE2: Actions are fluid, not awkward
					IE3: Things stay where you put them
					IE4: Accidental mistakes are unlikely
					IE5: Easier actions steer what you do
					IE6: It is easy to refer to specific parts
					TE1: You don't need to think too hard
					TE2: You can read-off new information
					TE3: It makes you stop and think
					TE4: Elements mean only one thing
					TE5: You are drawn in to play around
					PE1: The order of tasks is natural
					PE2: The steps you take match your goals
					PE3: You can try out a partial product
					PE4: You can be non-committal
					PE5: Repetition can be automated
					PE6: The content can be preserved
					CE1: You can extend the language
					CE2: You can redefine how it is interpreted
					CE3: You can see different things when you look again
					CE4: Anything not forbidden is allowed

■ Participant 1   ■ Participant 2   ■ Participant 3
■ Participant 4   ■ Participant 5   ■ Participant 6

Fig. 6. Participant responses for the 5 point agreement/disagreement Likert scale questions, considering the patterns of experience as statements about Cuscus.

(P5), whilst others mentioned lack of undo or the need for expertise in Excel *"Knowledge of spreadsheet formula is required to fully utilise the program"* (P1).

TE1: You don't need to think too hard The agreements included comments that the tool *"made sense"* (P3) and *"So easy to create, your imagination is the limit"* (P2), whilst two other participants felt that they did have to think quite hard.

PE3: You can try out a partial product/PE4: You can be non-committal Disagreements with these patterns primarily elicited feedback regarding the lack of an undo button, but also comments of agreement (*"The visualisation evolves at each step of development."* (P1))

PE5: Repetition can be automated Comments focused on the need for improved copy and paste and better fill down (*"The most repetitive task performed was dragging cells down. It would have been nice to have a keyboard shortcut to drag them to be as long as adjacent columns."* (P5)).

SE1: You can see relationships between parts Most comments mentioned positively the visibility of the relationship between spreadsheet and visualisation, whilst P3 mentioned that the visualisation needed to be responsive to screen size.

SE4: You can compare or contrast different parts Most of the feedback was general in nature (e.g. *"Each part of the interface serves a clear purpose."* (P5)), with only one participant mentioning a usability difficulty (*some of the lines are hard to click* (P3)), though rating it neutrally.

PE2: The steps you take match your goals Received positive and one neutral rating, with one participant mentioning skill transference (*"Able to follow the same basic process used on other applications"* (P2)), whilst P5 commented that *"Sometimes you have to do things in roundabout ways"*.

Usability Feedback. Using the PUX framework has allowed us to collect detailed usability feedback. For example, users noted slight differences in cell selection from Excel, some difficulty in select lines on the canvas, wanting to select a reference or range when editing a formula by pointing at the respective cell (which currently isn't implemented), the limited set of shapes, as well as some limitations in the properties available for the shapes.

6   Discussion

Cuscus is a spreadsheet-graphics editor hybrid system that aims to empower end-users to create data visualisations. It aims to be particularly useful in situations where the charts available in widely used data analysis tools such as Excel or Tableau are too constrained for the visualisation that an analyst wishes to create.

Expressive Power and Simplicity. In both user studies, participants commented often on the flexibility and expressive power afforded by Cuscus, in terms of the kinds of visualisations that could be created. However, a concern that arose several times throughout the studies was the way that the means of specifying the visualisation is quite complex, requiring familiarity with spreadsheet formulas and geometry. Other tools in this space also observe that in designing for expressivity, simplicity is a trade-off [29,31]. In their case, the loss of simplicity comes from the large number of widgets needed to make the system useful, whilst in Cuscus, it comes from the user needing to think about the relationships between the data and the graphical marks comprising the visualisation, and between the graphical marks themselves. Within the design space of end user tools for data visualisation, user response to Cuscus suggests that the abstraction level we picked may be low, while the level in the other tools is too high, requiring many specialised widgets.

Interaction Opportunities. Currently, modifying the shapes through direct manipulation allows changes only to the properties that are not yet bound to formulas. For example, in a column chart, the user is allowed to change the width of the bars, but not the height, since the height is specified by a formula. Unfortunately, this encourages users to work primarily in spreadsheets, and less with the graphics editor. To avoid this, we plan to explore alternative designs that better support PE2: The steps you take match your goals and increase directness of interaction. One option might be to consider the resizing of a data-bound property as the scaling of that property, which could be represented by adding a multiplicative factor in the spreadsheet formula. Implementation is not entirely straightforward however, as multiple edits should be merged into a single scaling factor.

Working with Individual Shapes. In Cuscus, a shape is the unit of interaction, and a visualisation is created by multiplying a shape over different data. A typical workflow would be to start the design of a visualisation from a few data points and then expand to the larger dataset, similar to the practice observed by Huron *et al.* for visualisation construction out of physical tokens [23]. Working with individual data points rather than with data fields can create repetition viscosity$_{CD}$, as noted in iVoLVER [29]. In Cuscus, the spreadsheet representation and the use of Excel-style fill down for multiplying shapes avoids such granular repetitions to some extent. However, in the current implementation, when a shape property is changed, the user still needs to copy the new formula across all other shapes in the group, an action that is repetitive after several adjustments. We are exploring several solutions, from offering the option of setting a formula template for a column of cells (as in CalculationView [33]), or automatically copying the formula across shapes in the same sheet.

7 Conclusion

In this paper we presented Cuscus, a spreadsheet-based tool for creating novel visualisations. In Cuscus, the properties of graphic elements drawn on a canvas are also represented in spreadsheet-like form, allowing the user to bind data to visuals through typical spreadsheet formulas. The design of this tool was informed by fieldwork with data analysts and data journalists, from which we briefly describe several findings. We also reported on two usability studies with participants from both of these domains, which found the tool promising, often highlighting the flexibility and ability to create a wide range of visualisations. They were able to quickly understand how the tool works, and when asked to create a visualisation, were able to use the tool successfully. We also received detailed usability feedback which we plan to incorporate before further iterations.

References

1. Adobe Illustrator. https://www.adobe.com/illustrator. Accessed 30 Apr 2019
2. Datawrapper. https://www.datawrapper.de/. Accessed 30 Apr 2019
3. Gapminder. https://www.gapminder.org/. Accessed 30 Apr 2019
4. Infogram. https://infogram.com/. Accessed 30 Apr 2019
5. Microsoft Excel. https://products.office.com/excel. Accessed 30 Apr 2019
6. OECD Better Life Index. http://www.oecdbetterlifeindex.org/. Accessed 30 Apr 2019
7. RAWGraphs. https://rawgraphs.io/. Accessed 30 Apr 2019
8. Tableau. http://www.tableau.com/. Accessed 30 Apr 2019
9. Bigelow, A., Drucker, S., Fisher, D., Meyer, M.: Reflections on how designers design with data. In: Proceedings of the 2014 International Working Conference on Advanced Visual Interfaces, pp. 17–24. ACM (2014)

10. Bigelow, A., Drucker, S., Fisher, D., Meyer, M.: Iterating between tools to create and edit visualizations. IEEE Trans. Vis. Comput. Graph. **23**(1), 481–490 (2017)
11. Blackwell, A.F., Burnett, M.M., Jones, S.P.: Champagne prototyping: a research technique for early evaluation of complex end-user programming systems. In: 2004 IEEE Symposium on Visual Languages - Human Centric Computing, pp. 47–54 (2004)
12. Blackwell, A.F.: A pattern language for the design of diagrams. In: Richards, C. (ed.) Elements of Diagramming. (Forthcoming)
13. Blackwell, A.F.: First steps in programming: a rationale for attention investment models. In: Proceedings - IEEE 2002 Symposia on Human Centric Computing Languages and Environments, HCC 2002, pp. 2–10 (2002)
14. Blackwell, A.F., Green, T.R.G.: A cognitive dimensions questionnaire optimised for users. In: Proceedings of the 12th annual meeting of the Psychology of Programming Interest Group (PPIG 2000), pp. 137–152 (2000)
15. Bostock, M., Ogievetsky, V., Heer, J.: D3: data-driven documents. IEEE Trans. Vis. Comput. Graph. **17**(12), 2301–2309 (2011)
16. Bracha, G., Bak, L.: Dart, a new programming language for structured web programming. In: GOTO Aarhus Conference, October 2011
17. Cairo, A.: The functional art: an introduction to information graphics and visualization. New Riders (2012)
18. Church, L.: Possum. https://github.com/lukechurch/possum. Accessed 30 Apr 2019
19. Fallman, D.: Design-oriented Human-computer Interaction. In: Proceedings of the SIGCHI Conference on Human Factors in Computing Systems, CHI 2003, pp. 225–232. ACM, New York (2003)
20. Grammel, L., Bennett, C., Tory, M., Storey, M.A.: A survey of visualization construction user interfaces. In: Hlawitschka, M., Weinkauf, T. (eds.) EuroVis - Short Papers, pp. 19–23. The Eurographics Association (2013)
21. Green, T.R.G., Petre, M.: Usability analysis of visual programming environments: a 'cognitive dimensions' framework. J. Vis. Lang. Comput. **7**(2), 131–174 (1996)
22. Huron, S., Carpendale, S., Thudt, A., Tang, A., Mauerer, M.: Constructive visualization. In: Proceedings of the 2014 Conference on Designing Interactive Systems, pp. 433–442. ACM (2014)
23. Huron, S., Jansen, Y., Carpendale, S.: Constructing visual representations: investigating the use of tangible tokens. IEEE Trans. Vis. Comput. Graph. **20**(12), 2102–2111 (2014)
24. Kandel, S., et al.: Research directions in data wrangling: visuatizations and transformations for usable and credible data. Inf. Vis. **10**(4), 271–288 (2011)
25. Kim, N.W., et al.: Data-driven guides: supporting expressive design for information graphics. IEEE Trans. Vis. Comput. Graph. **23**(1), 491–500 (2017)
26. Liu, Z., et al.: Data illustrator: augmenting vector design tools with lazy data binding for expressive visualization authoring. In: Proceedings of the 2018 CHI Conference on Human Factors in Computing Systems. ACM (2018)
27. Marasoiu, M., Blackwell, A.F.: User experiences in a visual analytics business. In: Proceedings of the 28th Annual Workshop of the Psychology of Programming Interest Group (PPIG 2017) (2017)
28. Marasoiu, M., Islam, S., Church, L., Lucero, M., Paige, B., Petricek, T.: Stories of storytelling about UK's EU funding. In: Proceedings of the 2nd European Data and Computational Journalism Conference, pp. 14–16 (2018)

29. Méndez, G.G., Nacenta, M.A., Vandenheste, S.: iVoLVER: interactive visual language for visualization extraction and reconstruction. In: Proceedings of the 2016 CHI Conference on Human Factors in Computing Systems, CHI 2016, pp. 4073–4085. ACM, New York (2016)
30. Myers, B.A., Goldstein, J., Goldberg, M.A.: Creating charts by demonstration. In: Proceedings of the SIGCHI Conference on Human Factors in Computing Systems, CHI 1994, pp. 106–111. ACM, New York (1994)
31. Ren, D., Höllerer, T., Yuan, X.: iVisDesigner: expressive interactive design of information visualizations. IEEE Trans. Vis. Comput. Graph. **20**(12), 2092–2101 (2014)
32. Saldaña, J.: The Coding Manual for Qualitative Researchers. SAGE, January 2015
33. Sarkar, A., Gordon, A.D., Jones, S.P., Toronto, N.: Calculation view: multiple-representation editing in spreadsheets. In: 2018 IEEE Symposium on Visual Languages and Human-Centric Computing (VL/HCC), pp. 85–93 (2018)
34. Satyanarayan, A., Heer, J.: Lyra: an interactive visualization design environment. Comput. Graph. Forum: J. Eur. Assoc. Comput. Graph. **33**(3), 351–360 (2014)
35. Satyanarayan, A., Russell, R., Hoffswell, J., Heer, J.: Reactive vega: a streaming dataflow architecture for declarative interactive visualization. IEEE Trans. Vis. Comput. Graph. **22**(1), 659–668 (2015)
36. Warth, A., Dubroy, P., Garnock-Jones, T.: Modular semantic actions. In: Proceedings of the 12th Symposium on Dynamic Languages, pp. 108–119. ACM (2016)

A Board-Game for Co-Designing Smart Nature Environments in Workshops with Children

Rosella Gennari[1] , Maristella Matera[2] , Alessandra Melonio[1(✉)] ,
and Eftychia Roumelioti[1]

[1] Free University of Bozen-Bolzano, Piazza Domenicani 3, 39100 Bolzano, Italy
gennari@inf.unibz.it, alessandra.melonio@unibz.it,
eftychia.roumelioti@stud-inf.unibz.it
[2] Politecnico di Milano, Piazza Leonardo da Vinci 32, 20133 Milano, Italy
maristella.matera@polimi.it

Abstract. In recent years, the Human Computer Interaction community has increasingly engaged children in the design process of technology for them as co-designers, and recently as protagonists in co-design. It has also recognised the need of "bringing children back to nature". This paper combines both lines of research, giving children the role of protagonist co-designers of smart nature ecosystems. In order to engage children as co-designers, the research reported in this paper has employed a playful solution: a board game for children for co-designing smart interactive objects for outdoors nature ecosystems. This paper illustrates the genesis and recent evolution of the board-game in two workshops with children of different ages and gender. Its conclusions draw lessons for involving children as protagonist co-designers of smart nature ecosystems.

Keywords: Smart nature · Children · Co-design ·
Cultures of participation and meta-design approaches

1 Introduction

Research indicates that time spent outdoors in nature is important for children's development, but children spend much less time outdoors today than in the past. Technology is considered to be one of the main causes of children's living indoors [6]. Some researchers believe that technology can also be used to bring children outdoors, in novel smart nature environments, that is, nature environments augmented with "smart" behaviours, e.g., [24]. Along this line of research, recent initiatives tried to make children the *protagonists* of the ideation of novel smart nature environments for them; e.g., researchers have organised co-design workshops with paper-based generative toolkits in order to engage children in the design of smart objects for spending time outdoors in nature

---

Members from the first institution were supported by the GeKI project.

A. Malizia et al. (Eds.): IS-EUD 2019, LNCS 11553, pp. 132–148, 2019.
https://doi.org/10.1007/978-3-030-24781-2_9

[22]. This paper also addresses the issue of how to make children the protagonists of the design of novel smart nature environments for them. In order to do so, this paper introduce a card-based board game for ideating smart nature environments with children through play, in which the children have the role of protagonists.

The paper starts by reviewing the relevant literature for co-designing with children for nature. Then it describes the latest version of the board game and what originated it. It continues with the two workshops in which the game board was used by two 4-member groups of 11 and 14 years old children, 4 males and 4 females. The game-play gave a rich set of data, qualitative and quantitative, which are reflected over in the paper conclusions.

2   Related Work and Background

Co-design protagonists. In the early days of Human Computer Interaction (HCI), children were involved as users or testers of technology for them. Subsequently, following a Participatory Design (PD) tradition, children started to be involved as co-designers in different stages of design, whether as design informants or full partners, e.g., [11,14]. Recently, a complementary perspective on children as co-designers has emerged. This perspective adds what motivates or gives children benefits in co-design, considering them the protagonists of design [21]. In this view, children guide the design process and are given the means to critically reflect on technology and its role in their lives. In this paper, we aim at engaging children as co-design protagonists.

Generative toolkits. Numerous generative toolkits are used to engage people and enable them to co-design, e.g., visual materials (e.g., photos), storytelling kits. Recent workshops have employed cards to both engage people and ideate smart solutions with them [5,23,33]. The systematic analysis in [30] lists different benefits of card-based design, such as to foster creative thinking and problem solving (e.g., [17,28]), support the design of a product or service considering users' needs (e.g., [4]), provide methods or information for specific domains (e.g., [8]), facilitate collaborative working in participatory and co-design sessions (e.g., [18]). Sets or decks of cards, such as the IoT Card Set [2], the IoT Design Deck [10] and the Tiles Cards [27], have been used for co-designing or augmenting every-day's objects with smart behaviours. Adapted versions of Tiles Cards were employed in co-design workshops with children as well [13,26].

However, the most useful cards (i.e., likely to lead to design outcomes) consider the environment's specificity, e.g., cards for co-designing smart cities should be different than cards for designing toys [19,30]. Moreover, rules for the usage of cards should support the purpose of the cards [25,30]. Cards and rules should be designed for their intended users, e.g., by considering children's characteristics [19]. In particular, rules for using cards with children can be conveyed as a game's rules; playfulness is widely recognised fundamental for engaging children, and triggering creativity, e.g., [28]. These are ideas also pursued in this paper.

From Smart Cities to Smart Nature. There are a number of workshops meant for co-designing smart cities with adults, some using cards or games. For instance, Tiles cards have been used in smart city workshops with different stakeholders [16]. There are less smart city initiatives with children, which use cards or games. LocaLudo, for example, is a board platform that involves families in the design of new architecture landscapes through playing [20].

Recently, HCI research is voicing the need to facilitate children's engagement in the design of smart natural environments, e.g., [3]. In this context, children have been involved as informants or users. For instance, contextual inquiries with children led to the emergence of the ABBOT smart toy to engage children in natural outdoors environments [7]. To the best of our knowledge, however, there are few workshops for co-designing smart nature environments with children. One of the few exceptions is the project by Smart Toy LLC, which engaged children in co-design sessions of a new app and smart toy that encourages them to empathise with nature [22].

The goal of our research is also to continue this line of investigation and co-design smart nature ecosystems with children through a board game with cards for nature environments. The origins of the game and its evolution are unravelled in the remainder of this paper.

3   The SNaP Board-Game

The *Smart Nature Protagonists* (SNaP) board-game is a cooperative game for co-design workshops, with ideas taken from traditional board-game design [31]. It considers children as co-designers in the design practice of augmenting outdoor environment objects with the use of tools and rules explained in the following.

3.1   Tools and Setup

The game is designed for 2–4 players, in the role of *Designers*, and a moderator, in the role of a city *Mayor*. It takes place in the central park of a city the Mayor administers, and Designers work for. Each player should design a smart interactive object, and fulfill the missions given by the Mayor. It consists of: 1 Scaffolding Map (see Fig. 1), 1 Game Board (see Fig. 2), 4 Mission Cards, 4 Tokens, a deck of Nature Cards (see Fig. 3), 1 Table with all the available cards (see Fig. 3), Coins, 1 Dice, 4 Note Sheets (see Fig. 4) and 1 one-minute Hourglass. Each Designer takes a note sheet and a token. The Mayor keeps a copy of the cards of each category and the coins. The rest of the cards are placed shuffled and faced down on the game board at the corresponding category spot.

Fig. 1. Scaffolding Map

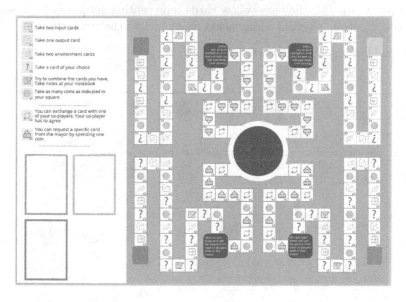

Fig. 2. Game board (Colour figure online)

3.2   Nature Cards

Nature Cards (see Fig. 3) have been created to inspire ideas for making outdoor
nature environments smart. With Nature Cards, we aim to make the design of
smart interactive objects for outdoor nature environments accessible to children,
so as to engage them as protagonists in the design process. The layout of the
cards is based on the Tiles Ideation Toolkit [27], a card-based design toolkit
for IoT user experiences. The original Tiles toolkit is meant to be generic with
no focus on a specific context or for specific card users [15]. In our work, we
focus instead on outdoor natural environments, and children, older than 8 years,

as main users of cards. Therefore, our Nature Cards are especially designed for outdoors, and to be used by children aged from 8 years old onward. For instance, easy-to-recognise icons and a suitable language have been used to make them comprehensible and easy to perceive by the targeted age.

For creating Nature Cards, we run contextual inquiries into parks and nature environments. Afterwards, we selected for cards a series of outdoor objects, inputs and outputs which children can ideate and prototype with. Currently, Nature Cards are composed of three categories:

1. Environment Cards (18): they are green cards representing artifacts (e.g., a bench) or natural elements (e.g., a tree) that can be usually found in a park or any other outdoor nature environment;
2. Input Cards (20): they are blue cards representing sensors (e.g., motion sensor) and other input physical components (e.g, buttons) that trigger an interaction;
3. Output Cards (5): they are yellow cards representing actuators (e.g., sound) or other output physical components that react to the interaction.

Figure 3 shows the entire Nature Card deck.

Fig. 3. Nature Cards: top green cards are environment Cards; middle blue cards are Input Cards; bottom yellow cards are Output Cards. (Colour figure online)

3.3   Rules and Game-Play

The game is supported by a narrative: the Mayor wants to organise a festival in the city's central park and needs Designers. Designers should carry out one of the following missions, and ideate smart interactive objects for the park:

1. Add playful and interactive attractions to the park;
2. Help visitors explore hidden spots of the park;
3. Make sure the visitors respect the park during and after the festival;
4. Make sure the park is accessible to everybody.

Players can choose a specific mission from start or during the game play. In the former case, each player should have a different mission. In the latter case, missions have an inspirational and non-restrictive role. Players place their tokens at different colored square (see Fig. 2) and play to reach the central grey circle.

First step: cards are collected. Each player, in turn, throws the dice and moves the token the number of squares indicated by the dice. Depending on the square the token reaches, the player may be entitled to get one or more cards from the decks of cards, get coins, try to combine the cards and take notes, exchange or buy a card. Each time a player's token lands on the notebook space, the Mayor turns the hourglass and all the players individually should start reflecting on how to combine the cards they already have and use their Note Sheets.

Each Note Sheet consists of colorful spots to organise the cards players have, write down the cards they need, take notes and place their coins (see Fig. 2). Players place the cards they do not need on the corresponding place on their Note Sheet, as an indication that they are willing to exchange them. They can also refer to the all-cards Table to note down the extra cards they may need. The Note Sheet and the all-cards Table can also be used individually at any time during the game. Some cards are blank: if a player receives a blank card, the player can use it as any other card of his or her choice from the same category.

Middle step: ideas are discussed. When a player lands on or passes over the grey square in the middle of the path, he or she has to stop there and wait until all the other players reach their own grey square. When all players have reached this point, they have to present their ideas in turn to the rest of the team and the Mayor. Each player should give their opinion to the one presenting, and advise

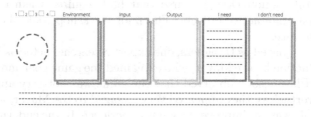

Fig. 4. Note sheet

this on how to improve ideas. In the end of each turn, the Mayor is entitled to deliver her or his final advice to the player. At the end of this, each player should have an idea and what cards the player may be still in need of.

Final step: ideas are finalised. After the end of the discussion part, the players keep on moving towards the central circle. When a player lands on the exchange icon, he/she can either exchange or buy a card from another player. When the player lands on the city-hall icon, he or she can buy a card from the *Mayor*. Each card costs 1 coin. When all the players reach the center, they should present their final smart interactive objects with the corresponding cards to the *Mayor*.

4   Pilot Workshops

4.1   Workshops with Adults and Children

Preliminary versions of the game incrementally evolved by playing it. We started with three pilot workshops: one with five adults, all experts of HCI; two workshops with 2 11-years old children and 2 adults with expertise in HCI. Thanks to these pilot workshops we reached a version of both the game board and the cards that we considered ready to be used in co-design workshops.

A subsequent co-design workshop was organised [12]. This involved four 10 to 13 years old girls, two of whom had no prior experience of co-design or making, and two HCI experts, one acting as Mayor and the other as observer. This workshop helped assess the game-play rules. It also helped identify issues, especially in the introduction phase in which cards were explained, as the Mayor should have taken care especially of participants without experience of co-design or making. The game-play rules and introduction phase were then reflected over.

4.2   Workshop with University Students

Before proceeding with new co-design workshops with children, we decided to conduct a workshop for evaluating the game-play rules with others knowledgeable of HCI. We also wanted to investigate to which extent the rules would enable participants to generate ideas. We enrolled Masters students of *Politecnico di Milano*: 3 males attending the Computer Engineering Masters; 1 female attending the Communication Design Master. Their age ranged from 21 to 23 years. They all had previous exposure to the design of smart objects as they had attended an Interaction Design course that had required them to design and prototype smart interactive objects. The pilot workshop took place in a quiet room of *Politecnico*.

The students played as Designers, one expert researcher acted as Mayor. After a short introduction by the Mayor, who explained the game goal and its rules, the play started. Players soon observed that the game was not very appropriate for their age. Nevertheless, they appeared very engaged to the Mayor, and willing to identify possible ways to improve the game experience. In the end, they generated three different ideas, which are reported in Table 1.

Table 1. Ideas generated during the pilot workshop with university students. Missions the ideas relate to are reported in italics; employed cards are in capital letters

Players	Interactive objects
1st	*In order to guide visitors towards hidden areas*, I would use STREET SIGNS which, thanks to a MOTION SENSOR, detect when people pass nearby and thus street signs become evident thanks to blinking LEDs
2nd	*In order to make sure the visitors respect the park during and after the festival*, I would equip STREET SIGNS with LEDs that are switched on when garbage is thrown on the ground
3rd	*In order to make sure the park is accessible to anybody*, I would install a DISPLAY on STREET LIGHTS close to some barriers, e.g., stairs, to indicate alternatives paths
4th	This player was not able to elaborate any idea

One player, with the mission "Add playful and interactive attractions to the park", was unable to generate any idea. The reason is that this player collected very few, redundant cards that did not enable the generation of any significant idea. Others experienced similar issues, e.g., in terms of available Input Cards or Output Cards. For this reason, the game rules were purposely revised, by including more squares in the game board that would enable players to gain further cards or exchange cards with other players.

5 Two Workshops with Children

With the version of the game presented in this paper, we organised two main co-design workshops. These workshops explored the following research questions: (1) children's ideas generated by playing the game; (2) children's engagement with the game; (3) children's overall experience with the game.

Fig. 5. Two game-play sessions from workshops 1 and 2, respectively

The workshops involved males and females, of different ages: Workshop 1 involved pre-teens; Workshop 2 involved young teens. Details on them are in the following. Figure 5 shows game-play sessions from both workshops.

5.1 Participants and Setting

Eight kids, aged 11–14 years, participated in the workshops. The participants in Workshop 1 were 4 children, 2 females and 2 males, all aged 11 years old. The participants in Workshop 2 were 2 girls and 2 boys, all aged 14 years old. All children participated on a voluntary basis and their participation was asked to their parents through a consent form.

The workshops were run in a room of *Politecnico di Milano*; both lasted about 1.5 h, also including the introduction parts (see the workshop format illustrated below). Children played the role of designers. In both workshops, the same two HCI experts were involved, one as Mayor, the other as observer.

5.2 Workshops Format

The workshops were organised into four main parts.

Part I: Introduction. This is the ice-breaker part. Its purpose is to help the Designers and Mayor of the game know each other, besides introduce the players to the the design of interactive solutions. Before starting the game play, children are asked whether they use technological devices in their everyday life and their experience with co-creating smart interactive objects. The Mayor briefly explains the goal of the workshop and what smart interactive objects, inputs and outputs are. For instance, a smart interactive object is introduced as follows: an object that can sense its environment (has sensing capabilities) or can be triggered by a person and subsequently has some sort of reaction.

Part II: Scaffolding. This is the warm-up part and its purpose is to familiarise players with the tools and the concept of the game. The Input and Output Cards and the Scaffolding Map (see Fig. 1) are presented and explained. As a first step, players are asked successively to choose a random card and try to think of what it represents. In case of difficulty in understanding, the Mayor suggests players to read also the description under the title. As a second step, players are asked to take randomly one Input and one Output Card, choose an Environment Card to place on the Scaffolding Map and think of an interaction scenario with them.

Part III: Board game. The rules of the game are explained to the children and they are given the necessary materials to start. At the end of the game-play, players share their ideas with the moderator, according to the rules. They can also be asked to write down their ideas.

Part IV: Questionnaires and interviews. As a last part, self-report questionnaires are given to children to fill in. Their impressions are also orally elicited.

5.3   Data Collection

Photos and Videos. Data related to the ideas generated by children with the game were collected via photos and video-recordings.

Questionnaires. Data concerning participants' engagement were collected via a self-report questionnaire with two instruments from the standardised Fun Toolkit for children [29]: the Smiley-o-meter and the Again-and-Again table. The questionnaire asked children: how much they liked playing with SNaP using the Smiley-o-meter 5-point Likert scale, ranging from "not at all" (1) to "very much" (5); whether they "would do it again", using the Again-and-Again-Likert scale with answers "definitely yes", "maybe", "absolutely no".

For quantitatively assessing children's overall experience with the game, beyond engagement, participants were asked to fill the Expectation Rating (ER) questionnaire. This asked two questions in relation to children's expectations before playing the game, and children's experience after playing it [32]. It is a questionnaire rapid to fill in and hence it could be administered to participating children before and after the game-play. Questions were of the following form:

- Before playing (expectation rating): "How difficult or easy do you expect this task to be?"
- After playing (experience rating): "How difficult or easy did you find this task to be?"

Tasks were as follows: learning the game rules; ideating smart interactive objects with the game. Answers were given on a 7-point Likert scale, ranging from "very difficult" (1) to "very easy" (7). The questionnaire also probed children concerning ideas for improving the game, with an open-ended question.

Observations and Interviews. Data related to children's experience of the game were also collected and integrated with observations and interviews. Observations were both direct and indirect in the form of videos. Direct observations were by two HCI experts: one acting as Mayor during the game play, and the other as observer. The HCI experts collected their observations independently and then compared their notes, resolving doubts through discussion or by referring back to videos. Interviews were unstructured, in the form of question-answering during the workshops.

5.4   Results and Reflections for Workshop 1

Ideas. At the beginning of the game, each player, in agreement with the others, selected a specific mission. As Table 2 shows, the ideas for the selected missions were simple and mostly described the interaction of few Input and Output Cards with Environment Cards. Interestingly, Players 2 and 3 augmented with smart capabilities the MOTION sensor and the CAMERA.

Table 2. Ideas generated during the workshop with 11-years-old children. Missions the ideas relate to are reported in italics; the employed cards are in capital letters

Players	Interactive objects
1st	*In order to guide visitors towards hidden areas*, STREET SIGNS point to hidden parts of the parks with LIGHTS. LIGHTS must be switched on when the DISTANCE input detects that somebody approaches the signs
2nd	*In order to make sure the visitors respect the park during and after the festival*, when a person throws garbage on the ground, a (VIDEO) CAMERA, which is always switched on, intercepts this situation. Thus, a red light (LIGHT UP) is switched on and a SOUND alarm is produced. A policeman, attracted by the alarm, goes there using a BICYCLE, and brings the person to the closest trash bin
3rd	*In order to make sure the park is accessible to anybody*, 1. there are ROCKS and SWINGS with MOTION sensors and SOUND actuators, to alert blind people of obstacles; 2. there is a BRIDGE with a MOTION sensor and a DISPLAY; the MOTION sensor detects a person on a wheelchair near the BRIDGE, thus the DISPLAY alerts other people to pay attention
4th	*In order to add playful and interactive attractions to the park*, there are MOTION and LUMINOSITY sensors on a BRIDGE over WATER, and LIGHTS to enlighten WATER under the BRIDGE. The MOTION sensor detects when people pass on the BRIDGE; thus WATER has brilliant LIGHT COLOURS that depend on the detected LUMINOSITY level

The generated ideas were coherent with the mission selected at the beginning of the game. Also, all the conceived combinations among the different cards were generally feasible. These two aspects can be considered indicators of the quality of the generated ideas through the game-play.

Experience. During the game all the players seemed to be very committed in identifying how each gained card could be exploited in combination with the others. This commitment was also confirmed by the adequate role they were able to assign to some jolly cards: all the players received at least one such card, and they exploited them coherently with the mission idea and in a way that enriched and gave value to the card combination already in place. This can be considered an indication of their level of comprehension of the cards (they were able to identify the right additional cards that could be combined with the others), as well as their commitment to generate rich, interesting ideas.

Player 1 and Player 3 experienced some troubles as they did not gain coins during the game path. For this reason, the Mayor decided to modify the game rules on the spot, to provide each player with 2 coins at the start of the game.

Also, nobody wanted to exchange cards with the other players when they reached the related square in the game path, as in fear they might need all their cards later. For tackling this situation, we decided, on the fly, to introduce penalties in case of missing card exchanges. However, generally, players were most willing to collaborate and help each other, without feeling in competition. For instance, when Player 4 was in trouble in generating an idea ("what can I make?"), all the others tried to give advice. This player, who during the game appeared the one with most difficulties in conceiving ideas, in the end was able to present an interesting and coherent idea, also thanks to the received help.

The data collected prior to the game-play through the ER questionnaire highlighted that players were worried about the complexity of the game: they had expected that learning the game would be complex enough ($\bar{x} = 3.25$, $min = 3$, $max = 4$) and that creating interactive games would be complex enough ($\bar{x} = 3.25$, $min = 2$, $max = 4$). However, after playing the game, they reported a better experience: learning the game had been easy enough or easy ($\bar{x} = 5.75$, $min = 5$, $max = 7$), and creating interactive games had been easy enough ($\bar{x} = 5$, $min = 4$, $max = 6$). Overall, such quantitative results seem to confirm the qualitative results concerning children's positive experience of the game.

Players' suggestions for the game were all related to having a longer game-board path with the opportunity to gain a greater number of cards, as they felt that the duration of the game-play was too short, e.g., they all loudly complained when the Mayor announced the end of the game-play.

Engagement. The data collected through the engagement survey were very positive: all the players said that they liked playing very much and that they would definitely like to play it again.

5.5 Results and Reflections for Workshop 2

Ideas. At the beginning of the game-play, each player, in agreement with the others, chose a specific mission. The conceived ideas are reported in Table 3. The ideas for the selected missions were less simple than those of younger children, using almost all cards collected during the game-play. Interestingly, some of their ideas seem to indicate the need of services, such as publishing data on a web site, which were not foreseen in the game.

One emerged problem was that participants exploited the elements represented by the Environment Cards just as ingredients of possible scenarios occurring at the park, not properly as objects to be augmented by means of inputs and outputs. This is evident, for example, in the idea generated by the fourth player (see Table 3): paths, benches, bicycles were used only as elements of the narration—no smart interactions were conceived for these objects. This led us to address the need to enforce a stronger scaffolding phase, already identified during one of the pilot workshops, by introducing digital examples that can show more effectively how nature elements can be augmented.

Experience. During the game session it was evident that participants tried hard to exploit as many cards as possible among those collected during the game-play; something which was not observed with the younger children. Contrary to

Table 3. Ideas generated during the workshop with 14-years-old children. Missions the ideas relate to are reported in italics; the exploited cards are in capital letters

Players	Interactive objects
1st	*In order to guide visitors towards hidden areas,* a MOTION sensor detects when a BICYCLE passes close to STREET LIGHTS. The LIGHT-UP actuator then switches on lights. The MOVE actuator makes lights rotate to indicate the path to an hidden point that is worth being visited
2nd	*In order to make sure the visitors respect the park during and after the festival,* a TOUCH sensor detects when somebody trows something into a TRASH CAN, thus the MAKE SOUND and LIGHT UP actuators create a joyful effect (as a reward)
3rd	*In order to make sure the park is accessible to anybody,* I would define a PATH that facilitates walking for disabled people. Along this PATH, BENCHES are augmented so that if a person feels sick she or he can sit on it, and the HEART RATE and TEMPERATURE sensors measure her or his body parameters. The person can call for help by pressing the TOUCH button; a LOCATION sensor communicates the precise position of the bench
4th	*In order to add playful and interactive attractions to the park,* there is a PATH with BICYCLES and BENCHES that is enlightened (LIGHT UP). Along the path, there is a TREE augmented with a button (TOUCH). By pressing the button, one can take a picture (CAMERA) with the beautiful nature landscape in the background. The picture is shown on a DISPLAY installed on the tree, and also on the web site of the park

younger children, the older children seemed to care less about generating ideas. This suggests that the game board for older children should enable for a more complex game-play, consistently with the literature on game design for teens [1].

Also in the case of this workshop, data collected before the game through the ER questionnaire highlighted that participants thought that learning the game would be complex ($\bar{x} = 3.5$, $min = 2$, $max = 6$) and to create interactive games would be also complex ($\bar{x} = 3.25$, $min = 3$, $max = 4$). However, after the game experience, they expressed that learning the game had been easy ($\bar{x} = 5$, $min = 3$, $max = 7$) and that creating interactive games had been easy enough ($\bar{x} = 3.5$, $min = 3$, $max = 5$).

Like younger players, also older players suggested to define a longer game-board path with more opportunities to gain Nature Cards.

Engagement. Like with younger children, also older children seemed to be highly engaged: through the post-game-play engagement questionnaire, also older children reported that they liked playing the game very much and that they would definitely like playing it again.

6 Conclusions and Future Work

This paper reports research in the area of meta-design with children, at the intersection of two research lines: children co-designing as protagonists; children co-designing smart nature ecosystems. The paper starts outlining the relevant literature and then moves on to its core matters. It describes the SNaP board game, which fosters children's participation as protagonists in the co-design of smart interactive nature ecosystems for them.

The genesis of the game is described and pilot workshops which led to the version presented in this paper are reported. Then the paper delves into the description of the two latest workshops with the game, one with 11-years old children and the other with 14-years old children. Both workshops enabled researchers to collect rich data, qualitative and quantitative, concerning ideas generated by children through the game-play, their engagement with the game, and their overall experience with the game.

Data were analysed and compared. Results are overall positive, indicating that the game enabled children to generate ideas for smart interactive nature environments. Moreover, all children, independently of their age group and gender, were engaged with the game. Differences were noted in the experience according to age: younger children seemed keen on their own ideas, and reluctant to sacrifice cards they could use for their ideas; older children seemed to be more interested in using as many cards as possible per se, and make their idea "as complex as possible". Such data were reflected over for improving the game.

The contextual nature of the conducted research limits its generality but produced a rich set of suggestions for improving the game and its toolkit. For instance, in line with the obtained results, future editions of the game will enable longer game-play sessions. Further cards, e.g., for web services, will be added to the deck of Nature Cards, in order to enable participants to add further smart behaviours (e.g., posting photos in a web app). The Scaffolding Map will be improved and made interactive, and show video examples to children. The game-board will be divided into diverse levels, of different complexity, to accommodate the different age or experience of the players in an adaptive fashion, e.g., [9].

Our future work will especially focus on the challenge of supporting the transformation of the ideas generated through the board game into concrete smart objects that can bring children back to the exploration of outdoor environments.

References

1. Adams, E.: Fundamentals of Game Design. Pearson-Allyn and Bacon, Bacon (2009)
2. Angelini, L., Mugellini, E., Couture, N., Abou Khaled, O.: Designing the interaction with the internet of tangible things: a card set. In: Proceedings of the Twelfth International Conference on Tangible, Embedded, and Embodied Interaction. TEI 2018, pp. 299–306. ACM, New York (2018). https://doi.org/10.1145/3173225.3173288

3. Anggarendra, R., Brereton, M.: Engaging children with nature through environmental HCI. In: Proceedings of the 28th Australian Conference on Computer-Human Interaction. OzCHI 2016, pp. 310–315. ACM, New York (2016). https://doi.org/10.1145/3010915.3010981
4. Baykal, G.E., Goksun, T., Yantaç, A.E.: Customizing developmentally situated design (dsd) cards: informing designers about preschoolers' spatial learning. In: Proceedings of the 2018 CHI Conference on Human Factors in Computing Systems. CHI 2018, pp. 592:1–592:9. ACM, New York (2018). https://doi.org/10.1145/3173574.3174166
5. Brandt, E.: Designing exploratory design games: a framework for participation in participatory design? In: Proceedings of the Ninth Conference on Participatory Design: Expanding Boundaries in Design. PDC 2006, vol. 1, pp. 57–66. ACM, New York (2006). https://doi.org/10.1145/1147261.1147271
6. Coyle, K.: Digital technology's role in connecting children and adults to nature and the outdoors (2017), retrieved in September 2018. https://www.nwf.org/~/media/PDFs/Kids-and-Nature/NWF_Role-of-Technology-in-Connecting-Kids-to-Nature_$6-30$_lsh.ashx
7. Delprino, F., Piva, C., Tommasi, G., Gelsomini, M., Izzo, N., Matera, M.: ABBOT: a smart toy motivating children to become outdoor explorers. In: Proceedings of the 2018 International Conference on Advanced Visual Interfaces. AVI 2018, pp. 23:1–23:9. ACM, New York (2018). https://doi.org/10.1145/3206505.3206512
8. Deng, Y., Antle, A.N., Neustaedter, C.: Tango cards: a card-based design tool for informing the design of tangible learning games. In: Proceedings of the 2014 Conference on Designing Interactive Systems. DIS 2014, pp. 695–704. ACM, New York (2014). https://doi.org/10.1145/2598510.2598601
9. Di Mascio, T., Gennari, R., Melonio, A., Vittorini, P.: The user classes building process in a TEL project. International Workshop on Evidence-Based Technology Enhanced Learning. Advances in Intelligent and Soft Computing, vol. 152. Springer, Berlin (2012). https://doi.org/10.1007/978-3-642-28801-2_13
10. Dibitonto, M., Tazzi, F., Leszczynska, K., Medaglia, C.M.: The IoT design deck: a tool for the co-design of connected products. In: Ahram, T., Falcão, C. (eds.) Advances in Usability and User Experience, pp. 217–227. Springer International Publishing, Cham (2018). https://doi.org/10.1007/978-3-319-60492-3_21
11. Druin, A.: The role of children in the design of new technology. Behav. Inf. Technol. 21, 1–25 (2002)
12. Gennari, R., Matera, M., Melonio, A., Roumelioti, E.: A board game and a workshop for co-creating smart nature ecosystems. In: Proceedings of the 9th International Conference in Methodologies and Intelligent Systems for Technology Enhanced Learning (mis4TEL 2019). Springer (2019)
13. Gennari, R., Melonio, A., Rizvi, M., Bonani, A.: Design of IoT tangibles for primary schools: a case study. In: Proceedings of the 12th Biannual Conference on Italian SIGCHI, Chapter. CHItaly 2017, . pp. 26:1–26:6. ACM, New York (2017). https://doi.org/10.1145/3125571.3125591
14. Gennari, R., Melonio, A., Rizvi, M.: The participatory design process of tangibles for children's socio emotional learning. In: Proceedings of End-User Development. IS-EUD 2017, pp. 167–182. Springer, Cham (2017). https://doi.org/10.1007/978-3-319-58735-6_12
15. Gianni, F., Divitini, M.: Designing IoT applications for smart cities: extending the tiles ideation toolkit. Interaction Design and Architecture(s) pp. 100–116, December 2017

16. Gianni, F., Divitini, M.: Designing IoT applications for smart cities: extending the tiles ideation toolkit. IxD&A **35**, 100–116 (2017)
17. Golembewski, M., Selby, M.: Ideation decks: a card-based design ideation tool. In: Proceedings of the 8th ACM Conference on Designing Interactive Systems. DIS 2010, pp. 89–92. ACM, New York (2010). https://doi.org/10.1145/1858171.1858189
18. Hildén, E., Ojala, J., Väänänen, K.: Development of context cards: a bus-specific ideation tool for co-design workshops. In: Proceedings of the 21st International Academic Mindtrek Conference. Academic Mindtrek 2017, pp. 137–146. ACM, New York (2017). https://doi.org/10.1145/3131085.3131092
19. Hourcade, J.P.: Child-Computer Interaction. self (2015)
20. Huyghe, J., Wouters, N., Geerts, D., Vande Moere, A.: Localudo: card-based workshop for interactive architecture. In: Proceedings of the Extended Abstracts of the ACM Conference on Human Factors in Computing Systems 2014, April 2014. https://doi.org/10.1145/2559206.2581348
21. Iivari, N., Kinnula, M.: Empowering children through design and making: towards protagonist role adoption. In: Proceedings of the 15th Participatory Design Conference: Full Papers. PDC 2018, vol. 1. pp. 16:1–16:12. ACM, New York (2018). https://doi.org/10.1145/3210586.3210600
22. Koepfler, J.: Connecting children with nature through smart toy design (2016), Retrieved in September 2018. https://www.smashingmagazine.com/2016/07/connecting-children-with-nature-through-smart-toy-design/
23. Kultima, A., Niemelä, J., Paavilainen, J., Saarenpää, H.: Designing game idea generation games. In: Proceedings of the 2008 Conference on Future Play: Research, Play, Share. Future Play 2008, pp. 137–144. ACM, New York (2008). https://doi.org/10.1145/1496984.1497007
24. Lechelt, Z., Rogers, Y., Marquardt, N., Shum, V.: Democratizing children's engagement with the internet of things through connectus. In: UbiComp 2016 Adjunct-Proceedings of the 2016 ACM International Joint Conference on Pervasive and Ubiquitous Computing (2017). https://doi.org/10.1145/2968219.2971435
25. Lockton, D., Harrison, D., Holley, T., Stanton, N.: Influencing interaction: Development of the design with intent method. vol. 350, p. 5, January 2009. https://doi.org/10.1145/1541948.1541956
26. Mavroudi, A., Divitini, M., Gianni, F., Mora, S., Kvittem, D.R.: Designing IoT applications in lower secondary schools. In: 2018 IEEE Global Engineering Education Conference (EDUCON), pp. 1120–1126, April 2018. https://doi.org/10.1109/EDUCON.2018.8363355
27. Mora, S., Gianni, F., Divitini, M.: Tiles: a card-based ideation toolkit for the internet of things. In: Proceedings of the 2017 Conference on Designing Interactive Systems. DIS 2017, pp. 587–598. ACM, New York (2017). https://doi.org/10.1145/3064663.3064699
28. Raftopoulos, M.: Playful card-based tools for gamification design. In: Proceedings of the Annual Meeting of the Australian Special Interest Group for Computer Human Interaction. OzCHI 2015, pp. 109–113. ACM, New York (2015). https://doi.org/10.1145/2838739.2838797
29. Read, J.C., MacFarlane, S.: Using the fun toolkit and other survey methods to gather opinions in child computer interaction. In: Proceedings of the 2006 Conference on Interaction Design and Children. IDC 2006, pp. 81–88. ACM, New York. https://doi.org/10.1145/1139073.1139096

30. Roy, R., Warren, J.: Card-based tools for creative and systematic design. In: Proceedings of the Design Research Society DRS2018 conference (TBC), vol. 3, pp. 1075–1087 (2018). http://oro.open.ac.uk/54650/
31. Salen, K., Zimmerman, E.: Rules of Play: Game Design Fundamentals. The MIT Press, Cambridge (2003)
32. Sauro, J., Lewis, J.: Quantifying the User Experience. Morgan Kaufmann, Burlington (2012)
33. Vaajakallio, K., Mattelmäki, T.: Design games in codesign: as a tool, a mindset and a structure. CoDesign 10(1), 63–77 (2014). https://doi.org/10.1080/15710882.2014.881886

An Internet-of-Things End-User Development Approach to Environmental Monitoring of Cultural Heritage Archives

Monica G. Maceli[✉]

Pratt Institute, School of Information, New York, NY, USA
mmaceli@pratt.edu

Abstract. End-user development (EUD) seeks to facilitate the extension and customization of systems during use, with increasing possibilities and complexities as the Internet-of-Things (IoT) computing paradigm becomes widespread. One domain that stands to benefit from adopting such an approach is that of environmental monitoring in cultural heritage archives. Monitoring environmental conditions in cultural heritage organizations is vitally important to ensure effective preservation of archives, though existing systems tend to be costly and/or limited in functionality. This research explores archivists' need for end-user development features in their environmental monitoring systems through a focus group, constructs a resulting prototype, and reflects upon the potential impact of IoT technologies on facilitating EUD behaviors within archival practice.

Keywords: End-user development · Cultural heritage · Archives · Environmental monitoring · Internet-of-Things

1 Introduction

The longstanding vision of end-user development (EUD) is to allow for flexible modification of information technology systems during use, by end users as their emergent needs arise [e.g. 1]. Though EUD has historically focused on the extension and customization of spreadsheet and web-mashup tools by end users, technology has become increasingly malleable in recent years, allowing for a diverse range of tools that facilitate EUD behavior [2]. A computing paradigm shift that has become increasingly meaningful to the study and practice of EUD is that of the Internet-of-Things (IoT), in which lightweight network-connected systems and sensors are dispersed throughout the environment, allowing for real-time data collection, analysis, and response. This shift has increased the complexity of system design, as IoT infrastructure typically consists of many layers of technology coordinating in data collection, transmission, storage, and retrieval activities. An area of practice that has many potential gains in features and functionality from taking an IoT approach is that of environmental monitoring of cultural heritage archives. Archivists typically seek to monitor and control conditions, such as temperature and humidity, to protect collections from environmental damage over time, though many of the devices used lack networked features [e.g. 3, 4].

© Springer Nature Switzerland AG 2019
A. Malizia et al. (Eds.): IS-EUD 2019, LNCS 11553, pp. 149–157, 2019.
https://doi.org/10.1007/978-3-030-24781-2_10

This paper explores the potential transformation in archival environmental monitoring practices through reconceiving the archives space as an IoT "smart environment" with archivist end users empowered to act as continuous designers of such a system. Though the bulk of prior EUD research emphasizes extending or modifying one primary technology, such as a spreadsheet tool, this study attempts to construct an EUD-facilitating system through low-cost, readily-available open source IoT solutions. To this end, the research questions investigated include: *What end-user development behaviors might archivists want to engage in? How well are these supported by current open-source Internet-of-Things technologies?* Through a "design time" exploratory focus group composed of archivist practitioners, requirements for future modifiability at "use time" are gathered from analysis of participants' transcripts, a final prototype is constructed, and the implications for the study and practice of end-user development are considered.

2 Background

Environmental monitoring, primarily of temperature and humidity, is a well-established best practice in cultural heritage archives as a means of overseeing and correcting the conditions established by heating, ventilation and air conditioning systems [3–6]. This monitoring is typically accomplished through independent data logging devices, placed strategically throughout archival spaces [e.g. 7]. Though a variety of commercial data logger devices are available, the lower-end systems typically lack any networked features and often require manual data retrieval from each standalone device. In contrast, research work in this area has investigated more complex solutions – such as wireless networks of sensors [e.g. 8] – and drawn inspiration from new approaches such as the Internet-of-Things [e.g. 9]. Little of this work, however, has yielded open and configurable solutions for the average archival practitioner outside of the research context.

More broadly, the Internet-of-Things (IoT) as a computing paradigm shift has drawn interest from a variety of research perspectives, notably those of end-user development and its allied fields of end-user programming and end-user software engineering, as well as within cultural heritage practice and applications more generally. End-user development (EUD), as the most expansive topic, seeks to involve users in the design and customization of systems, not solely at the time of design but throughout the life of the system [1]. Prior research has identified numerous IoT technology tools with promise in facilitating end-users acting as developers to craft their systems in use, such as in the context of the smart home [10], smart environments [11], or cultural heritage organizations [e.g. 12, 13]. Petrelli et al. [12] envision museums reconfigured with "adaptive smart exhibits", with embedded digital content that is responsive to end users' context. Though the authors note that such technology systems have been feasible for quite some time, there is a lack of hardware and software systems to support creation by museum staff. Ardito et al. [13] further explored the barriers to cultural heritage professionals and patrons in interacting with an extending museum smart objects, finding numerous areas for improvement in the composition of smart experiences.

Notably, Barricelli and Valtolina [14] suggest that EUD in the IoT era demands expanding our research attention to how users interact with an "ecosystem of elements" (pp. 10), and arrange and organize data from a variety of sources. In contrast, earlier EUD technology-focused work primarily explored extending a single existing system, such as a spreadsheet program, or developing novel tools for use in a particular domain [2]. To mitigate the challenges inherent to developing customizable IoT systems, such environments have been well-studied in recent years, with research work providing guiding design principles for the home and other "smart" environments. Davidoff et al. [15] presents a series of design principles oriented towards allowing smart home users to fully gain control over the system's design and operation. Though archival work may take place in a variety of workplace contexts, from offsite warehouse, to staff offices, or in museum galleries, several of the principles have broader relevance here, in particular "P.2 - Easily construct new behaviors and modify existing behaviors"; "P.3 - Understand periodic changes, exceptions and improvisation"; and "P.4 - Design for breakdowns" (Davidoff et al. [15]).

Schmidt and Herrmann [16] advocate for the need for "intervention user interfaces" allowing for users to intervene in automated system behaviors on an as-needed basis, suggesting six design principles for interventive systems. Their principles include: expectability and predictability, communicate options for interventions, exploration of interventions, easy reversal of automated and intervention actions, minimize required attention, and communicate how control is shared (p. 45). Both of these sets of principles provide a useful way to assess technologies for their ability to support EUD behaviors, particularly in the emergent, unanticipated contexts that may arise in IoT systems. Such systems have the potential to improve efficiency and flexibility of archival environmental monitoring, and bring systems more in line with popular commercial solutions for consumers, in the home and similar environments requiring monitoring and response.

3 Exploratory Focus Group

The research study consisted of an exploratory focus group including four archives practitioners, from a variety of types of cultural heritage organizations, including libraries, museums and galleries in the New York City area. Participants were first asked a series of background questions, to assess their data needs, current practices, and challenges in environmental monitoring. Then participants worked together to identify key system features and to sketch potential environmental monitoring system interfaces. The initial focus group findings (reported in more detail in [17]) described many data requirements, as well as sociotechnical and technical challenges encountered by participants in the course of their archival work. This research suggested a potential solution of integrating multiple sensors' data into a customizable data dashboard interface, which would be both remotely and locally-accessible to end users, including charts, export options, value ranges and exceeded alerts, real-time data, and a date range selector.

In pursuit of the research questions investigated within this paper, a secondary analysis of the focus group transcript was conducted, using qualitative coding to identify themes of relevance to a potential end-user development solution for archival environmental monitoring. These findings were employed in building a prototype system allowing for future end-user modification in use, with an emphasis on using open source and open hardware inasmuch as possible, to potentially facilitate deep customization. The resulting system and user requirements were assessed against design principles suggested by prior research (Davidoff et al. [15]) to explore their effectiveness in designing for the archival IoT context. The focus group transcript was assessed for themes of relevance to end-user development, namely those oriented towards future modification of the system by end users, in order to develop a coding scheme and overall themes in participant responses. Themes emerging from participant data are presented in Table 1, below, with selected illustrative quotes and mapped to EUD design principles. These end-user development themes were considered along with the base required features in the development of the final system prototype, discussed further in the following section.

Table 1. Themes of relevance to end-user development in focus group responses, categorized and mapped to design principles proposed by Davidoff et al. [15]

EUD-related theme expressed	Sample participant quote	Related EUD design principle(s)
Missing features, not anticipated and provided at "design time"	"…Although I like the [existing systems'] charts, I find their analysis to be unhelpful… suggestions for maintaining museums, libraries, and archives that have much broader range of acceptable limits." [P4]	*"P.2 - Easily construct new behaviors and modify existing behaviors"* [15]
	"To some degree the reporting tools work, but that's why I also supplement it with the email, with a list of a simplified version of where we're doing well and where we're not meeting our goals" [P2]	
Need to customize and design physical properties of devices and sensors	"There's definitely a need for a low-cost sensor…where you can easily change the sensor out every year, and put a new one in" [P4]	*"P.2 - Easily construct new behaviors and modify existing behaviors"; "P.4 - Design for breakdowns"* [15]
	"We can't use any of our [devices] in a public space because they're just so big" [P4]	

(*continued*)

Table 1. (*continued*)

EUD-related theme expressed	Sample participant quote	Related EUD design principle(s)
Need to customize and design system feedback	"For the normal devices, you really do have to go collect the data to see if something is wrong. I guess to see if the device has moved itself? You don't really know until you go look." [P2]	*"P.3 - Understand periodic changes, exceptions and improvisation"; "P.4 - Design for breakdowns"* [15]
	"I set it up so that I could get an alert, it would actually just make a noise when it's a high or low on a range, which is not so helpful because I don't actually work in the spaces." [P3]	
Need for real-time data monitoring and end user intervention features	"I know what's going on in the stacks, because I do visual exams once, if not twice a day, to just to see what the readings are." [P4]	*"P.3 - Understand periodic changes, exceptions and improvisation"* [15]
	"It doesn't interpret anything for you. You see this graph, and it's hard to say what it means" [P2]	

4   Prototype System Design and Discussion

The first research question sought to understand *what end-user development behaviors archivists may desire to engage in*. As detailed in Table 1, below, the archival practitioners described emergent needs that were poorly supported by the current systems. These ranged from modifying data reports to suit various stakeholders, to physically customizing the devices to change parts or integrate unobtrusively into the space. Many of the unmet needs discussed had been compensated for by performing additional manual work outside of the existing system, or by incurring greater cost to the organization.

To improve the mismatch between designed features and emergent needs expressed, the resulting prototype system allows for archival practitioners to monitor the environmental conditions of their collections, both in-person and remotely, with an emphasis placed on the ability for the system to be deeply modifiable by end users. The initial requirements of the focus group indicated that the features must include a data visualization interface with charts, export options, value ranges and exceeded alerts, web and mobile access, real-time data, and a date range selector. Data must also be able to be presented for a variety of audiences, from board members to other archivists. Data-collection devices must be customizable to include the ability to be housed in a range of enclosures, as well as easily replace parts, such as sensors.

As was detailed earlier, an additional requirement was that existing open source software and hardware be used when feasible to maximize future flexibility in unanticipated directions. Popular and well-supported hardware and software were considered for each layer of the system, with the author assessing customizability, ease of use by novices, and available documentation (such as active support forums, tutorials, and software libraries).

These characteristics were considered for end node devices, base station devices, data persistence and storage engines, and data visualization tools. The final designed prototype consisted of a Raspberry Pi™ single-board computer base station, which ran (1) a time series database to store sensor data and (2) a web-accessible data visualization tool for monitoring. Several wireless peripheral devices, constructed from Adafruit® microcontrollers and temperature/humidity sensors [18], were placed throughout the environment to monitor areas of concern and microclimates as needed. The sensing devices transmitted data over Wi-Fi or Bluetooth Low Energy (BLE) to the base station for storage and visualization. All software used was open-source, with many components employing open hardware as well, with the final choices made based on assessing the potential for end-user modification of the system. Users of the system are able to create, customize, and otherwise modify all data visualizations and alerting rules (Figs. 1 and 2, below). To allow for a customizable "intervention user interface" the data visualizing platform chosen for use was the open-source Grafana platform [19].

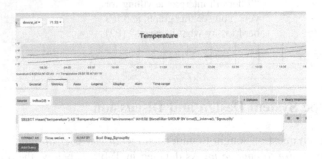

Fig. 1. Example of chart editing interface, displaying a database query which may be constructed through a graphical programming interface or by hand (shown).

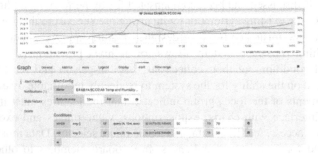

Fig. 2. Example of alert editing interface, in which alert rules may be configured, as well as means of communication, such as SMS text or email (not pictured).

Grafana allows end users to create, customize, and modify dashboards, which could consist of a variety of types of charts, custom text, and single statistics. Deeper customizable is possible, in the form of connecting data sources, writing database queries, and using variable-driven templating. End users may define and activate alerting rules based on data-driven conditions of their choosing (Fig. 2, below), which send alerts with a variety of mechanisms (e.g. email, web hooks) to individuals or groups of recipients. Over a period of several months, the system was employed to monitor the environmental conditions and to test functionality and stability. During the research, construction, and testing of the prototype, the second research question of - *how well are these supported by current open-source Internet-of-Things technologies?* – was considered. As detailed earlier, IoT systems encompass a range of technologies, devices, protocols, standards, and other characteristics. Thus, these systems move our historic EUD focus from one primary digital interface to a broader range of interaction and scenarios of use. Though the final system design sought to emphasis ease of end-user modification and customization, there was unavoidable complexity in the current IoT landscape's need to traverse multiple technologies, from sensors to microcontrollers, databases and wireless protocols.

This complexity requires, at a minimum, a high-level understanding of how the various components of such an ecosystem interact and serve in collecting, storing, and displaying data. On the positive side, for each layer of needed functionality, there were several popular open-source options, with active communities developing future functionality. Such communities would provide the necessary support for end-user developers that may desire to transition more fully into a developer role in the future.

Overall though, this work paints a promising picture of the trajectory of current IoT systems and emphases their potential impact in the cultural heritage realm. The ideas generated by archivists mapped well to existing end-user development design principles, and can assist in the creation of future-flexible systems. As system designers, this work suggests that attention to designing for future breakdowns, managing exceptions, and allowing for the construction of new behaviors may be the most meaningful dimensions in driving our focus towards future EUD customization and extensibility.

5   Conclusion and Future Work

This paper presents the results of a focus group of archival practitioners, employed in cultural heritage organizations, tasked with environmental monitoring of collections. Participants' critique of existing systems and desired future possibilities are considered through the lens of end-user development, resulting in the design and development of an open-source system prototype, giving an opportunity to reflect upon the challenges and opportunities of the intersection of Internet-of-Things technologies and end-user development behaviors. Future research work will deploy the designed system within cultural heritage archives to assess user feedback and ability to engage in EUD activities.

References

1. Lieberman, H., Paternò, F., Klann, M., Wulf, V.: End-user development: an emerging paradigm. In: Lieberman, H., Paternò, F., Wulf, V. (eds.) End User Development, pp. 1–8. Springer, Dordrecht (2006). https://doi.org/10.1007/1-4020-5386-X_1
2. Maceli, M.G.: Tools of the trade: a survey of technologies in end-user development literature. In: Barbosa, S., Markopoulos, P., Paternò, F., Stumpf, S., Valtolina, S. (eds.) IS-EUD 2017. LNCS, vol. 10303, pp. 49–65. Springer, Cham (2017). https://doi.org/10.1007/978-3-319-58735-6_4
3. Harvey, R., Mahard, M.R.: The Preservation Management Handbook: A 21st-Century Guide for Libraries, Archives and Museums. Rowman & Littlefield, Lanham (2014)
4. Temperature, relative humidity, light, and air quality: Basic guidelines for preservation. https://www.nedcc.org/free-resources/preservation-leaflets/2.-the-environment/2.1-temperature,-relative-humidity,-light,-and-air-quality-basic-guidelines-for-preservation. Accessed 31 Aug 2018
5. Wilsted, T.P.: Planning New and Remodeled Archival Facilities. Society of American Archivists, Chicago (2007)
6. Pacifico, M.E., Wilsted, T.P. (eds.): Archival and Special Collections Facilities: Guidelines for Archivists, Librarians, Architects, and Engineers. Society of American Archivists, Chicago (2009)
7. Morris, P.: Achieving a preservation environment with data logging technology and microclimates. Coll. Undergrad. Libr. 16(1), 83–104 (2009)
8. D'Amato, F., Gamba, P., Goldoni, E.: Monitoring heritage buildings and artworks with wireless sensor networks. In: Proceedings of 2012 IEEE Workshop on Environmental Energy and Structural Monitoring Systems (EESMS), Perugia, Italy, pp. 1–6. IEEE (2012)
9. Londero, P., Fairbanks-Harris, T., Whitmore, P.M.: An open-source, internet-of-things approach for remote sensing in museums. J. Am. Inst. Conserv. 55(3), 1–10 (2016)
10. Fogli, D., Lanzilotti, R., Piccinno, A.: End-user development tools for the smart home: a systematic literature review. In: Streitz, N., Markopoulos, P. (eds.) DAPI 2016. LNCS, vol. 9749, pp. 69–79. Springer, Cham (2016). https://doi.org/10.1007/978-3-319-39862-4_7
11. Desolda, G., Ardito, C., Matera, M.: Empowering end users to customize their smart environments: model, composition paradigms, and domain-specific tools. ACM Trans. Comput.-Hum. Interact. 24(2), 1–52 (2017)
12. Petrelli, D., Ciolfi, L., van Dijk, D., Horneker, E., Not, E., Schmidt, A.: Integrating material and digital: a new way for cultural heritage. Interact. New Vis. Hum.-Comput. Interact. 20(4), 58–63 (2013)
13. Ardito, C., Buono, P., Desolda, G., Matera, M.: From smart objects to smart experiences: an end-user development approach. Int. J. Hum. Comput. Stud. 114, 51–68 (2018)
14. Barricelli, B.R., Valtolina, S.: Designing for end-user development in the internet of things. In: Díaz, P., Pipek, V., Ardito, C., Jensen, C., Aedo, I., Boden, A. (eds.) IS-EUD 2015. LNCS, vol. 9083, pp. 9–24. Springer, Cham (2015). https://doi.org/10.1007/978-3-319-18425-8_2
15. Davidoff, S., Lee, M.K., Yiu, C., Zimmerman, J., Dey, A.K.: Principles of smart home control. In: Dourish, P., Friday, A. (eds.) UbiComp 2006. LNCS, vol. 4206, pp. 19–34. Springer, Heidelberg (2006). https://doi.org/10.1007/11853565_2
16. Schmidt, A., Herrmann, T.: Intervention user interfaces: a new interaction paradigm for automated systems. Interactions 24(5), 40–45 (2017)

17. Maceli, M., Villaespesa, E., Adams, S.A.: Environmental monitoring of archival collections: an exploratory study of professionals' data monitoring dashboard needs and related challenges. In: Taylor, N.G., Christian-Lamb, C., Martin, Michelle H., Nardi, B. (eds.) iConference 2019. LNCS, vol. 11420, pp. 777–784. Springer, Cham (2019). https://doi.org/10.1007/978-3-030-15742-5_73
18. Adafruit Industries. https://www.adafruit.com/. Accessed 21 Feb 2019
19. Grafana - The open platform for analytics and monitoring. https://grafana.com/. Accessed 21 Feb 2019

End-User Development in Speech Therapies: A Scenario in the Smart Home Domain

Fabio Cassano[1], Antonio Piccinno[2(✉)], and Paola Regina[1]

[1] Omnitech Research Group, Bari, Italy
{fabio.cassano,paola.regina}@omnired.eu
[2] Department of Computer Science, University of Bari, Bari, Italy
antonio.piccinno@uniba.it

Abstract. Smart home systems allow the connection and the communication between different Internet of Things devices under the same environment. Those are commonly used to support people in their daily life, but most of them have more than just "leisure or fun" purposes. As a matter of fact, if correctly configured, the smart home and all the devices connected to it, can assist people in medical contexts. In this paper we propose a scenario where the smart home acts as active supporter and as an "emotion generator" for children with speech problems and that follow a specific speech therapy. As a matter of fact, emotions and speech capabilities are strictly connected in babies and young boys. The smart home environment can orchestrate the global devices functioning and improve the children emotional involvement in such therapy. On the other side, the speech therapist, through the EUD, can organize the smart home behaviour to better support the child.

1 Introduction

Nowadays Smart Home (SH) systems are able to connect and control many different Internet of Things (IoT) devices at the same time. They are mainly used to support people in their daily routine activities; however an increasing number of researcher all over the world are trying to use SH systems to improve the assistance to patients and physicians for therapies far from specialized centers. This concept of "home hospitalization" can improve the life of the patients because they do not have to move from home, trying to reduce the healthcare costs. In the described context, the SH plays a fundamental role in the scheduling and monitoring the different therapies that people have to follow. Moreover, it acts as a "deus ex machina" that supports the physicians during the patient's therapy. In this scenario, the End-User Development (EUD) could be the key for the creation or the modification of the different software artifacts that caregivers use at home.

One of the most common medical situation involving different caregivers is the "speech therapy". It comprises a set of exercises and games aimed at

© Springer Nature Switzerland AG 2019
A. Malizia et al. (Eds.): IS-EUD 2019, LNCS 11553, pp. 158–165, 2019.
https://doi.org/10.1007/978-3-030-24781-2_11

stimulating the child's language, convincing him/her to concentrate and show a collaborative attitude. Being widely based on a creative and empathetic approach, it does not follow a specific treatment path. Moreover, with children patients there is no treatment protocol capable of fitting everyone's needs, especially given the variety of the disorder with the patient's age. To better support the children therapeutical path, empathizing with them and providing them confidence, it is common that the speech therapy may occur in a domestic environment. In this paper, a scenario about the joint use of EUD and IoT technology to support children that follow a speech therapy is proposed. To do so, we have studied in literature which are the most used approach to improve a person health condition at home, using the available IoT devices, managed all together by the SH. On one hand, the speech therapists focus their attention to the encouragement and improvement of the children activity [1]. On the other, the SH could act like a magnification lens of the speech therapy where each success can boost the child emotional response and improve his/her speech capability over the time. Finally, EUD allows the creation and the modification of the speech therapies that the parents can administer without the constant presence of the speech therapist.

The paper is structured as follows: Sect. 2 present the background study to better understand the proposed scenario. Section 3 describes the scenario and Sect. 4 draws the evolution and the test of this work.

2   Background Study

The needs of developing strategies to cope with speech disorders is motivated by the fact that sometimes patients, especially children, have difficulty improving despite the standard therapeutic approaches [2]. This happens because there are many cases in which the cause of the disorder is not organic but rather psychogenic, caused by emotional or psychological factors. In this cases, acute or chronic emotional stress are some of the symptoms that characterize these kind of patients [1]. Moreover, the speech disorder itself may lead to psychological side effects. For these reasons, giving a treatment that can affect the emotional level is of fundamental importance. For children, many approaches have been proposed, most of them in the form of serious games. In [3] a voice-controlled serious computer game for the sustained vowel exercise is proposed, combining real time speech processing with both the gamification of the speech therapy exercises and the parameterization of the difficulty level. In [4], a serious game in which children can learn to speak specific words was designed and implemented, allowing the gamer to control an avatar by voice. The aim of this game was to engage the child longer, compared to classical clinical approaches, keeping him in a familiar environment.

Many solutions have been proposed to cope with people's diseases by supporting them with SH technologies. Speech recognition techniques have been already explored in SH environments. In addition, the benefits of voice activated smart home technology were outlined, with a particular emphasis on persons with disabilities, using techniques for speech recognition [5,6]. Moreover, nowadays, among many applications for voice assistance, few tech companies are opening up the power of voice to end users with speech impairments: it is the case of Voiceitt[1], GoogleAssistant[2] and Tecla[3] [7]. How the SH environment can be used to cope the assistance needs of users that have to follow some therapies is a well known field of research. Moreover, recent studies have uncovered how the EUD and its related concepts are increasing in popularity in a wide variety of domains, including the medical field, the robotic or the IoT [8]. In this area, a study on how the EUD can support physician's therapies is also addressed [9].

Finally, to merge IoT technology with EUD and SH domain, methods for treating data collected from sensors have been studied. In literature it has been presented a model that shows how users' needs, capabilities and the smart home (supported by the IoT devices) meet and play together a key role of supporting people with EUD techniques [10]. In this research, Authors describe the usage of four different nodes on a connected graph, each belonging to a different application domain. By assessing the patient health's status and the technology available in the SH, they setup the IoT devices with the aim to improve his/her International Classification of Functionalities (ICF) value [11]. Further examples on EUD and IoT being used together to support people's life and activities are also reported in [12,13].

There are many techniques available to allow the communication between the devices. One of the most used is the "middleware" one, which allows external software to access sensor data [14]. A model like this could be integrated within the services offered by the SH domain. A methodology to acquire real-time sensor data along with data management techniques is also applied in IoT domains belonging to different research fields [15].

3   The Proposed Scenario

In this paper, we present a scenario involving children with speech problems and their parents, as well as the speech therapists with the therapy. Using a SH environment that evokes some positive emotions in the children, the speech therapies are more effective than the classic ones, which are mainly focused on the treatment of the disorder. In addition, EUD techniques are used to facilitate the creation and therapy management. The benefits deriving from the use of IoT technology for childhood education or disorders is proposed in some studies [16,17]. By "instantiating" the model proposed in [10] on this proposed scenario, the first node is evaluated on a child that needs an improvement of the ICF value in the "participation" domain. In the second node, the therapist has defined a therapy at home using some smartphone and tablet applications specifically built for children with that kind of problems. In the third node of the cycle it is defined how the IoT technology and the SH can better support the therapy. In particular

---

[1] http://www.voiceitt.com/.

[2] https://assistant.google.com/.

[3] https://gettecla.com/pages/tecla-e.

it has been found that the SH, through some lamps, an audio speaker and the smart TV, can improve the engagement of the children to the therapy.

The idea on the basis of this scenario is the improvement of the child's engagement in the daily therapies as well as increasing the desire to well perform through all the therapy. The parent's support role is as fundamental as the therapist one. As a matter of fact, they act as "caregivers", replacing the physician during the home therapy which can be easily defined by the physician through specific apps built for mobile devices (e.g.: tablets and smartphones). Figure 1 represents the scenario with the SH that is going to support the speech therapy. It presents six rooms with seven different areas of interest numbered from 1 to 7. The room labelled with the number 1 in Fig. 1 is the child room, where he/she spends most of the time and where it is supposed to be at the time of the therapy. In this room, a changing color lamp (e.g.: Philips Hue Lamps) is installed as well as in the corridor and partially in the lounge room. Figure 1a shows the initial status of the SH, where the child is waiting (or playing) in the room 1. Once the time of the therapy has come, the entire SH system enables the different IoT devices, orchestrating them with the specific aim of increase the child emotional response. The lights start glowing with different colours, catching the child's attention, as well as the speaker plays a music that invite the child to start the therapy in the lounge room (Fig. 1b, room 3). Note that this room has two areas of interests catching the child's attention, one with the fireplace and one with the smart TV. Also the parents get caught by the changing of the state of the SH and prepare all the different devices that are needed to perform the speech therapy. When they are all together in the lounge room, the colour of the light changes to green and the therapy can start. The behaviour of the SH is edited and configured by the speech therapist using EUD techniques. Through a remote interface the speech therapist can easily add/edit or remove games to the child therapy as well as add/edit or remove some smart home behaviour in

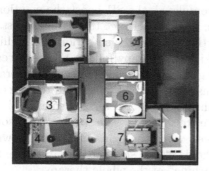
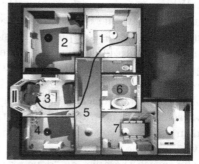

(a) The SH in its "non-activated" status: the child is located in the room 1, waiting for the therapy to start.

(b) The SH in its "activated" status, the lights in the hall are activated to recall the child attention.

Fig. 1. The SH in its "non-activated" status: the child is located in the room 1, waiting for the therapy to start.

case of the successful completion of the task. By using both a tablet, which is able to edit all the available configurations of the different IoT devices, and the Event-Condition-Action (ECA) paradigm, the speech therapist can create rules in order to improve the children and the parent engagement in the therapy [18]. In addition to this, the gamification technique facilitates the therapy completion. As a matter of fact, children are more engaged when they see the support coming from the different fantasy characters they love. Figure 2 shows a scenario with a child and his mother taking the speech therapy at home with the support of the smart TV, showing the favourite child character. Through two different views of the same scene, it has been highlighted the elements of the smart environment: on the left the attention is focused on the presence of the child and the parent, while the figure of the right shows how the virtual character is played on the TV.

Fig. 2. The scenario where a child is involved in the speech therapy at home

Figure 3 draws the general way that the speech therapist has to control and configure the SH behaviour. In the described scenario, the green dragon is currently used by the speech therapy to react when a task is successfully completed by the child and its reactions and behaviour are set by the speech therapist. When an assignment is correctly completed, the SH boost the emotional "reward" by activating the smart devices: the lights change the colour and start glowing, while the speaker plays a music that catches the attention of the child, evoking good vibes. Also the tablet used for the therapy follows the same reaction pattern, with the mobile app showing the child success. When the therapy is harder to be completed some suggestions are required by the child to correctly complete the task. Rather than showing the fantasy character, the smart TV can display some different graphical suggestions to the child. The speaker plays some sound in order to evoke the correct answer, while the lights may start glowing slowly to help the child concentration. The described scenario comprises the SH with the speech therapist as "deus ex machina" of the whole therapy.

To test the proposed SH solution, an EUD has been implemented that allows the physician to remotely control the therapy. Precisely, the speech therapist can create or edit through a smartphone or a web interface a wide variety of therapies that are collected in a personal database. Those are easily sent to the child's SH system that is going to control the different smart devices such as the Smart TV,

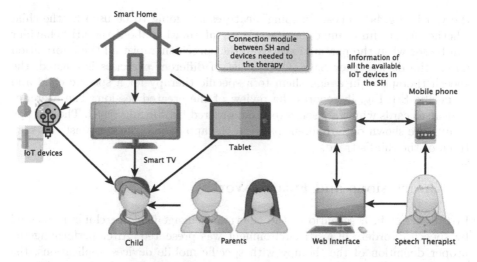

Fig. 3. The diagram describing the speech therapy approach using the SH

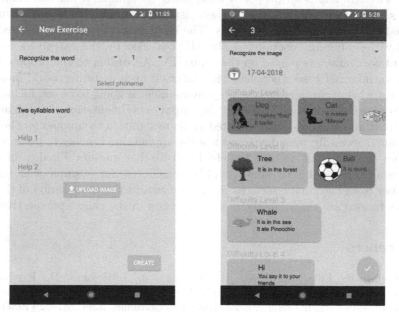

(a) The speech therapist can add a new (b) Review of the created speech exer-
exercise   cises

Fig. 4. The EUD speech therapist app

the lights etc. Figure 4 shows an example of the mobile application: the speech
therapist creates a new exercise, firstly choosing its type and, consequently, filling the required fields: the specific word, the phoneme, the syllables and some
optional hints, along with an image which can visually help the child to identify

the word (Fig. 4a). Those "helping" features are going to be used by the child whether he/she finds any difficulties. More information about the SH behaviour can be set when the parents have given the speech therapist all the information about the devices they have. Once a list of different exercises is created, the speech therapist can assign them to a specific therapy for a specific child and a specific SH: Fig. 4b reports the review of the created session. The exercises appear as cards which are selectable and ordered by difficulty level. The therapy results are shown on a different panel in the app, where the therapist can keep track of the child's trend.

4   Conclusions and Future Works

In this research, a scenario of the emotional engagement for children affected by speech disorders in a SH environment was presented. After performing the proper definition of the therapy with specific mobile devices applications, the engagement of the child to the therapy is provided by offering support through IoT devices. It has been proposed that, using a configured SH and some IoT devices connected to it, the speech therapist can adopt EUD techniques to create and edit many specific therapies. The child involvement is supported not only by the different reactions of the SH, but also by the caregivers and by the fantasy characters played on the smart TV. According to the proposed scenario, an informal case study has been followed and, as future work, manifold aspects are being considered: a testing environment is going to be set, including a sample with real users and collecting data from experimentation through an IoT infrastructure and applying automated audio recognition techniques for the data processing. Secondly, an enhancement of the application is going to be provided, both for the therapist and for the child and his/her parents. Finally, an automatic speech recognition system could be considered, for example with the aid of proper conversational interfaces [7], as well as a further integration of the IoT devices to increase the attractiveness of exercises in the child's perspective [17].

References

1. Butcher, P., Elias, A., Raven, R., Yeatman, J., Littlejohns, D.: Psychogenic voice disorder unresponsive to speech therapy: psychological characteristics and cognitive-behaviour therapy. Br. J. Disorders Commun. **22**(1), 81–92 (1987)
2. Bernthal, J.E., Bankson, N.W., Flipsen, P.: Articulation and Phonological Disorders: Speech Sound Disorders in Children. Pearson, Boston (2009)
3. Lopes, M., Magalhães, J., Cavaco, S.: A voice-controlled serious game for the sustained vowel exercise. In: ACE, p. 32-1 (2016)
4. Nasiri, N., Shirmohammadi, S., Rashed, A.: A serious game for children with speech disorders and hearing problems. In: SeGAH, pp. 1–7. IEEE (2017)
5. McLoughlin, I., Sharifzadeh, H.R.: Speech recognition for smart homes. In: Speech Recognition. Intech (2008)
6. Busatlic, B., Dogru, N., Lera, I., Sukic, E.: Smart homes with voice activated systems for disabled people. TEM J. **6**(1), 103 (2017)

7. Baldauf, M., Bösch, R., Frei, C., Hautle, F., Jenny, M.: Exploring requirements and opportunities of conversational user interfaces for the cognitively impaired. In: Proceedings of the 20th International Conference on Human-Computer Interaction with Mobile Devices and Services Adjunct, pp. 119–126. ACM (2018)
8. Barricelli, B.R., Cassano, F., Fogli, D., Piccinno, A.: End-user development, end-user programming and end-user software engineering: a systematic mapping study. J. Syst. Softw. **149**, 101–137 (2019)
9. Cassano, F.: EUD models and techniques for the smart-home. In: IS-EUD, pp. 103–106. Technische Universiteit Eindhoven (2017)
10. Caivano, D., Cassano, F., Fogli, D., Piccinno, A.: EUD4SH: a EUD model for the smart home. In: Novais, P., et al. (eds.) ISAmI2018 2018. AISC, vol. 806, pp. 86–93. Springer, Cham (2019). https://doi.org/10.1007/978-3-030-01746-0_10
11. World Health Organization: International Classification of Functioning, Disability and Health: ICF. World Health Organization, Geneva (2001)
12. Buono, P., Cassano, F., Legretto, A., Piccinno, A.: A homemade pill dispenser prototype supporting elderly. In: Garrigós, I., Wimmer, M. (eds.) ICWE 2017. LNCS, vol. 10544, pp. 120–124. Springer, Cham (2018). https://doi.org/10.1007/978-3-319-74433-9_10
13. Costabile, M.F., Fogli, D., Lanzilotti, R.: Supporting work practice through end-user development environments. J. Organ. End User Comput. (JOEUC) **18**(4), 43–65 (2006)
14. Casale, A., Spadafina, L., Porcelli, A., Matrino, D., Sarcina, V.: A water meter reading middleware for smart consumption monitoring. In: EESMS, pp. 1–6. IEEE (2016)
15. Blonda, M., Calabrese, A., Cardellicchio, A., Casale, B., Di Lecce, V., et al.: Innovative methodology for detecting of possible harmful compounds for wastewater treatment the MAUI project. In: Workshop on Metrology for Industry 4.0 and IoT, pp. 1–6. IEEE (2018)
16. Sula, A., Spaho, E., Matsuo, K., Barolli, L., Xhafa, F., Miho, R.: A new system for supporting children with autism spectrum disorder based on IoT and P2P technology. Int. J. Space-Based Situat. Comput. **4**(1), 55–64 (2014)
17. de la Guía, E., Camacho, V.L., Orozco-Barbosa, L., Luján, V.M.B., Penichet, V.M., Pérez, M.L.: Introducing iot and wearable technologies into task-based language learning for young children. IEEE Trans. Learn. Technol. **9**(4), 366–378 (2016)
18. Caivano, D., Cassano, F., Fogli, D., Lanzilotti, R., Piccinno, A.: We@Home: a gamified application for collaboratively managing a smart home. In: De Paz, J.F., Julián, V., Villarrubia, G., Marreiros, G., Novais, P. (eds.) ISAmI 2017. AISC, vol. 615, pp. 79–86. Springer, Cham (2017). https://doi.org/10.1007/978-3-319-61118-1_11

Evaluation of a Visual Tool for Early Patent Infringement Detection During Design

Salvatore Sorce[1(✉)], Alessio Malizia[2,3], Vito Gentile[1], Pingfei Jiang[4],
Mark Atherton[4], and David Harrison[4]

[1] Università degli Studi di Palermo, Palermo, Italy
{salvatore.sorce,vito.gentile}@unipa.it
[2] University of Hertfordshire, Hatfield, UK
a.malizia@herts.ac.uk
[3] Molde University College, Molde, Norway
[4] Brunel University London, Uxbridge, UK
{pingfei.jiang,mark.atherton,david.harrison}@brunel.ac.uk

Abstract. Patent infringement detection usually implies research among documents in different forms, in both natural and unstructured language, often involving a lot of human resources and time. In order to ease this patent check process, we previously presented a visual tool to be used by designers themselves at any stage of the design process, providing them with useful and reliable information for deciding whether to steer their design away from potential patent infringements. In this work, we report on a usability study carried out on such a tool with 21 professional designers from industry in the field of mechanical engineering. The outcome of our study shows that our tool is very well accepted by designers, and felt useful and helpful even by legal experts.

Keywords: Visual interfaces · Visual programming ·
Block programming · End-user programming ·
Patent infringement detection

1 Introduction

Product design mainly relies on the capability of inventors to produce suitable products or parts for the task they have to accomplish. Unfortunately, in the industry world functionalities and geometry are not the only drivers of the inventors' design. Indeed, there are patents to deal with, which cover products, parts, and even functionalities. Patents are often represented in the form of PDF documents, possibly scanned from their original hard copies, thus making any search difficult. Furthermore, the features covered are often described in natural, unstructured, language, with no technical details, aiming at not clearly revealing the covered design itself. Last, but not least, the patent check process occurs only at a stage of design by which it has already involved a lot of human resources

© Springer Nature Switzerland AG 2019
A. Malizia et al. (Eds.): IS-EUD 2019, LNCS 11553, pp. 166–173, 2019.
https://doi.org/10.1007/978-3-030-24781-2_12

and time, which is too late for re-design to be economically feasible. For this reason, legal disputes on patents are time- and money-consuming, and even if only a small percentage of disputes reach the court, they strongly affect the life of both the supposed infringers and infringed.

Based on this situation, during a project on intellectual property defence we were involved in [11], we set up a visual software tool to be used unobtrusively by designers at any stage of the design process, in order to give them useful and reliable information for deciding whether to steer their design away from potential patent infringements [17]. The visual tool is based on portable web technologies, and relies on an available semantic database for patent representation [2].

In this paper, we report on a user study we carried out with participants from industry in the field of mechanical engineering, who were neither part nor aware both of the tool and of the project before the study itself. For our study, we involved 21 professional designers, and we used well known questionnaires to assess perceived usability, usefulness and workload of the tool. The outcome of our study shows that such a tool is very well accepted by designers, and felt useful and helpful even by legal experts. In particular, for our tool we obtained good values for all the metrics we used, and also a good overall acceptance as a side-instrument to be used even since the beginning of the design process.

2 Background and Related Work

Patent infringement is the commission of a prohibited act with respect to a patented invention without permission from the patent holder. The test for infringement requires that the infringing party's product falls within one or more of the claims of the patent. The first claim defines the distinguishing technical features that set the invention apart from the prior art. When designers make judgements on intellectual property their analysis usually relies on the graphical/visual descriptions of the patented invention (e.g. images, sketches) in addition to the textual information provided with the patent. Indeed, patent analysis has been proved to be able to provide an efficient way to study and understand prior art, allowing to gather valuable information such as technological details and market opportunities [8,14]. Research conducted by Cascini and Zini used function trees to represent components of an invention in order to measure patent similarities [7]. Other researchers investigated effective ways of visualising patent analysis [8,12]. Li et al. worked on patent claim mapping in identifying patent claim conflicts [15]. The majority of research on patents serves professionals who work closely with patents such as patent analysts, Research and Development specialists, suggesting that research in assisting designers to understand patents and identify emerging design-prior art conflict has been overlooked to date.

In order to assess on patent infringement, experts often use text-based patent search or retrieval systems [1,5], which typically involves a keyword search. The semantics of these keywords will affect the quality of the results obtained, and so other techniques including natural language processing (NLP), statistical inference and machine learning (e.g. IBM Watson SIIP platform [10]) are used to improve results. However, text-based techniques are problematical [4] and generic patent image retrieval approaches (e.g. [19]) do not effectively capture the important working principle of the design [15]. Patent image retrieval systems such as Patseek and PatMedia [4] search for visual similarity of images, which is not necessarily a similar working principle, whereas a common working principle between designs suggests a potential conflict with the prior art.

It is worth noting that many of the systems and tools for patent analysis mentioned above require additional knowledge for designers to deal with query languages or patterns that normally are not part of their background.

To solve these issues, and in contrast with prior work, we previously presented a visual interface for helping designers to access prior art via a semantic database without requiring any specific background on query languages [17]. The interface design allows users to exploit block-oriented programming [18], presenting a program logic based on compositions of visual blocks. In this paper we report on a usability study on such a tool.

3   The Visual Tool

The automatic patent analysis follows a well-established workflow [1], which is based on a suitable machine-readable patents representation, and on a further patent analysis system, which in turn could be full- or semi-automatic.

Our visual tool represents the front-end for a patent analysis framework that focuses on mechanical engineering and is based on a semantic database. The database includes mechanical products covered by patents, and it is composed of a patent functional representation and a domain-specific ontology [2]. The functional representation aims at expressing patents in terms of geometric features and their functional interactions. The domain-specific ontology enables knowledge sharing and conceptualisation, providing a standardised vocabulary for

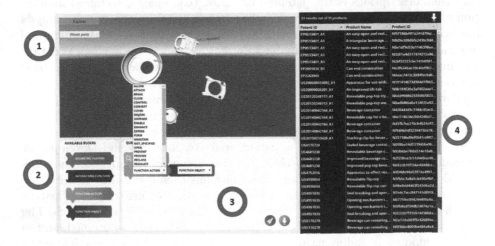

Fig. 1. The interface layout.

describing patented designs. The vocabulary, the relationships among geometric features and their functional interactions are encoded in a semantic database; this structured representation models similar working principles between an emerging design and prior art. The whole framework allows for early identification of potential conflicts and thereby can help designers steer their emerging designs away from overlapping patents.

Figure 1 shows the interface layout, whose symbols meaning and operational principles are described in [17].

4 Study Design

After the encouraging results of a preliminary evaluation of our visual tool [17], we decided to carry out a more structured study in order to assess the perceived usability, usefulness and workload. To this end, we recruited 21 professional designers from five industries as participants (3 females, 18 males, age ranging between 20–62 y.o., $M = 35.7$, $SD = 13.0$). This allowed us to collect a suitable amount of data for a meaningful analysis. In the following, we name the industry partners with five labels: BB, SN, CT, WFO and JR.

None of the participants were colourblind, while 11 were visually impaired (wearing glasses or contact lenses). 7 participants were involved in the patent infringement detection process; in particular:

- BB users were all involved in the process, mostly for legal aspects;
- only one SN user out of two was involved, for legal aspects;
- two CN users out of five were involved, for design and legal aspects;
- none of the three WFO users were involved in the process;
- none of the seven JR users were involved in the process.

We prepared 3 scenarios with 5, 5, and 7 tasks each respectively, and all participants were asked to accomplish them. All the participant industries allowed us into their premises upon appointment, and they let their employees leave their workplaces for the time needed for the test. The apparatus consisted of a laptop PC running our web-based visual interface. The users came up one after the other, and we asked the tested user to not reveal what we asked them and what they did to upcoming ones. For each test, after a brief explanation of the context, the experimenter started asking the user to complete each of the three scenarios one after the other, with a short pause between them. For each scenario, the final goal consisted of subsequent tasks, each depending on the previous one, except the first. The experimenter asked users to accomplish the planned tasks, by reading the goals in terms of queries expressed in natural language (e.g.: "Search for products that provide opening"; "Search for products having rivets on a plate"). The users were also asked to comment aloud their actions, in order to give the experimenter the opportunity to take note of them. The goal of each task was to compose the corresponding query on the visual tool, with no hints on the tool and in particular on how to start. The whole test took 5 sessions along three days (2 sessions a.m. and p.m. in the first two days,

1 session all day long for the third day). There was no time limits for each test, and they lasted 21 min at least and 45 min at most.

At the end of each test, we submitted 5 questionnaires to each user, both structured and free-text:

– Raw NASA Task Load Index (NASA-TLX - workload assessment) [9]
– System Usability Scale (SUS - usability assessment) [6]
– Usability Metric for User Experience (UMUX-Lite - usability assessment) [13]
– Net Promoter Score (NPS - satisfaction assessment) [16]
– Demographic + personal free suggestions

We let users complete the questionnaires all alone, being available for any request of clarification if needed. We also collected the experimenter's notes taken during the tests, for an additional qualitative cognitive walkthrough.

5   Results

The **NASA-TLX** questionnaire allows to evaluate the overall perceived workload in terms of mental demand, physical demand, temporal demand, achieved performance, required effort, and frustration level. Table 1 shows the results of the NASA-TLX questionnaire. It is worth noting that we had the highest counts in the positive parts of each scale, showing a positive evaluation of the perceived workload in terms of its components. Indeed, we had the highest counts on values less or equal than 30 for mental demand, physical demand, temporal demand, effort and frustration level, and on values greater or equal than 80.

Concerning the overall perceived workload across the 21 users resulting from the values of each dimension, we had an average value of 44/100. We observed higher counts on low values of perceived workload in the age range 29–65, with 15 questionnaires resulting in values in the range 29–47, and 6 resulting in values in the range 47–65.

The **SUS** questionnaire allowed us to obtain a usability level, which is also comparable to any other outcome from SUS questionnaires. We obtained an overall average SUS score of 70.36 (SD = 17.56), which is considered acceptable [3].

The **UMUX-Lite** questionnaire provides a measure of perceived usefulness and usability. Figure 2 shows a two-dimensional quadrant in which values of

Table 1. Workload values count, resulting from the NASA-TLX questionnaires.

	Min	AVG	Max	5	10	15	20	25	30	35	40	45	50	55	60	65	70	75	80	85	90	95	100
Mental Demand	15	47.14	90	0	0	1	0	3	5	1	1	0	3	0	2	0	1	0	2	1	1	0	0
Physical Demand	5	22.38	55	4	5	2	2	1	1	1	2	0	1	2	0	0	0	0	0	0	0	0	0
Temporal Demand	5	36.43	85	1	0	2	2	4	1	3	1	2	1	0	2	0	1	0	0	1	0	0	0
Performance	20	76.67	100	0	0	0	0	1	0	1	0	0	0	0	0	1	1	3	6	2	5	0	1
Effort	10	42.38	80	0	1	1	0	2	4	2	2	3	0	0	3	0	1	0	2	0	0	0	0
Frustration Level	10	40.71	90	0	2	4	0	0	3	2	2	1	1	1	1	0	0	2	0	1	1	0	0

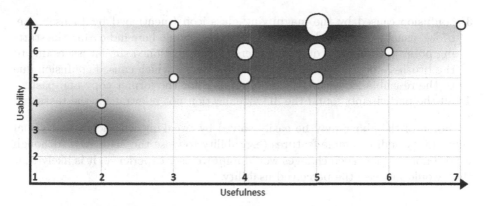

Fig. 2. UMUX-Lite results quadrant. Bigger points correspond to higher number of users who answered with that combination of usability and usefulness levels.

perceived usability and usefulness are reported for each user. In this case, we had an overall positive feedback, with 5 users in the bottom-left part of the quadrant, and 16 in the top-right part. In more detail, concerning the usefulness, we had 16 users who rated our tool with a 4 or more. As far as the usability is concerned, we had even more satisfying results, with 19 users who rated our tool with a 4 or more (18 users rated the usability with 5 or more).

The **NPS** is based on a single 11-point scale, and it aims at assessing the users' satisfaction by means of how much they would likely recommend the tool to their colleagues. In this case, we had 6/21 detractors (29% - scored 0–6), 10/21 promoters (48% - scored 9–10) and 5/21 passive (24% - scored 7–8), leading to an overall positive NPS [16]. We obtained the highest average evaluation from youngest users, who were also not involved in the legal aspects of patent infringement detection. Above all, participants who found the tool very useful reported that they would check for a possible patent infringement before the legal department would take care of it. In other words, they would enjoy the possibility to have some early hint on possible patent infringement, in order to decide whether to steer their design away, or to consciously pursue the current idea.

5.1 Cognitive Walkthrough

During the tests users mentioned some issues that may have had an impact in lowering the perceived usability:

1. inability to immediately understand how to interact for the very first task (mentioned by 18 users, i.e. 86%), although proceeding quickly thereafter
2. inability or difficulty in guessing the drag-and-drop feature (mentioned by 13 users, i.e. 62%), or where to drop the selected block (8 users, i.e. 38%)

3. confusion caused by the magnifying glass icon (mentioned by 14 users, i.e. 67%), usually associated with search features, while here indicating the starting point to compose a query. 14 users (67%) mentioned similar issues due to the brush-shaped button used to clear the query, which caused confusion due to the resemblance with the icon often used for the format copy-and-paste
4. all the participants found the 3D visualisation not relevant for the tasks

Some of the above may be easily solved by tweaking with icons and visual clues, or by adding simple features (e.g. ability to close the 3D view). Although we did not test how such changes would improve user experience, it is likely that they would increase the perceived usability.

5.2 Discussion

The analysis of the study results gave us some useful hint on both the current design choices and how to change them, where needed. In particular, we observed that most of the "negative" evaluations or comments were related to the very starting phase of the interaction. Once users filled the cognitive gap, they proceeded very fast, thus showing that such gap was very little and the learning path very short. This means that in a real scenario, where users would be suitably trained in using such a tool, they would only enjoy the features of the tool they appreciated. It is worth recalling that in our tests we did not give any hint on how to interact just because we wanted to have the most critical evaluation as possible.

6 Conclusion and Future Work

In this paper we reported on a study to assess the effectiveness a visual tool for early patent infringement detection, in terms of perceived workload and usability, shortly discussing the study results and extracting some general suggestion.

Based on the relevant and useful suggestions, we plan to slightly re-design the interface, by replacing the "magnifying glass" icon with a textual hint, and a shaded area as a visual hint on where to drop a block, which appears whenever a block is dragged into the "query composition" area. We plan to implement the new design and to carry out a further study on a greater number of users, aiming at obtaining some useful and significant guidelines for interface designers in the field of visual tools for professionals.

References

1. Abbas, A., Zhang, L., Khan, S.U.: A literature review on the state-of-the-art in patent analysis. World Pat. Inf. **37**, 3–13 (2014). https://doi.org/10.1016/j.wpi.2013.12.006
2. Atherton, M., Jiang, P., Harrison, D., Malizia, A.: Design for invention: annotation of functional geometry interaction for representing novel working principles. Res. Eng. Des. **29**(2), 245–262 (2018). https://doi.org/10.1007/s00163-017-0267-2

3. Bangor, A., Kortum, P., Miller, J.: Determining what individual SUS scores mean: adding an adjective rating scale. J. Usability Stud. **4**(3), 114–123 (2009). http://dl.acm.org/citation.cfm?id=2835587.2835589

4. Bhatti, N., Hanbury, A.: Image search in patents: a review. Int. J. Doc. Anal. Recognit. **16**(4), 309–329 (2013). https://doi.org/10.1007/s10032-012-0197-5

5. Bonino, D., Ciaramella, A., Corno, F.: Review of the state-of-the-art in patent information and forthcoming evolutions in intelligent patent informatics. World Pat. Inf. **32**(1), 30–38 (2010). https://doi.org/10.1016/j.wpi.2009.05.008

6. Brooke, J.: SUS - a quick and dirty usability scale. Usability Eval. Ind. **189**(194), 4–7 (1996)

7. Cascini, G., Zini, M.: Measuring patent similarity by comparing inventions functional trees. In: Cascini, G. (ed.) CAI 2008. TIFIP, vol. 277, pp. 31–42. Springer, Boston, MA (2008). https://doi.org/10.1007/978-0-387-09697-1_3

8. Chen, R.: Design patent map visualization display. Expert Syst. Appl. **36**(10), 12362–12374 (2009). https://doi.org/10.1016/j.eswa.2009.04.049

9. Hart, S.G., Staveland, L.E.: Development of NASA-TLX (task load index): results of empirical and theoretical research. In: Hancock, P.A., Meshkati, N. (eds.) Human Mental Workload, Advances in Psychology, vol. 52, pp. 139–183. North-Holland (1988). https://doi.org/10.1016/S0166-4115(08)62386-9

10. IBM: IBM Strategic IP Insight Platform (SIIP). https://researcher.watson.ibm.com/researcher/view_group.php?id=2134. Accessed 15 Mar 2019

11. Jiang, P., Atherton, M., Sorce, S., Harrison, D., Malizia, A.: Design for invention: a framework for identifying emerging design-prior art conflict. J. Eng. Des. **29**(10), 596–615 (2018). https://doi.org/10.1080/09544828.2018.1520204

12. Kim, Y.G., Suh, J.H., Park, S.C.: Visualization of patent analysis for emerging technology. Expert Syst. Appl. **34**(3), 1804–1812 (2008). https://doi.org/10.1016/j.eswa.2007.01.033

13. Lewis, J.R., Utesch, B.S., Maher, D.E.: UMUX-LITE: when there's no time for the SUS. In: Proceedings of the SIGCHI Conference on Human Factors in Computing Systems, CHI 2013, pp. 2099–2102. ACM, New York (2013). https://doi.org/10.1145/2470654.2481287

14. Li, Z., Tate, D., Lane, C., Adams, C.: A framework for automatic triz level of invention estimation of patents using natural language processing, knowledge-transfer and patent citation metrics. Comput.-Aided Des. **44**(10), 987–1010 (2012). https://doi.org/10.1016/j.cad.2011.12.006

15. Li, Z., Atherton, M., Harrison, D.: Identifying patent conflicts: TRIZ-Led patent mapping. World Pat. Inf. **39**, 11–23 (2014). https://doi.org/10.1016/j.wpi.2014.07.002

16. Reichheld, F.F.: The one number you need to grow. Harv. Bus. Rev. **81**(12), 46–54 (2003). http://europepmc.org/abstract/MED/14712543

17. Sorce, S., Malizia, A., Jiang, P., Atherton, M., Harrison, D.: A novel visual interface to foster innovation in mechanical engineering and protect from patent infringement. J. Phys. Conf. Ser. **1004**, 012024 (2018). https://doi.org/10.1088/1742-6596/1004/1/012024

18. Turbak, F., Bau, D., Gray, J., Kelleher, C., Sheldon, J.: Foreword. In: 2015 IEEE Blocks and Beyond Workshop (Blocks and Beyond), pp. vii–viii, October 2015. https://doi.org/10.1109/BLOCKS.2015.7368986

19. Vrochidis, S., Papadopoulos, S., Moumtzidou, A., Sidiropoulos, P., Pianta, E., Kompatsiaris, I.: Towards content-based patent image retrieval: a framework perspective. World Pat. Inf. **32**(2), 94–106 (2010). https://doi.org/10.1016/j.wpi.2009.05.010

Natural Language Data Queries on Multiple Heterogenous Data Sources

Alexander Wachtel$^{(\boxtimes)}$, Dominik Fuchß, Matthias Przybylla,
and Walter F. Tichy

Karlsruhe Institute of Technology, Karlsruhe, Germany
{alexander.wachtel,walter.tichy}@kit.edu,
{dominik.fuchss,matthias.przybylla}@student.kit.edu

Abstract. Motivated by a real-world scenario, we enable end users to query data due natural language from different sources like spreadsheets and databases. We provide a natural language user interface (NLUI) solution on how real-world entities and relations between them can be interpreted as a model to allow end user questions on the data. Therefore, the system enables end users to give instructions step-by-step, to avoid the complexity in full descriptions and give directly feedback of success. An evaluation is conducted with human users who had to perform a series of tasks using natural language. Overall, 13 end user took part in our survey with ten questions. 94.9% of all answers in the first part could be resolved on spreadsheet data, and 62,5% on SQL database.

Keywords: End user development · Natural language user interfaces ·
Natural language processing · Relation extraction · Dialog systems

1 Introduction

We aim for a breakthrough by making computers programmable in ordinary, unrestricted, written or spoken language. Rather than merely consuming software, users of the ever-increasing variety of digital devices and software building blocks could develop their own programs, potentially leading to novel, highly personalized, and plentiful solutions. With natural language, programming would become available to everyone. End users describe algorithms in their natural language and get a valid output by the dialog system for given description, e.g., selection sort of a set. The functionality is aimed at users with no programming knowledge, as the system enables simple routines to be programmed without prior knowledge. This makes it easier for users to get started with programming. The system also illustrates the relationship between a natural statement and its code representation, so it can also help to understand and learn a programming language [1]. At the end, the system is enabled for the object-oriented programming. Based on this, the system interprets the end user descriptions searching for classes, attributes, and methods. In general, classes represent entities from the real world, attributes specify different properties of an entity, and methods

© Springer Nature Switzerland AG 2019
A. Malizia et al. (Eds.): IS-EUD 2019, LNCS 11553, pp. 174–182, 2019.
https://doi.org/10.1007/978-3-030-24781-2_13

are functions or algorithms that allow to manipulate these attributes. Furthermore, end users will also be able to interact with already existing objects, e.g., Excel tables, images, graphs, but also external connections, such as connecting to SQL tables. Such objects should be addressed directly and manipulated by natural language input. In this case, our system analyses the data and allows user queries to different resources like tables, charts, and databases. End users could ask for information in their natural language on disconnected data that cannot be looked up in one step by the human.

2   Relation Extraction

In general, there are two obvious approaches to adaptation in a dialog system that works on data. On the one hand, we can adapt the system to the user. This means that we make it possible to resolve synonyms or the like. The other option is to adapt to the data. Exactly this adaptation of the data will be carried out in the following. As we have seen above, we can understand descriptions of relationships, classes and objects. But what about relationships that already exist in models, such as in and between tables. We also take a simple approach to extract from these tables. For this we abstract underlying platforms such as Excel or SQL and transfer the tables into a common model. Then we extract the contained elements and their relations from the tables.

Transformation of Tables. In a first step, we transform the different types of tables into a simplified table model. The first row represents all attributes. Each further row represents one object. A class is assigned to each table. Each cell represents either a primary key, a foreign key or simply an attribute. We transform the different tables into the common format via an interactive process. First, the user is asked for the class name for each table. Depending on the source the user will be asked to provide the identifying attribute for the elements of the table. In a last question, the user can specify which columns are to be used to create the object names. An object is built later from each line of the table. The information obtained in this way is used to establish connections between the tables in a follow-up step. In the last step, possible join relationships are searched. A join relationship results from the dissolution of a foreign key relationship (See Table 1). These tables show a set of owners in the first table. The second table shows different houses with their street, the number of parties and an entry to their owner. The entries in the *Owner* column represent a foreign key to the table of owners. This means that there is a relationship between the classes. To set up such join relationships between tables, the system asks the user during loading, whether the relationship is correctly recognized. If this is the case, the relationships are created automatically for each class and object. Adding SQL databases as a data source and transforming it into the table model is fairly easy. A lot of the concepts used in our table model exist in SQL databases as well. In the SQL metadata is all the information stored, necessary to answer all the questions mentioned in the subsection above. Currently only the primary key is extracted out of the metadata, since every table in SQL has a primary key.

Table 1. Houses and owners

Name	Reputation	Street	Parties	Owner
Smith	A+	2 Piper St	9	Smith
Miller	A	1 Piper St	6	Smith

Relationships, Classes, and Objects. After we have seen in Subsect. 2 that such join relationships can be resolved through interaction with the user, the next step is to form the relationships at the class and object level. For this purpose, a class is built from each of the tables. Columns that are not marked as foreign keys are used as attributes. Then the join relationships are converted to associations. The tables are transformed into the two classes *Owner* and *House*. These contain the attributes *Name*, and *Reputation* or *Street*, and *Parties*. Finally, one sees the association *owns*. The name of this is determined by the user in dialog with him or her. In the last step, an object is created for each row in the tables. In our example, the objects *Smith*, *Miller*, *HouseNo1* and *HouseNo2* are created. The names of the last two are generated automatically, since no name giving columns are selected (See Fig. 1).

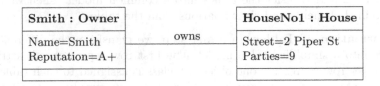

Fig. 1. Houses and owners: objects

Once a join relationship between tables has been established, the tables can be extended by new rows without having to rebuild the structures. The deletion of rows is also supported. In this respect, the synchronization of the underlying model with the data of the tables is possible without any further action on the part of the user. Semi-automatic extraction of models from tables allows the system to use existing data. Since data is available in various formats, we are looking forward to import data from various sources. As a first step, data from SQL databases will be processed. We support the combination of the different bases and abstract from them. For this we use the already known meta-format. Each data modification is synced by the converter incrementally. Our prototype operates on the abstract data. For this reason, it is independent on the underlying data source. For the demonstration of the compatibility with SQL databases a part of a help desk ticket system, based on a real-world scenario, is used. Before getting into details, some major differences between the two used knowledge bases have to be discussed. Generally the User can work on the Excel data better than a program, for SQL is the applies the opposite. In Excel no unnecessary information, like keys, are added and nothing is encoded. SQL on the contrary is based on encoding objects and its tables to maintain a clear structure, for an easy extraction of information. The simple conversion into the abstract data model is described in the following steps.

3 Natural Language Query Handling

Section 2 has shown how these models can also be obtained from tables. We are providing a concept to deal with different types of knowledge bases. The following scenario shows how these relationships between entities can be used to resolve user requests. We will show why adaptation in the direction of the data makes sense and how this can be used. The concept of countries and states is used for this, whereby we use the Austrian provinces with their capital, population and area as example. A human could simply answer the question "What is the overall area of Austria?" by calculating the sum of areas of all provinces. For this, the computer needs knowledge of the connection between the countries, states, Austria and the states of Austria. We can simply explain the concept by writing "A country consists of states" into the system. Afterwards, we can use the extraction process as shown in Sect. 2 to load the data from the table. As a last step we have to explain that Austria is a country which has the states listed in the table. This is also possible by using natural language interface of JustLingo. Afterwards, the system is ready to answer user requests. Some simple requests are shown in Fig. 2. We see three questions and the provided answers of the system. Currently, two groups of questions and a fallback is implemented to answer simple questions.

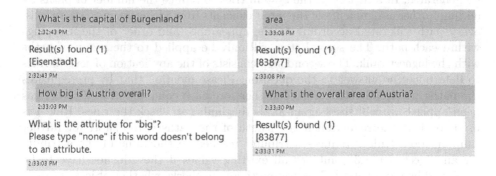

Fig. 2. JustLingo NLUI: example interaction

User Queries. The first type of request is the direct query of attributes. These are queries that refer directly to an attribute and a set of objects. E.g. "What are the capitals of the states of Austria?" To generate the answer, we first map the linguistic elements of the query to the elements in the model. After that we identify the *start* of the query. In the example case this would be the object Austria. As soon as this has been identified a search for the *target* will start.

In our example the target would be the linguistic element *capitals*. With this information the search of connecting paths will be invoked. After this step the system obtains a set of 9 possible paths starting at the object Austria and ending at an element which represents the linguistic element *capitals*. These are the paths from the object Austria to the capitals of all 9 states of Austria. E.g. the path defined as [*Austria → country-has-state-relation → Styria → Capital → Graz*]. To discard paths that are not necessary for the result, the paths will be rated. To do this, the other mappings are compared with the paths. In our example, the mapping of the linguistic element *states* to the class State would be used. The evaluation of the paths found this way is explained detailed in Subsect. 3. The second type of queries are those in which the user paraphrases an attribute with an adjective. These are called indirect query of attributes. E.g. "How big is Austria overall?" To resolve this kind of queries the system uses the possibility of interaction with the user. Therefore, the system asks for which property is meant. After the answer of the user the system has learned the meaning of *big* for this context. Thus, the system would not ask the user again, about the meaning of *big*. All follow-up steps are performed in the same fashion as performed in the approach to resolve direct requests. We have made the resolution of requests extensible. In particular, we have created a fallback handler in case a request does not fit into any schema. This fallback tries to analyze a given request by extracting all possible mappings between linguistic elements of the query and all entities. After extraction, the candidates of each element are sorted by the type of entities. The idea here is, for example, to prefer named objects to classes in order to limit the size of the later answer.

Evaluation of Paths. In this last step the final answer of the system will be generated. In a first step, the system tries to reduce the number of paths by adding further assignments of the input elements to model elements. Afterwards, every path will rated according to the appearance and order of the mappings within each path. The second step will only be applied to the group of paths with the highest rank. The second step consists of the application of several rules to determine the answer to the question. Please mention that by prerequisites the paths are equally structured and therefore have equal *lengths*. If a rule has been applied, we will start again at the beginning to check the rules. Rule 1 is used to abort the reduction if the length of the paths is too short for further simplification. Rule 2 reduces attributes reached to the value of the attribute for an object. Rule 3 combines all existing values if they do not have to be combined by any relation. The system therefore checks whether objects precede these values as the last element. Rule 4 simplifies the paths, if a value has already been created at the end of the paths, and the corresponding objects precede them by deleting the affected objects. Rules 5 and Rule 6 deal with the occurrence of relationships. If only one path exists, no function is used to merge the values, since only one value exists. Otherwise, a function is used that summarizes the values according to the relationships found. Rule 7 intercepts the case that the user did not ask for an attribute, but for objects. In this case, the objects are replaced by the values of the names. User interaction may needed to find the function which shall be used to aggregate the values if the function could not be determined in Rule 7. Afterwards, the result is presented to the user.

Rebuilding Path Search. Since adding the compatibility of using different kind of knowledge bases, the amount of Data has grown significantly. A deep search for paths between tables couldn't keep up with the growing data. To avoid searching for too long paths, which would be either way eliminated in the evaluation of paths (See Sect. 3), a quicker way of searching is a simple routing algorithm, in this case Dijkstra. As a first step, the program looks through the data with generated hints, to categorize hits into classes, object, attributes name or attributes value. If data in at least two categories is found, the search for a path can be done. Connections between the tables have been defined as in Sect. 2 mentioned, therefore performing a routing between the two tables, in which the data was found, is a simple operation. Because of that only the shortest possible connections between the two tables are found. This allows now the answer that there is no answer to that question, instead of finding an answer, which has a too long path. The paths found still will be Evaluated as mentioned in Sect. 3.

Using Results for Complex Functions. As we have seen, our system can answer a user's simple question. We have extended the natural language interface so that the answers to such questions can be linked further. For this purpose, functions that we define in natural language can be used. For this we use the already known mechanisms for creating algorithms from natural language. Thus, we achieve a great flexibility in the way of linking. For example, intermediate results can be used as parameters for stochastic functions, or they can be ordered by sorting algorithms. This makes it possible to split more complex queries that the system would otherwise not understand into individual operations that the system understands.

4 Evaluation

As a first user study we designed a study in which undergraduate computer science students were asked to solve tasks in two different classes of complexity. This approach is used to evaluate the question and answering module and test its limits. The user study should show to what extent the system discussed in Sects. 2 and 3 can answer user requests. In the first exercise of the user study, the 13 participants are given the task of asking questions to the system. As data basis the model from Sect. 3 is used here, which contains the relationship from countries and federal states, as well as Austria with its states as data [3]. In the evaluation, the participants were then given tasks such as *Determine the average population of all Austrian states* and had to use the system to get the answer. First, the *query error rate* for a set of queries Q and a set of answers A is defined as follows:

$$QER(A, Q) = \frac{\#(answer\ wrong) + \#(no\ answer)}{|Q|}$$

This measure is based on typical measures of NLP. Secondly, we consider the number of *not understood inputs* ($\#(NUI)$) to the system. In the study, nine participants were able to solve all six tasks of this first part. The remaining four participants were each unable to solve one of the tasks. In total a QER of 0.051 was achieved. The average for $\#(NUI)$ was 2.62. The second part of the study examined how these results change when several tables are linked. In addition, the participants should define their own task after they have solved the all set tasks. For this part of the evaluation, two tables have been adopted by Eurostat and relations between them have been established [17,18]. All in all, the participants received three tasks for which they had to formulate a question and were allowed to create a task themselves. A predefined task in this context was exemplary *Determine the average population in Belgium in 2012 and 2013*. Here the QER was 0.26 and the $\#(NUI)$ was 2.31. These values are based on the fact that all participants, if they have formulated their own task (12 participants), have made a more complex request, which the system did not understand. These complex questions were characterized by comparisons or orders of data.

Multiple Datasources. To be able to compare the changes made, the same input from the user study was used. The evaluation of this part only focuses on questions for data. Evaluating the generation of UML diagrams is neglected. For the same user input, the following results were produced: QER was 0.72 and the NUI was 2.70. Compared to the previous results a worsening in finding the correct answer is clearly visible. With these results the new answer finding got tuned to make the final evaluation. The final evaluation represents our intuition to include other kind of databases into the program. Since there are no other programs available to connect cross-platform databases and ask questions in natural language. In this evaluation tables in excel sheets and a SQL-database are used. Real data is used for this.

5   Related Work

Paternò [13] introduces the motivations behind end user programming defined by Liberman [9] and discusses its basic concepts, and reviews the current state of art. In 2006, Myers [12] provides an overview of the research in the area of End-User Programming. As he summarized, many systems for End User Development have already been realized [8]. During a study in 2006, Ko [8] identifies six learning barriers in End User Programming: design, selection, coordination, use, understanding and information barriers. In 2008, Dorner [16] describes and classifies End User Development approaches taken from the literature, which are suitable approaches for different groups of end users. Implementing the right mixture of these approaches leads to embedded design environments, having a gentle slope of complexity. Such environments enable differently skilled end users to perform system adaptations on their own. Sestoft [15] increases expressiveness and emphasizing execution speed of the functions thus defined by supporting recursive and higher-order functions, and fast execution by a careful choice of data representation and compiler technology. Cunha [5] realizes techniques for model-driven spreadsheet engineering that employs bidirectional transformations to maintain spreadsheet models and synchronized instances. The idea of programming in natural language was first proposed by Sammet in 1966 [14]. One of the difficulties is that natural language programming requires a domain-aware counterpart that asks for clarification, thereby overcoming the chief disadvantages of natural language, namely ambiguity and imprecision. [7] describes a method for the automatic acquisition of the hyponymy lexical relation from unrestricted text. This approach avoids the need for pre-encoded knowledge and also applicability across a wide range of text. The method discovers patterns and suggests that other lexical relations will also be acquirable in this way. In recent years, significant advances in natural language techniques have been made, leading, for instance, to IBM's Watson [6] computer winning against the two Jeopardy! world champions, Apple's Siri routinely answering wide-ranging, spoken queries, and automated translation services such as Google's becoming usable [10,19]. In 1979, Ballard et al. [2] introduced their Natural Language Computer (NLC) that enables users to program arithmetic calculations using natural language. Metafor introduced by Liu et al. [11] has a different orientation. Based on user stories the system tries to derive program structures to support software design. NLP2Code [4] enables developers to request for code snippets from the Stack Overflow, and integrates these snippets directly into the source code editor.

6 Conclusion and Future Work

In this paper, we presented a solution on extracting the real-world entities from human descriptions. From the meta representation we then create meta models and generate source code. After that, our system allows end user to query data in disconnected tables in natural unrestricted language. However, programming in natural language remains an open challenge [19]. There are several user inputs $i_2, \ldots, i_N$ that are similar to i_1 and also map to the known action a_1. There is also a problem on the classification of required system action or skill. The match of the user input i_1 to system action a_1 is unique until the function of the system could be clearly divided by the syntax of the user input. In case of object-oriented programming, the user input can be referenced to the Algorithm skill or Class interpretation skill. They have similar inputs but different actions on execution. For this reason, it is not enough to check the language on the syntactical level. Furthermore, the syntax matching should also be extended by the interpretation on the meta level. These methods should combine syntax, semantic and context classification. In our next paper, we will present the classification with several different classifiers. The result of the individual classifiers is summed and forms the overall similarity of the input to the skill. Ordinary, natural language would enable almost anyone to program and would thus cause a fundamental shift in the way computers are used. Rather than being a mere consumer of programs written by others, each user could write his or her own programs [20].

References

1. Wachtel, A., Eurich, F., Tichy, W.F.: Programming in natural language building algorithms from human descriptions. In: The Eleventh International Conference on Advances in Computer-Human Interactions, March 2018
2. Ballard, B.W., Biermann, A.W.: Programming in natural language: NLC as a prototype. In: Proceedings of the 1979 Annual Conference, pp. 228–237. ACM (1979)
3. Bundesanstalt Statistik Österreich: Regional Atlas Austria (Online Atlas). http://statistik.at/web_de/services/regionalatlas_oesterreich/index.html
4. Campbell, B.A., Treude C.: NLP2Code: code snippet content assist via natural language tasks. In: ICSME (2017)
5. Cunha, J., Fernandes, J., Mendes, J., Pacheco, H., Saraiva, J.: Bidirectional transformation of model-driven spreadsheets. In: ICMT (2012)
6. Ferrucci, D., et al.: Building Watson: an overview of the DeepQA project. AI Mag. **31**(3), 59–79 (2010)
7. Hearst, M.A.: Automatic acquisition of hyponyms from large text corpora. In: Proceedings of the 14th Conference on Computational Linguistics - Volume 2 (1992)
8. Ko, A.J., Myers, B.A.: Designing the whyline: a debugging interface for asking questions about program behavior. In: Proceedings of the SIGCHI Conference on Human Factors in Computing Systems (2004)
9. Lieberman, H., Paterno, F., Klann, M., Wulf, V.: End-user development: an emerging paradigm. In: Lieberman, H., Paternó, F., Wulf, V. (eds.) End user development, pp. 1–8. Springer, Heidelberg (2006). https://doi.org/10.1007/1-4020-5386-X_1
10. Liu, H., Lieberman, H.: Toward a programmatic semantics of natural language. In: IEEE Symposium on Visual Languages and Human Centric Computing (2004)
11. Liu, H., Lieberman, H.: Metafor: visualizing stories as code. In: Proceedings of the 10th International Conference on Intelligent User Interfaces. ACM (2005)
12. Myers, B., Ko, A., Burnett, M.: Invited research overview: end-user programming. In: CHI Extended Abstracts on Human Factors in Computing Systems (2006)
13. Paterno, F.: End user development: survey of an emerging field for empowering people. ISRN Softw. Eng. (2013)
14. Sammet, J.E.: The use of English as a programming language. Commun. ACM **9**, 228–230 (1966)
15. Sestoft, P., Sørensen, J.Z.: Sheet-defined functions: implementation and initial evaluation. In: Dittrich, Y., Burnett, M., Mørch, A., Redmiles, D. (eds.) IS-EUD 2013. LNCS, vol. 7897, pp. 88–103. Springer, Heidelberg (2013). https://doi.org/10.1007/978-3-642-38706-7_8
16. Spahn, M., Dorner, C., Wulf, V.: End user development: approaches towards a flexible software design. In: ECIS, pp. 303–314 (2008)
17. Statistical Office of the European Union: Population on 1 January by age and sex (2017). http://appsso.eurostat.ec.europa.eu/nui/show.do?dataset=demo_pjan
18. Statistical Office of the European Union: House price index - annual data (2018). http://appsso.eurostat.ec.europa.eu/nui/show.do?dataset=prc_hpi_a
19. Ortiz, C.L.: The road to natural conversational speech interfaces. IEEE Internet Comput. **18**, 74–78 (2014)
20. Tichy, W.F., Landhäußer, M., Körner, S.: Universal programmability - how AI can help. Artificial Intelligence Synergies in Software Engineering, May 2013

Open Piping: Towards an Open Visual Workflow Environment

Charles Boisvert[(✉)], Chris Roast, and Elizabeth Uruchurtu

Department of Computing, Communication and Computing Research Centre,
Sheffield Hallam University, City Campus, Howard Street, Sheffield S1 1WB, UK
{c.boisvert,c.roast,e.uruchurtu}@shu.ac.uk

Abstract. The most popular visual programming tools focus on procedural, object-oriented and event-based programming. This paper describes a boxes-and-wires functional programming tool, aimed to be accessible to novice programmers, while also supporting open access to the specified processes, executable programs and results for study and deployment.

Keywords: Computer science education · Data science ·
Functional programming · End-user programming

1 Introduction

Visual, block-based environments such as ALICE [4] or Scratch [17] have recently transformed the teaching of computing [1,9].

Yet this development in procedural and object-oriented programming tools has not disseminated to analysing and processing data. For example, the nifty assignments repository of computing assessment ideas [14,15] contains 107 assignments, collected for their quality, but only eight of these incorporate work with a real data set.

Of particular concern to us, at Sheffield Hallam University, is adapting our tools, teaching methods and resources in order to facilitate access to and process of data by students at any level. Specific interest areas have been working with open data advocacy groups [12] and making data analytic tools more available [19].

The Open Piping project pursues this idea with an open-source functional programming environment and visual data flow interface for data processing[1].

2 Project Motivations

Open Piping is a visual functional programming environment, based on a boxes and wires model, intended for data processing applications.

---

[1] http://boisvert.me.uk/openpiping.

© Springer Nature Switzerland AG 2019
A. Malizia et al. (Eds.): IS-EUD 2019, LNCS 11553, pp. 183–190, 2019.
https://doi.org/10.1007/978-3-030-24781-2_14

Visual boxes and wires environments are common [11,13], including some in commercial [8] and scientific [7] use. But in many cases, the value of the tools is limited due to the poor transparency of the processes and technology they implement.

Take the case of the popular - until its end in 2015 - Yahoo pipes [13]. To execute pipes on systems of their choice, users had to go through a complex export process. This was their only option when Yahoo support ended.

Open piping aims to propose an ease of use comparable to commercial tools, in an open architecture to facilitate development flexibility, reuse and allow richer exchanges between users.

2.1   Open by Design

Our ambition is to propose a graphical tool for user-defined data processes, which would include, by design, the transparency and flexibility needed to apply user-defined processes in a range of languages and environments. Open piping aims to be at once:

Open. That is, Open Source; the system's source code is available under the GNU licence. But so is the notation used to define processes. Any user process can then be transformed from this notation into executable code in a target programming language.

Interoperable. The process specification format is openly available, and uses a human-readable, JSON formatted S-expression. This is needed to ensure the interoperability of the system with any manner of services, such as alternative end-user interfaces, new languages or process hosting and remote execution tools.

Easy to use. The user interface makes it easy to define data flows and shows clearly the relation between data flow, resulting S-expression, and executable functionality.

With resulting processes easy to deploy. The ability to choose from multiple languages and standards for services and content integration, would facilitate the re-use of user-defined processes in different environments, such as within content-management systems, as web or application widgets, or within a service-oriented architecture.

Altogether, these characteristics aim to ensure that users can easily define the processes they want to operate on data, while also retaining control of these processes to use them in new environments.

3   Open Piping Operation

3.1   System Architecture

The boxes-and-wires model describes the directed acyclic graph for a function, with the boxes representing functions and the wires, the data to which they apply.

Configuration data defines base functions available to the end-user. This information at once determines primary graphical blocks, provides access to basic processing capabilities, and limits that access, for security, to a chosen set with defined functionality.

The end-user defines a function by wiring elementary blocks. This function is translated into an S-expression in JSON, which can be compiled into an executable function in any number of languages, provided that calls to the primitive functions can be defined.

The interface elements presented Fig. 1 sum up the use of Open Piping. The end-user chooses elementary blocks (1) to define a flow (2) which is translated to a symbolic expression (3) encoded in JSON to use the many existing tools for this format. The expression is then interpreted (4) and executed (5).

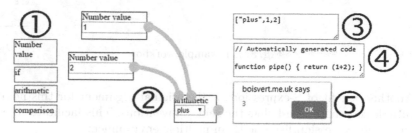

Fig. 1. Open piping main interface elements

3.2   Defining and Encoding a Data Flow

The block description and interface configuration also uses the JSON format. For instance, Fig. 2 shows the configuration lines to define the box representing arithmetic operations. The user can choose add, subtract, divide, or multiply from a single 'arithmetic' box.

Fig. 2. Defining and representing graphically a box of arithmetic functions

An example data flow is presented Fig. 3. The web interface uses the JSPlumb library [10] to manipulate and represent the screen objects. Traversing the graph recursively provides a symbolic expression. An advantage of symbolic expressions is that code remains close to existing languages such as LISP or Scheme. For instance, in a LISP-like language, the workflow Fig. 3 results in the structure:

```
(if (isNumber 15) (plus 1 15) "not a number")                    [1]
```

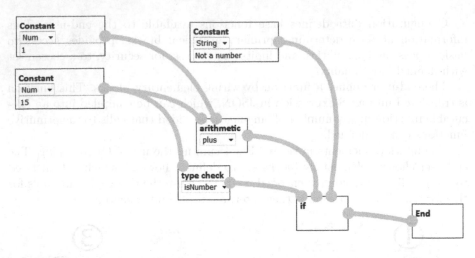

Fig. 3. An example workflow

Another benefit of S-expressions is the original argument for this notation: executable code and data follow the same conventions. This facilitates the processing of an expression like line [1] in multiple environments.

The expression is encoded in JSON, to provide to the interpreter. JSON's wide use and readability make it particularly suitable to this purpose. The encoding follows these simple rules:

- JSON notation defines *objects*, *arrays*, *strings*, *numbers* and the values true, false, and null. Our encoding relies on all but *objects*.
- Atomic values are *strings*, *numbers* and the values true, false, and null.
- Lists are represented by a JSON array. Each element of the list can be an atomic value or a list, and so on recursively.

Respecting this convention, the process shown Fig. 3 is written:

```
["if", ["isNumber",15], ["plus",1,15], "Not a number"]
```
[2]

3.3   Interpret a Symbolic Expression in Executable Language

To allow the execution of the same expression in diverse environments, we rely on characteristics present in most programming languages - use of variables, of a means of conditional execution, of functions - but we must provide elementary information to support the interpretation in each language. These data are themselves written in JSON.

To illustrate the interpretation process, let us study the case of interpreting expression [2] above in JavaScript and JQuery.

The interpretation relies on a list of predefined functions and string substitutions for the language:

```
"plus": {"args": "a,b", "sub": "(@a+@b)"}
"if": {"args": "a,b,c", "sub": "@a?@b:@c"}                        [3]
"isNumber": {"args": "n", "body": "return $.isNumeric(n);"}
```

Some operators are interpreted by substituting character chains to form the target code. Arithmetic operators like + use this technique, but so do conditionals, which we interpret in JavaScript with the ternary operator. Functions are identified and composed from arguments and body information. So [4] contains all the information needed to interpret the example completely.

Using this data, the expression is interpreted recursively. First the expression

```
["isNumber", 15]                                                 [4]
```

results in the definition of function isNumber,

```
function isNumber(n) {return $.isNumeric(n);}                    [5]
```

and into one function call. The plus function is then interpreted by substituting strings, and finally if to compose the overall result:

```
process(isNumber(15)?(1+15):"Not a number");                    [6]
```

We can see that the interpretation of a user-defined function is simple; to be able to execute a process in a given language, we simply need to define and execute safely the primitive functions required.

3.4 Overcoming Visual Limitations

The graphical model shown above should support end-user's understanding and programming of simple processes. However, based on our experience and prior research such as [2,3,18], we speculate that several aspects of the visualisation are not easily represented in ways that end-users spontaneously understand. Here, we present a number of potential solutions to support end-users as programs become more complex.

Coordinating Visual Code with Results. Visual programming can support end-users with a number of displays - the results of a program, of its code, of its execution. The wires and boxes model is a form of visual code, but many systems show a visual representation of execution results.

Coordinated views can also apply to viewing code. Yahoo pipes [16] is an example of this approach: its visualisation showed code, in boxes and wires form, along with a sample of the data resulting from it. Users could also select subsets of the code to view its result. This supported end-users with a presentation of the code, of some results, and of execution information (as partial execution results), as well as debugging support by means of choosing code subsets to test.

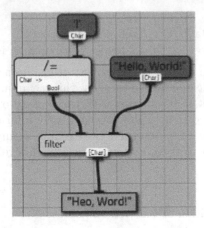

Fig. 4. Viskell shows data type explicitly

Data Typing. The boxes and wires model shown in our example Fig. 3 does not show any type information. Typing has many advantages for novice programmers, in particular limiting errors by constraining the validity of constructs, ensuring security, and facilitating debugging.

Typing can be presented in textual form, a solution adopted by Viskell as shown in Fig. 4 [20]. An alternative is visual clues, such as colour, shape, or icons: languages like MIT Scratch [17] adopt this approach, and use the added advantage of shape as a metaphor for syntactic validity. Type can also be implemented in the language and enforced in the interaction, yet not presented visually: that is the solution adopted by Yahoo pipes, which enforces type checking with the impossibility of connecting a wire to a box if types do not match, but give no visual typing clue.

Representing Conditionals. Conditional execution is one of the basic elements of programming. A three-argument function, for the Boolean that determines which branch is executed, and each of the two branches, is a suitable technical answer, but as the prototype workflow shown earlier in Fig. 3, visual clues in support of the user are clearly lacking.

Prograph [5] solves this problem by adding to boxes and wires a third construct, *frames*, for sections of code that are end-users should consider separately.

First Class Functions. First-class functions are a fundamental benefit of functional programming, but also a difficult concept to represent in ways that users can understand and control. The earlier illustration of Viskell (Fig. 4), shows a lambda-expression within the model, supported by textual type annotation: not every end-user will find it clear.

An alternative relies on the same notion of frames as for conditionals: a function that accepts another as a parameter, represents that parameter within

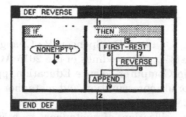

Fig. 5. Prograph shows the conditional branches within two frames for clarity.

a frame. Yahoo pipes adopts that solution, albeit for a limited use of first-class functions: it implements user actions to drop a box into a functional parameter slot. [6] have investigated the primitives needed to represent completely the power of first-class functions within frames, but the solution is not an easy visualisation of the notion.

4   Conclusion and Future Work

The structure of our system lets users retain control of their processes. In particular:

Limits to processing capabilities are not inherent to the system, but instead to the environment in which the process is deployed, for example by setting a processing time limit.

The visual language is loosely coupled to the execution environment, by producing a function definition in an open intermediate representation; this ensures that changes to the visual interface, to the target language, and to the execution environment are independent.

Risks of code injection are limited by transmitting the symbolic expression to an interpretation environment hosted with the execution environment, rather than communicate executable code, as well as by defining in the interpreter what primitive functions are allowable.

We believe that these characteristics can support adoption and self-learning through greater open access to computation.

Currently our prototype ensures that end-users can define processes, and demonstrates the compilation from the S-expression to JavaScript and execution. Multiple environments common on web servers and clients are considered - e.g. JQuery, PHP, node.js, etc, as well as deployment of executable results in new systems.

Developing this prototype's capabilities to support users further, will require a balance of technical feasibility, theoretical clarity and empirical evidence to identify the most appropriate solutions.

References

1. Adshead, D., Boisvert, C., Love, D., Spencer, P.: Changing culture: educating the next computer scientists. In: Proceedings of the 2015 ACM Conference on Innovation and Technology in Computer Science Education, pp. 33–38. ACM (2015)
2. Blackwell, A.F.: Pictorial representation and metaphor in visual language design. J. Vis. Lang. Comput. **12**(3), 223–252 (2001)
3. Blackwell, A.F.: The reification of metaphor as a design tool. ACM Trans. Comput.-Hum. Interact. **13**(4), 490–530 (2006)
4. Cooper, S., Dann, W., Pausch, R.: Alice: a 3-d tool for introductory programming concepts. J. Comput. Sci. Coll. **15**, 107–116 (2000). Consortium for Computing Sciences in Colleges
5. Cox, P., Pietrzykowski, T.: Advanced programming aids in PROGRAPH. In: Proceedings of the 1985 ACM SIGSMALL Symposium on Small Systems, pp. 27–33. ACM (1985)
6. Fukunaga, W. Pree, A., Kimura, T.D.: Functions as objects in a data flow based visual language. In: Proceedings of the 1993 ACM Conference on Computer Science, CSC 1993, pp. 215–220. ACM, New York (1993)
7. Hull, D., et al.: Taverna: a tool for building and running workflows of services. Nucleic Acids Res. **34**(suppl 2), W729–W732 (2006)
8. Instruments, N.: What is labview. http://www.ni.com/en-gb/shop/labview.html. Accessed 30 Apr 2019
9. Jones, S.P., et al.: Computing at school. International comparisons (2011). Accessed 7 May 2013
10. JSPlumb, I.: Jsplumb toolkit documentation. https://jsplumbtoolkit.com/docs.html. Accessed 13 Apr 2017
11. Le-Phuoc, D., Polleres, A., Tummarello, G., Morbidoni, C.: Deri pipes: visual tool for wiring web data sources. In: Book DERI Pipes: Visual Tool for Wiring Web Data Sources, 2008 edn. (2008)
12. Love, M., Boisvert, C., Uruchurtu,, E., Ibbotson, I.: Nifty with data: can a business intelligence analysis sourced from open data form a nifty assignment? In: Proceedings of the 2016 ACM Conference on Innovation and Technology in Computer Science Education, ITiCSE 2016, pp. 344–349. ACM, New York (2016)
13. O'Reilly, T.. Pipes and filters for the internet. http://radar.oreilly.com/2007/02/pipes-and-filters-for-the-inte.html. Accessed 10 Oct 2016
14. Parlante, N.: Nifty assignments. http://nifty.stanford.edu. Accessed 12 Jan 2016
15. Parlante, N., et al.: Nifty assignments. In: ACM SIGCSE Bulletin, vol. 35, pp. 353–354. ACM (2003)
16. Pruett, M.: Yahoo! pipes. O'Reilly, Sebastopol (2007)
17. Resnick, M., Maloney, J., Monroy-Hernández, A., Rusk, N., Eastmond, E., Brennan, K., Millner, A., Rosenbaum, E., Silver, J., Silverman, B., et al.: Scratch: programming for all. Commun. ACM **52**(11), 60–67 (2009)
18. Roast, C., Leitão, R., Gunning, M.: Visualising formula structures to support exploratory modelling. In: Proceedings of the 8th International Conference on Computer Supported Education, CSEDU 2016, pp. 383–390. SCITEPRESS - Science and Technology Publications, Lda, Portugal (2016)
19. Roast, C., Patterson, D., Hardman, V.: Visualisation – it is not the data, it is what you do with it. In: Kommers, P., Isaías, P. (eds.) e-Society 2018 Conference Proceedings, pp. 231–238. IADIS (2018)
20. Wibbelink, F.: Interacting with conditionals in viskell (2016)

Designing Troubleshooting Support Cards for Novice End-User Developers of Physical Computing Prototypes

Tracey Booth[1]([✉]), Jon Bird[3], Simone Stumpf[1], and Sara Jones[2]

[1] Centre for Human-Computer Interaction Design,
City, University of London, London, UK
{tracey.booth.1,simone.stumpf.1}@city.ac.uk
[2] Centre for Creativity in Professional Practice,
City, University of London, London, UK
s.v.jones@city.ac.uk
[3] Department of Computer Science, University of Bristol, Bristol, UK
jon.bird@bristol.ac.uk

Abstract. Previous work has shown that end-user developers (EUDs) find diagnosing and fixing circuit bugs in physical computing prototypes challenging. This paper reports on the design of a card deck to support troubleshooting by novice EUDs. The deck provides EUDs with ideas for different troubleshooting tactics and guides them in their use by encouraging reflection to help build EUDs' troubleshooting knowledge and skill. We describe the design process and the resulting card deck. Our work contributes a new way of supporting EUDs in troubleshooting physical computing prototypes.

Keywords: End-user development · Physical computing · Troubleshooting · Cards · Support tools

1 Introduction

Previous work [3] has established that end-user developers (EUDs) experience numerous problems when developing physical computing prototypes and that circuit bugs, rather than software bugs, are most likely to prevent successful development of a working prototype. EUDs often choose speculative, unproductive troubleshooting strategies, rather than performing systematic inspection or focused tests to narrow in on the cause of a problem. While support tools such as the Idea Garden [4] exist for end-user programmers (EUPs) only limited support is available for end-user developers of physical computing prototypes to overcome these challenges, e.g. [7].

The contribution of our paper is a set of troubleshooting support cards for physical computing. In the next section we summarise the key findings from our analysis of EUDs troubleshooting physical computing prototypes and describe what support they need. In Sect. 3, we explain our decision to use cards to provide the support needed by

© Springer Nature Switzerland AG 2019
A. Malizia et al. (Eds.): IS-EUD 2019, LNCS 11553, pp. 191–199, 2019.
https://doi.org/10.1007/978-3-030-24781-2_15

EUDs, and outline some of the key considerations that guided the development of our card set. We also describe and report the findings from two focus groups that informed the design of the final card set. Finally, we describe the resulting deck of cards, and discuss how it may be further developed.

2   What Support Do EUDs Need When Troubleshooting?

Our earlier work [3] investigated the problems that EUDs encounter when developing physical computing prototypes using Arduino [1]. We found that participants experienced many obstacles and that the majority who did not complete their prototype did so due to unresolved circuit bugs. Further analysis showed that two thirds of the changes that EUDs made to their prototypes when troubleshooting were speculative—they did not know what or where the error was, or were not sure how to fix it. On average, speculative changes led to three times as many new bugs being introduced into the prototypes compared to the number of bugs that were fixed.

On the basis of our earlier work, we have identified three overarching principles to support EUD troubleshooting. First, we need to encourage EUDs to be more reflective when troubleshooting and to avoid making speculative changes that typically result in more new bugs being introduced than fixed. Drawing on the work of Dewey [12], and Fleck and Fitzpatrick [8], our focus is on supporting EUDs to enter a reflective problem solving cycle (defining the problem; diagnosing and formulating a working hypothesis; reasoning; and testing the hypothesis through action) in which they think about what they should do and why—generating hypotheses, considering alternatives and the potential impact of their actions, questioning their assumptions—and evaluate their fix attempts. Secondly, support should facilitate EUDs persisting with systematic troubleshooting. Several EUDs in our study gave up troubleshooting and continued building, even when they had not solved their problems, because they ran out of ideas for things to investigate or try. This added further complexity to their prototypes, making problem diagnosis even more challenging. Finally, EUDs would benefit from support in planning and tracking their troubleshooting. This would help them to carry out all necessary steps and enable them to remember what they had tried and what the results were.

We also believe EUDs require specific support for different troubleshooting activities. Particular aspects of diagnosis/evaluation that require support include recognising symptoms of failure (determining whether something is or is not doing what it is supposed to), defining the problem/failure (identifying the symptoms and running tests to establish under what conditions failure occurs), inspection (closely and systematically inspecting a prototype for bugs and being aware of different bug types to look for), problem decomposition (breaking down a complex prototype into smaller, isolated parts which can help to establish the boundaries of failure and home in on the cause), and testing (knowing what tests to perform and how to evaluate the results).

3 Developing Cards to Support Troubleshooting

Software tools such as the Idea Garden [4] provide support for end-user program-mers, while other tools, e.g. [7], help learners debug electronic circuits. To our knowledge there is no tool to support EUDs troubleshooting both programming and electronics.

To develop our tool for supporting EUDs in troubleshooting physical computing bugs in a more reflective manner, we looked to other domains for inspiration. A popular method used to generate ideas and provide low-tech, process support in other domains, either in general, or for particular activities, involves the use of *physical cards*.

3.1 Why Cards?

Numerous card-based tools exist to support the generation and development of ideas within a creative or design process and/or to provide specific knowledge during one. Domain, problem or activity-specific card tools include: MRG Cards (mixed reality games design [15]), DSD Cards (designing technology for children [2]), Exertion Cards (exertion games design [14]), PLEX Cards (design for playfulness [11]), Tango Cards (tangible learning games design [6]), Envisioning Cards (considering human values during design [9]), and Tiles IoT Toolkit (designing IoT prototypes [13]).

Cards afford several benefits. For example, they externalise ideas [13] and act as memory prompts [6], of relevant information or where a user is in a process. As cards can be moved next to one another or grouped, they facilitate comparisons [2] and can also help to break down a problem into steps [14] or to plan actions in order of priority. Arranging cards can support the framing and reframing of a problem, leading to hypotheses, while cards containing less-specific information can also help spark ideas [15]. As EUDs can easily arrange physical cards to explore relations or configure them into meaningful spatial arrangements, we feel this to be an appropriate medium for encouraging reflective troubleshooting, and planning and tracking activity.

3.2 Considerations When Designing Cards

To gain insight into designing our card-based tool, we looked to both the academic literature (design, creativity, HCI and education) and non-academic examples. Our intention was to gain an understanding of how the design of these tools supported their purposes, and to uncover the different factors important in the process of designing a card-based tool and delivering information in this medium. Based on our review of the academic literature, we identified four key categories of design considerations:

Physical Form. This should take usage into account, for example, handling and placement during activities. Properties such as size and thickness of cards matter [2], and card orientation has potential implications for both handling and positioning, as does sidedness: only one side of a card can be seen unless the user turns it over.

Information Content. Information on a card should support its purpose and reinforce desired behaviour. Questions—particularly open—are commonly used to prompt thought or reflection [2, 9, 14], as is providing minimal information [11], or evocative imagery [14]. Cards can also provide context or knowledge [2, 9, 13], concrete examples [6, 13] or instructions [9], however, too much information can overwhelm the user and be time-consuming to read [15], potentially disrupting the activity flow [6]. Descriptions should therefore be succinct and easy to digest [11] and information should be written in simple, everyday language, avoiding jargon [2, 6, 14].

Visual Appearance. Visual design can reinforce information architecture and improve searchability [6], by using spatial layout, colour, iconography and typography to make it easy to find specific cards, categories or content types [2]. It should be easy to differentiate cards (and categories) from one another [6] and if a card is double-sided, the two sides should be visually distinct [2]). Care should be taken with imagery— some can be confusing or open to misinterpretation [6, 11].

Structure. An effective information architecture will aid users in navigating a card set and finding the information they need. It should support visual scanning [6] of the deck and of the information types on a card. Categories should be simple and understandable; tabs are a way to physically separate different card types or categories [6].

3.3 A Study to Inform the Card Deck Design

Building on our review of the literature, we conducted a small study to help design our card deck. We ran two focus group sessions, each involving a pair of EUDs (30-42 years old; one female pair, one male-female pair) who were new to Arduino, and therefore representative of the intended users of our card deck. All had limited experience of both programming and electronics. Prior to the focus groups, we developed some example cards and content. From our literature review (e.g. [5]), we had identified a set of 34 tactics that novice EUDs might be encouraged to use when troubleshooting Arduino-based prototypes, and tentatively grouped these into seven categories. During the sessions, participants were asked for feedback in terms of information content, physical form and visual appearance, as well as categorisation. We video-recorded the focus groups and took notes during them. We used the notes and transcripts of the video recordings for analysis.

Physical Form, Information Content, and Visual Appearance. Participants considered four physical formats—playing card size and double that size, in both landscape and portrait orientations—and ranked these by preference, given the physical limitations of an environment of prototype development. Participants much preferred the smaller cards, in portrait orientation, being a standard playing card size and easier to handle than the larger cards: *"All card games are this size. There is a very good reason for it. They feel very nice in the hand and you can flick through them very easily. (PB1)"*. They felt that smaller cards would take up less space and be laid out more easily, and that landscape cards would be harder to hold and flip through.

We created information content for two tactics: one a lower-level tactic (*Inspect for poor connections*), intended to prompt an EUD to inspect their circuit for a particular bug type; the second a higher level tactic (*Isolate part of the system*), requiring an EUD to think about how they might simplify and test their prototype to narrow in the location of the bug. Participants were asked to consider three different types of information content, and rank these by preference:

- *'Questions to ask'*—Designed to encourage thought or reflection. For example: "How could this help narrow in on the cause of failure, or rule something out?".
- *'Can apply to'*—Information to guide troubleshooting to the bug location. For example: "Jump wire ends in breadboard holes or Arduino pins".
- *'Ways to apply'*—Things to do, supporting specific trouble-shooting activities. For example: "Check component legs in the breadboard".

'Questions to ask' was ranked as most useful, followed by 'Ways to apply'. Encouraging reflection was appreciated *"[...]to spark some thinking in myself, so I could kind of direct my investigations. (PB2)"* However, some novices may simply prefer to be told what to do: *"No, I want it to tell me 'do this, do this' (laughs) (PA1)"*.

Participants then considered 30 different designs, each for a potential front or back of a card. As well as in size, orientation and information, designs differed in colour coding, typography, titling, and iconography. Each pair chose three potential 'whole card' designs, ranked by preference. All felt that, as novices, having iconography and colour coding would aid understanding, recognition and selection, and that single-word titles were too ambiguous. The top-ranked card created by each pair was identical: a smaller-sized, portrait-oriented, double-sided card, with a distinct, uncluttered front (full title, large icon, brief summary) and more detailed information on the rear.

Categorisation (card deck structure). Finally, participants performed a sorting exercise, using the set of 34 tactic titles and seven category titles, in order to inform the information architecture of our card deck. Participants discussed each tactic and, as a pair, agreed on which category to put it into. If unsure, they could also place tactics into a "?" category. While both pairs sorted the majority of tactics into the categories to which we had originally assigned them (Pair A 26/34; Pair B 20/34), this exercise helped us to identify some confusing or ambiguous wording, for example, "type" and "look for", and the need for some categorisation changes.

4   The Final Card Set

Informed by the focus group findings, we revised the card set. Twelve tactics and two categories were renamed, to make them easier to understand. We also reassigned five tactics to different categories and removed two categories. Further discussion within the research team led to a new category of tactic: 'Stop... think'. Although not used in the focus group study, the final card deck also contains two other card types: *Best Practice* cards, which have their own category, and *Component Information* cards, currently assigned to the 'Get Help' category, as they hold factual information about components.

The troubleshooting card set now comprises 46 cards: 36 tactics and four component cards in five categories, as well as six best practice cards. Figure 1 shows the front of a card from each category. The full set of cards can be viewed at http://traceybooth.com/tscards.

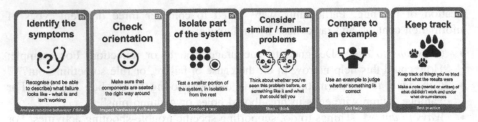

Fig. 1. Example cards from each category

4.1 Tactics Categories

The tactics we have chosen for the card set—drawn from a review of both academic and non-academic debugging and troubleshooting literature, and our previous work—aim to guide novice EUDs in diagnosing their problems instead of making haphazard speculative changes to their prototypes, as our previous work has shown they tend to do. The first three categories present three broad tactical approaches EUDs might take: The *'Analyse run-time behaviour/data'* category contains eight tactics to guide users in using what is—or can be made—visible at run-time to diagnose their problems, suggesting specific things they might look for. The *'Inspect hardware/software'* category contains 14 tactics that suggest different types of visual checks EUDs might do, i.e. inspecting the circuit, program, IDE or computer connection—several of the bugs we observed in our previous study could have been identified through visual inspection, had participants known where to look and what to look for. The *'Conduct a test'* category contains seven tactics that involve making changes, however the aim is to encourage novices to be more systematic in these, conducting focused tests with an idea of what they are looking for. As well as electronics-specific tactics, such as swapping working and non-working components, this category contains higher-level tactics, for example, decomposing problems into smaller ones, to isolate cause of failure to a particular area of the prototype. In contrast, the *'Stop...think'* category contains four tactics that encourage novices to step back from <u>doing</u> and focus on <u>thinking</u>, especially if they are stuck. Finally, the *'Get help'* category suggests three ways in which novices might use external information, rather than their own knowledge alone, to diagnose and fix their problems.

4.2 Card Designs

Tactic Cards. The tactic cards (see Fig. 2) are a standard playing card size (64 mm × 89 mm), double-sided, with a clean, impactful design on the front, and detailed information on the back. Both sides are portrait-oriented, and corners are rounded. The front contains the tactic title in large, bold text above a large icon and a brief summary of the tactic—enough to give a novice EUD an indication of what the tactic is about.

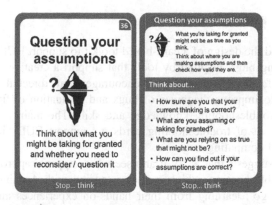

Fig. 2. Tactic card design, front (left) and rear (right)

The top panel of the card rear repeats the icon in a smaller size, for continued visual recognition if the card is turned over, flanked by a short description of why/how the tactic might be useful. The lower panel contains a list of open questions, which aim to prompt reflection. The category name appears at the bottom of both sides and the title of the card is repeated at the top of the rear, so the card can still be identified when turned over. Categories are colour-coded, using a colour scheme designed for maximum visual difference [10]; cards are bordered in their category colour and a band of the same colour visually separates the two information panels on the rear.

Best Practice, Component Information and Category Cards. The best practice cards follow a similar design to the tactic cards but are currently single-sided and contain a description rather than questions, as the aim is to inform, rather than to prompt thinking something through. The component information cards are larger (89 mm × 128 mm), as they contain far more information and more complex imagery, including component pinout images, specifying correct connection types, and basic circuit wiring information, as well as other information key to using or controlling the component. The category cards are the same width as the tactic and best practice cards but are slightly taller, so that their titles are visible above the other cards, making it easy to see and select cards from a particular category. On the rear of each category card is a bulleted list of the cards it contains.

Additional Materials: Playmat and Cards Stand. Our previous work suggests that EUDs could benefit from support in structuring and planning their troubleshooting. Inspired by boardgames, we designed a playmat, which provides a 'shortlist' area where EUDs can place a selection of tactics to try and an 'active' area, for the current card(s). It also reinforces the cycle of 'diagnose, fix, evaluate', encouraging EUDs to diagnose before attempting fixes, and to evaluate the result of any fix attempts.

We modelled and 3D printed a three-tiered stand to hold and display the cards in a structured, space-efficient way. This provides EUDs with visual prompts of the different tactical approaches available and makes the cards in a category easier to access.

5 Discussion and Conclusion

We have described the design of a card-based toolkit to support EUDs troubleshooting physical computing bugs, inspired by tools that support a creative or design process. Our aim was to facilitate reflection and encourage more directed exploration when troubleshooting, to improve diagnosis of bugs and evaluation of fixes, and build up novices EUDs' troubleshooting knowledge and skill. The main contribution of this paper is a novel set of troubleshooting cards, to support EUDs in diagnosing and resolving physical computing bugs.

Our research suggests that a 'try it and see what happens' approach is generally a poor way of troubleshooting, which creates a tension with Arduino's philosophy of people 'having a go', learning from their hands-on experiences and 'tinkering' [1]. How to strike the right balance between this and a more structured approach to troubleshooting is still an open research question.

While it is possible to create software-based support, we feel that a card-based, physical tool not only affords the benefits described in Sect. 3.1, it additionally does not give novice EUDS more technology to contend with when troubleshooting problems. The format also encourages flexibility of use, for example, the cards could be used by individuals or collaboratively, and in formal or informal learning environments. We have already received interest from educators teaching physical computing in schools and adult education.

We are currently evaluating our toolkit in an empirical study with EUDs, to investigate the effects of using the cards in hands-on troubleshooting tasks. We intend to refine the cards in light of the results of this study, and make the toolkit available for download, extension, and customisation. We see toolkits such as ours as a vital step towards greater adoption and continued use of physical computing technology by novices.

References

1. Banzi, M.: Getting Started with Arduino. O'Reilly Media Inc, Sebastopol (2009)
2. Bekker, T., Antle, A.N.: Developmentally situated design (DSD): making theoretical knowledge accessible to designers of children's technology. In: Proceedings of CHI 2011, pp. 2531–2540. ACM, New York (2011)
3. Booth, T., et al.: Crossed wires: investigating the problems of end-user developers in a physical computing task. In: Proceedings of CHI 2016, pp. 3485–3497. ACM, New York (2016)
4. Cao, J., et al.: Idea Garden: Situated support for problem solving by end-user programmers. Interact. Comput. 27(6), 640–660 (2015)
5. Craft, B.: Ten troubleshooting tips. In: Arduino Projects For Dummies, pp. 359–367. Wiley, Chichester (2013)
6. Deng, Y., et al.: Tango cards: a card-based design tool for informing the design of tangible learning games. In: Proceedings of DIS 2014, Vancouver, Canada, pp. 695–704. ACM, New York (2014)
7. Drew, D., et al.: The Toastboard: ubiquitous instrumentation and automated checking of breadboarded circuits. In: Proceedings of UIST 2016, pp. 677–686. ACM, New York(2016)

8. Fleck, R., Fitzpatrick, G.: Reflecting on reflection: framing a design landscape. In: Proceedings of OzCHI 2010, pp. 216–223. ACM, New York (2010)
9. Friedman, B., Hendry, D.: The Envisioning cards: a toolkit for catalyzing humanistic and technical imaginations. In: Proceedings of CHI 2012, pp. 1145–1148. ACM, New York (2012)
10. Harrower, M., Brewer, C.A.: Colorbrewer.org: an online tool for selecting colour schemes for maps. Cartographic J. **40**(1), 27–37 (2003)
11. Lucero, A., Arrasvuori, J.: PLEX Cards: a source of inspiration when designing for playfulness. In: Proceedings of the 3rd International Conference on Fun and Games. ACM, New York (2010)
12. Miettinen, R.: The concept of experiential learning and John Dewey's theory of reflective thought and action. Int. J. Lifelong Educ. **19**(1), 54–72 (2000)
13. Mora, S., et al.: Tiles: a card-based ideation toolkit for the Internet of Things. In: Proceedings of DIS 2017, pp. 587–598. ACM, New York (2017)
14. Mueller, F., et al.: Supporting the creative game design process with exertion cards. In: Proceedings of CHI 2014, pp. 2211–2220. ACM, New York (2014)
15. Wetzel, R., et al.: Developing ideation cards for mixed reality game design. In: Proceedings of 1st International Joint Conference of DiGRA and FDG, pp. 175–211, Dundee, UK (2016)

End-User Development Goes to School: Collaborative Learning with Makerspaces in Subject Areas

Anders I. Mørch[1]([⊠]), Kristina Torine Litherland[1], and Renate Andersen[2]

[1] Department of Education, University of Oslo, Oslo, Norway
{andersm, kristitl}@iped.uio.no
[2] Department of Primary and Secondary Teacher Education,
Oslo Metropolitan University, Oslo, Norway
renatea@oslomet.no

Abstract. Norwegian K-12 curriculum reform for 2020 aims to integrate programming in different subject areas, especially math, natural sciences, arts and crafts, and music. There are challenges and opportunities associated with this scenario. A challenge is that students need to learn two topics simultaneously, and an opportunity is that teachers can adopt computer science skills gradually by building on their domain expertise and the notion of different levels of modification since most teachers are not yet fluent in computer science. We present an exploratory case study to show that end-user development (EUD) is a possible solution for the Norwegian situation. The case study demonstrates evidence of collaborative learning with EUD in a makerspace in an advanced placement science classroom for a mixture of gifted underachievers and high-achievers.

Keywords: Collaborative learning · Empirical research ·
End-user development · Makerspace · Programming (blocks vs. text) ·
School · Qualitative study

1 Introduction

In many European countries, educational policy is under way to integrate computer science (programming, coding, computational thinking) in schools. The report "The Nordic approach to introducing computational thinking and programming in compulsory education" [3] reveals that in the last five years, programming or coding has emerged as a skill that young people should have. As a result, computational thinking [5] has emerged as a concept to prepare children for future challenges in an increasingly digital society [3].

EUD originated as an umbrella term for research and development in end-user tools for application development, such as spreadsheets [8] and design environments [4]. EUD researchers were inspired by easy-to-use programming languages and tools to improve computer applications, such as visual languages [15], scripting languages, and multiple representations [12]. EUD gained broader visibility and became a research

A. Malizia et al. (Eds.): IS-EUD 2019, LNCS 11553, pp. 200–208, 2019.
https://doi.org/10.1007/978-3-030-24781-2_16

topic with its own agenda in the European EUD-Net project (2002–2003), which defines EUD as "a set of methods, activities, techniques, and tools that allow people who are nonprofessional software developers, at some point to create or modify a software artifact" [14]. EUD researchers have developed tools and environments and tested them in laboratories, organizations, and homes. We study EUD in educational institutions (schools).

The "gentle slope" to programming is a relevant concept when using EUD in education. Namely, to modify an application through its user interface, end users should only have to increase their knowledge by an amount in proportion to the complexity of the modification [9]. Furthermore, simple modifications should not require programming, and more complex modifications should be possible with user-oriented programming languages and higher-level building blocks [4, 9]. To ease the burden of programming for novices, two techniques are useful: "direct activation" and "different levels of tailoring." Direct activation means accessing tailoring tools from the ordinary user interface with a simple keyboard command. Different levels of tailoring refers to interfaces for making changes at different levels of complexity or to views of an application, ranging from editing attribute values of visual objects to creating new behavior by integrating high-level building blocks, to creating new behaviour by general-purpose programming [10].

The usefulness of EUD for educational purposes can be assessed with regards to the ways these environments balance programming and domain-orientation: on one hand, providing the right amount of flexibility for making changes to software artifacts possible, and on the other hand, ensuring usability in specific domains of teaching and learning. We address the following research questions:

1. How can EUD help end users in makerspaces create their own software artifacts?
2. How can EUD help teachers engage students in subject-related learning activities?
3. What theoretical frameworks help to integrate the learning activities (RQ1 + 2)?

We use empirical data and review previous work to address the research questions. The rest of the paper is organized as follows. In Sect. 2, we review related research. In Sect. 3, we describe the case study (method, participants, data analysis), and in Sect. 4, we discuss our results by answering the research questions. Finally, we summarize our findings and suggest some directions for further work.

2 Literature Review: History, Scope, and Focus

Three lines of previous work have stimulated our research. First, domain-oriented, programmable design environments are software applications consisting of a domain-oriented user interface in the foreground and a programming environment in the background [4, 15]. Second, visual programming languages starting with the BLOX methodology [7] and Fabrik user interface [6] made it easier for non-expert and disabled users to learn textual programming languages (Pascal, Smalltalk, or C) by using direct manipulation (drag-and-drop program structures analogous to solving a jigsaw puzzle). Third, we were inspired by the line of research that started with Papert's work on Logo [13] and continued with Resnick, who developed new user-oriented languages

and led the development of Scratch; pioneered connecting VPLs to physical components in construction kits [16]; and provided an online library of reusable applications,
such as games and animations [17].

In recent years, there has been a growing interest in programming as part of a
school context. This is based on the understanding that programming is a necessary
competence for the 21st century. Consequently, to enable more people to learn programming, there has been an increased focus on programming languages that are more
visual. Visual programming languages, and more recently block-based programming,
enable young people to construct running programs by greatly simplifying the interface
[1]. The environments or tools along with a repository of helpful examples available
through the internet are an important success factor in the continued interest in programming in schools.

We focus on visual programming that learners find interesting and teachers consider relevant. An example is a toy vehicle connected via a circuit board to motors and
sensors that children use with other children during play, which is a type collaborative
learning environment for combining discursive and hands-on activities. Programming
in these environments allows the learners to control motors, sensors, lamps, and so on,
and some of the languages are Scratch, MakeCode with Micro:bit, and Blockuino
(Blockly with Arduino). We have used Blockuino and Micro:bit in this case. We argue
that with access to a range of tailoring tools between user interfaces and program code,
learners can modify software artifacts at different levels of abstraction to solve per-
sonally interesting problems and at the same time learn subject matter knowledge.

Bevan [2] argues that makerspaces in educational settings need better pedagogical
foundation. According to Bevan, key aspects of such pedagogy are design failure and
sense making, borrowing two terms from Papert's Constructionism [13]. Bevan suggests that "assembly activities" (step-by-step instructions) should precede "creative
construction" (open-ended exploration), as the former are often a prerequisite for
successful transitioning to the latter. Bevan says less about the role of the teacher in a
makerspace classroom but argues that schools can participate in this important area. We
argue that makerspaces must be aligned with teachers' practices, so that the two
agendas meet (students' interest-driven learning and schools' responsibility for a shared
curriculum).

3   Makerspace Case Study: Method, Participants, Data Analysis

Our study is an exploratory case study employing qualitative methods for data collection and analysis [18]. The aim of the study is for middle school pupils to learn
about and engage with science, but the makerspace course is only loosely connected
with the official curriculum in the science subjects. The pupils had all been identified as
either gifted underachievers or high-achievers. Every second week, they were taken out
of school to participate in the makerspace for four hours arranged at a nearby high
school. The makerspace teachers are science and technology enthusiasts.

The participants (N = 19) were pupils in school years 7 to 10 (12–15 years old).
We interviewed 17 of the pupils, using a semi-structured interview guide (246 min).

We observed six makerspace sessions and wrote field notes using pen and paper. Two of these sessions were video-recorded (535 min, one shown in Fig. 1). To collect and manage the data (spoken utterances, video footage, and verbal interviews), each session and interview was stored in a separate file and transcribed. The pupils were assigned a reference number stored in a table separate from other data. Three researchers were working together to categorize the data: first, according to an open coding process (data-driven) and then informed by our research questions. We identified a number of data extracts according to a number of codes and we have reproduced two extracts below, representative of our findings, and formatted for a short paper.

Fig. 1. Setting of makerspace case: Four pupils (aged 12–15) working to solve an assignment to program an Arduino board to light lamps and play music. The numbers refer to the informants.

The extracts are named "programming (blocks vs. text)" and "subject area relevance." In the first extract, the pupils were given a brief introduction to Arduino and Blockuino, a block-based programming language made from Blockly, which generates C code and communicates with an Arduino circuit board to control lamps and sounds. The pupils have created code to make the lamps flash in different patterns and start to create light and sound patterns when we enter here (95 min into the session).

Extract 1: Programming (Blocks vs. Text)

Pupil 3:	It seems tedious to write down all the commands as text
Pupil 1:	It is much better to write code in text than to use blocks
Pupil 4:	Yes, it is indeed a lot of work [supporting Pupil 3]
Pupil 1:	I think it is hard to find the blocks and how they fit together…
Pupil 2:	I think blocks are the better alternative
Pupil 1:	That's because you don't know how to write code; when you do, you'll find it's better
Pupil 3:	Nooooo, it's not!
Pupil 1:	Okay, right

The four pupils in Extract 1 debate what is better: textual or block-based programming (see Fig. 2). Pupil 1 argues for text-based programming, whereas the other three prefer blocks. Pupil 1's argument against blocks is that it is difficult to find the blocks in the inventory and combine them into working assemblies; he replies to Pupil 3 that the latter does not know how to program if he does not write program text, but Pupil 3 is not convinced, and Pupil 1 eventually stops arguing.

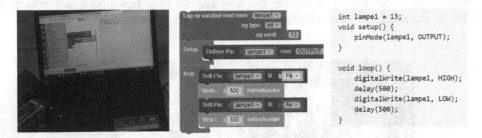

Fig. 2. Bridging the gap between hardware and software by EUD with interfaces at different levels of abstraction: Arduino board (wiring physical components), Blockuino (software blocks to program Arduino in Norwegian), and C (textual code generated from blocks assembly).

The second extract is an interview with a pupil who was working on a Micro:bit project concerning the measurement of velocity of egg in free fall without breaking it.

Extract 2: Subject Area Relevance

Researcher:	Is there anything you don't like in the makerspace?
Pupil 14:	I am not sure. It could be that we are not learning enough about subjects, in a way. We do not stick to a topic over time. It's like... You now... I know what we do is based on math and natural science or sciences in general [referring to the latest assignment to compute the velocity of an egg in free fall with techniques to lower acceleration], but we have so much freedom to explore... [seven minutes later in the transcript]
Researcher:	... can you come up with any suggestions for how teaching could be different?
Pupil 14:	It would be good to have subject-related knowledge better integrated with our exploratory activities. For example, the project we do now, we could also be learning about velocity and acceleration and similar things: how to compute values and set up formulas, or the way Micro:bit works out its computations, or whatever is happening with what we are doing

Pupil 14 is one of a few we have interviewed who explicitly identifies a shortcoming in the advanced placement course, as most of the other pupils are more than happy to engage in explorative learning assignments based on their own interests and pace. However, we found this criticism relevant to bring up, as it echoes a concern shared by many science teachers who are not makerspace enthusiasts. Pupil 14 would like a better integration of subject area knowledge and explorative makerspace learning activities to constrain the space of possibilities, which for many seem endless. Measures can be taken to address the issues, as revealed above: teachers pointing out relevant concepts and formulas when there is an opportunity for engaging pupils in deepened understanding, but it requires common background knowledge, which was not the case in our study as the pupils came from school years 7 to 10.

4 General Discussion

We discuss our results in terms of the three research questions we asked in the beginning of the paper and by comparing our results with those reported in the literature.

4.1 How Can EUD Help End Users in Makerspaces Create Their Own Software Artifacts?

The tasks required the pupils to create different types of software artifacts and they were highly motivated to do so. However, the pupils' background and skills in programming varied as they came from different schools and class levels. EUD can help their entrance to programming by multiple representations or levels of abstraction [10]. For example, Extract 1 illustrates how students modified software by composing blocks (integration) and textually (extension) to program an Arduino board. When the technology provides interfaces at different levels, i.e., hardware and software and between block-based and textual programming, it makes the tasks easier for novice users. The notion of mixed textual/graphical interfaces was introduced in the BLOX program methodology [7] but it did not attract a large user population of its time. Our informants were all novice programmers and the majority of them (especially the youngest) preferred block-based programming. Some of the older pupils, such as Pupil 1 in Extract 1, preferred to write code, but the quality of the written code varied among the more experienced pupils.

4.2 How Can EUD Help Teachers Engage Students in Subject-Related Learning Activities?

The organization of teaching was not optimized for engaging the pupils in curricular learning. They are middle school students who were taught outside the curriculum at a nearby high school. EUD can help to bridge the gap between these pupils' interests and curricular learning with the notion of "domain orientation," which means the artifacts the users interact with should resemble both the artifacts associated with a subject area (e.g. electric motors) and learners' prior experiences and interests (e.g. toy vehicles). Many of the artifacts the pupils interacted with revealed such connections or the potential for making connection. One example is the electric motor of a robot car, which uses the theory of electromagnetism to oscillate. Extract 2 shows that scaffolding could have helped the pupils to connect subject area knowledge and technological artifacts. Pupil 14 gave an example of how the teacher could intervene to constrain exploratory learning in the makerspace by providing scientific formula and concepts to help the pupils better understand the principles of what they were making and measuring (in Extract 2, Pupil 14 refers to the concepts of velocity and acceleration).

4.3   What Theoretical Frameworks Help to Integrate the Learning Activities (RQ1 + 2)?

Constructivism and sociocultural theory are two theories with concepts for understanding the different aspects of learning with technology we have observed. Constructivism proposes that knowledge is not passively received but actively built on an individual's prior experiences. It also considers the main function of cognition as adaptive in order to organize and make sense of the experiential world. Constructionism developed by Papert and colleagues [13, 16] builds on Piaget's constructivist theory and emphasizes the active role that students can take in constructing their own learning through hands-on activity with physical or visual objects. An aim is to create "objects to think with," which are computational artifacts embedding culture, knowledge, and personal identity [13, 16].

The sociocultural perspective on learning is concerned with learning by social interaction and scaffolding and originated with Vygotsky. The "tool and sign" concept [19] is especially interesting in this regard. On the one hand, in human development, there is a focus on tools and actions involving them as part of practical work, and on the other hand, there are (intellectual) concepts or verbal means to make sense of the actions without using the tools.

Building on the tool-sign dichotomy, the evolving artifacts framework (EAF) conceptualizes learning with technology as a combination of technology adaptation (tool development), and knowledge adaptation as sign/concept development [11]. The former is synonymous with EUD, and the latter is development of shared knowledge in a small group of collaborators, which is mainly a verbal activity but includes the use of EUD tools. Whereas EAF focuses on novice learners and their transitioning to experienced learners by contributing to the evolution of two types of objects (technology and shared knowledge), Constructionism suggests that one learns by building objects-to-think-with, which we consider integrated objects and a goal of evolving artifacts. This is currently a hypothesis that will be investigated in more detail in further work.

5   Conclusions and Directions for Further Work

We have reported from a case study in end-user development in an educational setting, a makerspace with learning activities involving computational technology at different levels of abstraction, from hardware to software, and using block-based and textual programming, with a mixture of gifted underachievers and high-achievers. We have collected video data of pupils' interaction with each other and with the technology, and we conducted interviews afterward. We have found tentative evidence that intermediate representations (e.g. block-based programming) can aid learning of more advanced programming and that pupils prefer it when they can see the relevance of what they do in school to their actual lives. Future work includes a more rigorous longitudinal study at different schools with an observation protocol based on theoretical frameworks for coding verbal data in collaborative learning activities in makerspaces, taking EUD and collaborative learning into account, as separate processes and as integrated process.

Acknowledgements. The authors are grateful to Research Council of Norway (RFF) for funding GT-Make project. We thank Elena Biuso for helping to collect and transcribe data, and Ellen Egeland Flø and Louise Mifsud for comments on an earlier version of this paper.

References

1. Armoni, M., Meerbaum-Salant, O., Ben-Ari, M.: From Scratch to "real" programming. Trans. Comput. Educ. **14**(4), Article 25 (2015)
2. Bevan, B.: The promise and the promises of making in science education. Stud. Sci. Educ. **53**(1), 75–103 (2017)
3. Bocconi, S., Chioccariello, A., Earp, J.: The Nordic approach to introducing Computational Thinking and programming in compulsory education. Report prepared for the Nordic@Bett2018 Steering Group (2018). http://www.itd.cnr.it/doc/CompuThinkNordic.pdf
4. Fischer, G., Girgensohn, A.: End-user modifiability in design environments. In: Proceedings CHI 1990, pp. 183–192. ACM, New York (1990)
5. Grover, S., Pea, R.: Computational thinking in K–12: a review of the state of the field. Educ. Researcher **42**(1), 38–43 (2013)
6. Ingalls, D., Wallace, S., Chow, Y., Ludolph, F., Doyle, K.: Fabrik: a visual programming environment. In: Proceedings OOPSLA 1988, pp. 176–190. ACM, New York (1988)
7. Kopache, M.E., Glinert, E.P.: C2: a mixed textual/graphical environment for C. In: Proceedings Workshop on Visual Languages, pp. 231–238. IEEE Press, Los Alamitos (1988)
8. Lewis, C.: NoPumpG: creating interactive graphics with spreadsheet machinery. University of Colorado, Department of Computer Science, Technical Report CU-CS-372-8 (1987)
9. MacLean, A., Carter, K., Lövstrand, L., Moran, T.: User-tailorable systems: pressing the issues with buttons. In: Proceedings of CHI 1990, pp. 175–182. ACM, New York (1990)
10. Mørch, A.: Three levels of end-user tailoring: customization, integration, and extension. In: Computers and Design in Context, pp. 51–76. MIT Press, Cambridge (1997)
11. Mørch, A.I., Caruso, V., Hartley, M.D.: End-user development and learning in Second Life: the evolving artifacts framework with application. In: Paterno, F., Wulf, V. (eds.) New Perspectives in End-User Development, pp. 333–358. Springer, Berlin (2017). https://doi.org/10.1007/978-3-319-60291-2_13
12. Mørch, A.I., Mehandjiev, N.D.: Tailoring as collaboration: the mediating role of multiple representations and application units. Comput. Support. Coop. Work **9**(1), 75–100 (2000)
13. Papert, S., Harel, I.: Constructionism. Ablex Publishing Corporation, Norwood (1991)
14. Paterno, F., Klann, M., Wulf, V.: Research Agenda and Roadmap for EUD. Technical report. IST-2001-37470, EUD-Net Network of Excellence, December 2003
15. Repenning, A., Sumner, T.: Agentsheets: a medium for creating domain-oriented visual languages. IEEE Comput. **28**(3), 17–25 (1995)
16. Resnick, M., Martin, F., Sargent, R., Silverman, B.: Programmable bricks: toys to think with. IBM Syst. J. **35**(3), 443–452 (1996)

17. Roque, R., Rusk, N., Resnick, M.: Supporting diverse and creative collaboration in the Scratch online community. In: Cress, U., et al. (eds.) Mass Collaboration and Education, pp. 241–256. Springer, Heidelberg (2016). https://doi.org/10.1007/978-3-319-13536-6_12
18. Silverman, D.: Doing Qualitative Research: A Practical Handbook. Sage, London (2005)
19. Vygotsky, L.S., Luria, A.R.: Tool and symbol in child development. In: Valsiner, J., van der Veer, R. (eds.) The Vygotsky Reader, pp. 99–175. Blackwell, Oxford (1994)

Virtual Assistants for End-User Development in the Internet of Things

Barbara Rita Barricelli(✉) ⓘ, Elena Casiraghi ⓘ,
and Stefano Valtolina ⓘ

Department of Computer Science, Università degli Studi di Milano, Milan, Italy
{barbara.barricelli,elena.casiraghi,
stefano.valtolina}@unimi.it

Abstract. The spread of Virtual Assistants (software and hardware) on the consumer market deeply changed the way Internet of Things (IoT) is implemented and used today. Such devices, and related applications, are becoming more and more integrated within smart environments and this might pave the way to potential new approaches to End-User Development activities, which can be performed in IoT environments. This paper discusses the evolution of the IoT ecosystem definition that has been studied by the authors in the last years.

Keywords: End-User Development · Internet of Things · Virtual Assistants · Natural Language Interfaces · Chatbots · Voicebots

1 Introduction

During the last years, Internet of Things (IoT) has become popular, and its success has spread out rapidly all over the world. Today we are witnessing a change in the way IoT is implemented due to the introduction and ubiquitous availability of affordable and trustable Virtual Assistants, also called Virtual Personal Assistants (VPAs), or Intelligent Virtual Assistants. The enablers of this technology are IoT, Artificial Intelligence applications, and Semantic Web. Precisely, thanks to IoT, users can be continuously connected with their VPA, by exchanging data describing current status, inquiry, or preference. Basically, VPAs are Intelligent Natural Language User Interfaces (NLUI), born as the evolution of voice assistants, which were basic NLUI responding to simple needs such as dictation, setting alarm clocks, responding to user commands, and chatbots or voicebots, diffused text GUI (chatbots) or NLUI (voicebots) interacting with users to provide first simple solutions to problems. The main difference between a chatbot and a voicebot is the way users can interact with them. A chatbot provides users with a text-based dialog like the one typically used on messaging platforms, including SMS, social network systems and web-based applications. This means users interact with chatbots on a screen by using rich user interfaces endowed with buttons, menu or other graphic items. On the other hand, users interact with a voicebot using their voice, i.e. in natural language. The voicebot then answers back using pre-recorded messages, text-to-speech responses or a combination of both. Voicebots conversation design (and therefore interaction design) needs to consider and control nuances of

A. Malizia et al. (Eds.): IS-EUD 2019, LNCS 11553, pp. 209–216, 2019.
https://doi.org/10.1007/978-3-030-24781-2_17

dialogue that people sometimes take for granted when speaking to others. These precursors of VPAs have to embed the typical person's voice, on which the conversational tone is modulated. Voicebots and chatbots are generally used by a group of users to respond to simple needs. VPAs have been developing by leveraging voicebots, with the aim of creating machine with an intelligence that allows them to adapt to their owner and principal users. VPA's intelligence and their potential to become sensitive companions motivate their continuous improvement and diffusion and motivate a shift in the way IoT is implemented. This shift does not only rely in the use of technologies such as VPAs, but also in the way users interact with them. VPAs essentially become intermediaries between users and the actual IoT environments. As defined by Cypher [1], the end user is a "user of an application program", someone who is not a computer programmer and who "uses a computer as part of daily life or daily work, but is not interested in computers per se". Today, thanks also to IoT, this definition evolves because IT devices and sophisticated software are becoming more and more part of the social tissue, and their use is common in almost every cultural context: with the growing diffusion of mobile devices, like smartphones and tablets, pervasive computing is spreading. IoT allows end users to manage physical devices, interactive systems, and personal data by deciding how to create new usage scenarios. This empowers them more than ever, making them evolve, as explained later in the paper, to become end-user developers [2]. As widely reported in literature, End-User Development (EUD) can be enabled by offering the end users tools that allow them to develop without having specific programming skills and knowledge about programming languages. This paper reports the preliminary results of an undergoing research work that aims at discussing new approaches to EUD activities, which can be performed in IoT environments through the use of VPAs. In this way, VPAs play real time connector role between human, sensors, IoT services, and data. According to the flow of dialog with the user, VPAs can activate specific APIs for communicating with users about daily workflows, technical problems and work related topics. VPAs becomes a new paradigm for human-IoT communication that leveraging on a natural interaction such as our own language can allows users to query or manage IoT services or devices. Under this perspective, VPAs are used to triggering EUD activities focused to help the users in personalizing the behavior of connected devices to orchestrate them and adequate them to the evolving users' needs and choices.

2   From Traditional GUIs to Virtual Assistants

Interface Design is never an easy task. As Norman said in the 90s, "The real problem with the interface is that it is an interface. Interfaces get in the way" [3]. Interfaces should provide an easy-to-use visual bridge and connection between the underlying system and the end-user. However, in the user's mind, the interface becomes the system itself and it is the one blamed when the system does not work correctly or does not behave as expected. Since the 90s, many other researchers and practitioners pointed out the problems related with the use of interfaces and their design. In 2015, Golden Krishna, published the book "The best interface is no interface" [4] and launched the so-called "no UI" (i.e., no User Interface) movement. The rationale behind this movement is that users think in different ways and therefore solve problems in different ways; when interfaces are used, the users are expected to adapt to specific interaction rules imposed by the interface. Traditional Graphical User Interfaces (GUIs) have been invented to support the interaction between human and computer; however, most of the time the human attention has to focus on the interface, rather than on the problem to solve. It follows that a more natural human-like interaction is needed: the closer we get to a natural human interface, the more comfortable it will be to solve problems by using machines. The three principles behind the No UI movement are: Embrace Typical Processes Instead of Screens, Leverage Computers Instead of Serving Them, and Adapt to Individuals. Following these principles several Natural User Interfaces (NUI) have been developed; they are user interfaces that you interact with using (natural to humans) modalities such as touch, gestures or voice. They are called "natural" because users feel natural to interact with them. When designing a NUI, developers should take advantage of the skill the users already possess. If users could apply their natural skills, they would be saved from the trouble of learning something completely new. Two different approaches to NUI design can be considered: (1) capitalizing on domain-specific skills; (2) capitalizing on common human skills, e.g. speaking, earing, and touching. While domain-specific skills allow to build NUI oriented to specific users (domain experts), the design of NUIs by exploiting common human skills leads to an interface design that is customized to almost all users (developers can indeed assume that most of the potential users have the needed skills simply because they are human). Based on the fact that, for most people, speaking and hearing are natural skills, often easier to practice than touch (e.g. writing and reading text messages is dangerous while driving; instead, dictating them or listening to them is easier), in the past twenty years Natural-Language User Interfaces (LUI or NLUI) have been designed and developed. The firstly developed LUIs/NLUIs have been generally called "Voice Assistants", "Digital Assistants", or "Virtual Voice Assistants" (VVA). VVAs exploit signal processing and Artificial Intelligence (AI) applications for natural language processing and understanding; they are designed to capture, understand, and execute simple voice commands expressed in a natural language; they complete simple tasks such as taking dictation, reading text or email messages aloud, looking up phone numbers, scheduling, placing phone calls, and reminding about appointments. Since their advent, VVAs have gained a lot of success, and their usage has spread, thus substituting, where possible, the use of traditional GUIs. Indeed, though traditional GUIs allow some freedom in navigation of the information architecture, and usually have the advantages of offering a (highly) interactive experience, often leading to serendipity, VVAs offer personalized and smart suggestions, shortcuts to frequent or recurring tasks, and are designed to retrieve specific answers very quickly. So, since timing has always been one of the most important characteristics of an interactive application, since their creation it has soon been clear that VVAs' importance would have rapidly grown; for this reason, in the past years a great deal of research effort has been devoted to their improvement. This brings to the establishment of a novel name, which includes the adjective "Personal": "Virtual Personal Assistants" (VPAs) [5]. VPAs are able to collect user data stored in the cloud, process the acquired data to learn from the users' preferences, and express sentiments. For this reason, nowadays we are increasingly likely to interact with a VPA than ever before.

3 A New Paradigm for EUD in a New IoT Ecosystem

More than ten years ago, Lieberman et al. [2] defined End-User Development as "a set of methods, techniques, and tools that allow users of software systems, who are acting as non-professional software developers, at some point to create, modify or extend a software artefact". More recently [6], the definition has been extended: "EUD encompasses methods, techniques, methodologies, situations, and socio-technical environments that allow end users to act as professionals in those domains in which they are not professionals". Here is where EUD steps in: to provide people with the capability to create and modify software will help them in achieving successful results in their daily activities. EUD represents the ideal approach for empowering end users and let them become unwitting developers in their own IoT environment [7–10]. As widely reported in the literature, EUD can be enabled by applying methods and techniques and by offering specific tools that support end users in the development of solutions with limited programming skills and knowledge about programming languages. Specifically, the solutions offered by EUD are focused to help the users in personalizing the behavior of connected devices to orchestrate them and adequate them to the evolving users' needs and choices. The systematic mapping review on EUD presented in [6] pointed out that the rule-based technique is mostly aimed at supporting the end users in the personalization of the behavior of smart devices in Ambient Intelligence systems and Internet of Things applications. The same paper discusses natural language as another technique for EUD, that was proposed more than fifty years ago [11] but is today used mainly for VPAs. This important use of natural language-based constructs on which VPAs are designed allows studying the interaction between humans and VPAs from a semiotic point of view Semiotic Engineering [12] views interactive software systems as artefacts through which the communication between users and systems takes place. The major problems that IoT applications have to deal with are related with the fact that they have to monitor a huge quantity of data collected by sensors and services that need to be exchanged together with their users' needs and/or preferences, in order to keep track and influence behaviors and critical situations. In this context, it becomes difficult to express conditions, spatial-temporal and thematic relations that typically affect the sensors' data-stream management. In general, besides spatial and temporal information, sensors provide thematic information in order to discover and analyze data.

3.1 VPAs and New Communication/Interaction Protocols in IoT

The application of Tondl's theory on analogic communication [13], and particularly its adaptation of digital communication [14] to the specific context domain described in this paper, may suggests that VPAs have a twofold role: the devices become the communication channels through which the user sends and receives messages, while the bots becomes the proxies of the IoT ecosystem. The communication process is depicted in Fig. 1.

User's messages are first sent to a device via voice or textual chat and then the device sends them to its general-purpose bot that, in turn, activates the dialogue with the domain-specific bot requested by the user. At the current stage of this study, the

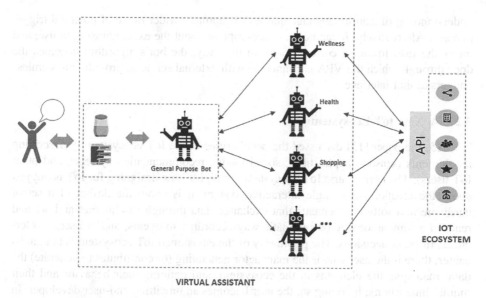

Fig. 1. The communication process between the user and the IoT Ecosystem by means of a VPA. The General Purpose Bot is the one that activates the domain-specific bot that the user wants to use. The domain-specific bot follows a flow of conversation with the users and interrogates the APIs needed to answer to their questions.

VPAs are not considered parts of a multi-agents system but are explicitly invoked through the communication with the general-purpose bot. Each domain-specific bot is in charge of interacting with the IoT ecosystem's elements by means of specific events API (for example API used for accessing the alarm clocks, the weather forecasting services, or other IoT-based services). The Events API is a VPA's equivalent of eyes and ears. It gives a bot a way to react to sent/received messages, changes to channels, and other activities that may happen during a conversation with users. When these events happen, a data payload is sent to the domain-specific bot, and it can use that data to compose a useful response. The dialog flow on which the VPA interfaces (voice- or chat-based) is built, acts as gateway between the user and the IoT services and applications by exploiting the events API they provide. The flow of dialogue that can be followed in using VPAs is designed with applications called conversational design editors, typically visual tools. A conversation's aim is to intercept users' intentions and consequentially activate the right API actions on a specific IoT ecosystem. The flow specifies the way VPA reacts, that can range between static and dynamic responses. The former is the simplest, much like a template filling: to every input, there is one corresponding answer. The latter is a kind of knowledge base, which returns the list of possible responses with the score of relevance computed using rule-based or AI strategies. The algorithm on which the bot is built exploits the dialog flow and the related retrieving strategies for accessing the events API. The event API accesses are orchestrated according the type of conversation. Through this orchestration, the context-specific bot's algorithm can get even more complex by broadening its understanding of natural language queries to capture a wider range of potential trigger phrases. Alternatively, it can be more prescriptive about the exact phrasing to use, and trains the user toward a correct usage. In this way, the bot's algorithm becomes the door through which the VPA is connected with external services, providing a seamless conversational interface.

3.2   A New IoT Ecosystem

In 2015, the paper [15] discussed the peculiarities of the IoT ecosystem by describing its elements (sensors, applications, social media, recommendation systems, and other IoT users). The user-centric IoT ecosystem highlights how designing for IoT is not just about the creation of a single interactive system: it is about the design of a set of hardware and software elements that exchange data through the Internet and act and react in a semi-automatic or automatic way according to events, and/or users' preferences, rules, or decisions. The peculiarity of the envisioned IoT ecosystem is that, at its center, there is the user who is the main actor generating (or contributes to generate) the data, managing the elements in the ecosystem, and defining their behavior and their mutual interactions; by doing so, the user becomes an unwitting end-user developer. In [15], the authors proposed a sensor-based rule language aimed at supporting the end user in composing space/time-based rules for extending the well-established but not powerful IF-THIS-THEN-THAT paradigm. The language follows syntax, semantics, and grammar of a Policy Rule Language proposed in [16], and is based on the ECA (Event, Condition, and Action) paradigm. It allows to specify rules stating policies for triggering actions (one or a set). Together with the language, in [16] SmartFit Rule Editor was presented: an environment designed to offer the possibility to exploit the expressivity of the language specification through visual interaction. Besides overcoming the complexity of IoT data, SmartFit enables the end user to implement personalized rules without having to learn programming. As made explicit by the rule language, each rule has a unique identifier, i.e. a name that can be used to recall the rule any time after its creation. This means that the rule can not only be called within the SmartFit environment, but it can also be exported and imported in other applications. This means that, with the introduction of VPA between the end user and the so-called IoT ecosystem, the EUD activities that can be implemented evolve.

4   Conclusions

The dramatic evolution of IoT, together with the spread of VPAs, brings the authors to reconsider the definition of IoT ecosystem reported in [15] and [16] in order to bring to light what is to be considered an important shift in the role played by the user and the elements as well. The new ecosystem is depicted in Fig. 2. The reader can note that the user still plays a central role in the ecosystem; however, they are elevated to a higher position, from which flows of data and interactions with the elements below are now mediated by a Virtual Assistant, i.e. the devices and the bots. In the picture, two bots are present in the flow of interaction: the first (grey background) is the general purpose bot that natively accompanies the device (e.g., Alexa for Amazon Echo, Google

Assistant for Google Home); the second (dark blue background) is the bot that is built upon a specific IoT application, i.e. a context-specific bot. It is worth to underline that VPAs are often described as a single technological entity; on the contrary, they are constituted by software – bots – and hardware counterparts, which could be voice detection devices or screen-based devices, like a smartphones or a tablet. Therefore, the communication between the user and the IoT ecosystem become even more complex but at the same time, the potentials of IoT grow significantly.

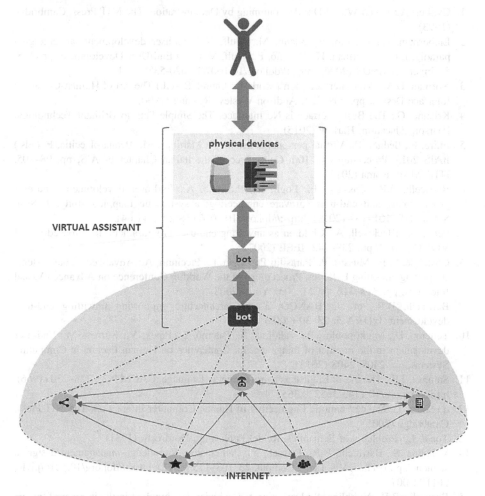

Fig. 2. The new ecosystem. The user still has a central role but elevated over the IoT ecosystem, and interacts with it by means of a Virtual Assistant, i.e. devices and bots. Icons made by Freepik from www.flaticon.com are licenced by CC BY 3.0.

The research done in the last years in the context of End-User Development in Internet of Things was motivated by the necessity of finding ways to support end users in controlling their own IoT ecosystem. The diffusion of Virtual Assistants and related bots deeply changes the communication protocols that have been previously studied, identified and implemented. This paper illustrates and discusses the changes that occur to the IoT ecosystem with the establishment of VPAs and therefore of conversation-based interaction.

References

1. Cypher, A.: Watch What I Do: Programming by Demonstration. The MIT Press, Cambridge (1993)
2. Lieberman, H., Paternò, F., Klann, M., Wulf, V.: End-user development: an emerging paradigm. In: Lieberman, H., Paternò, F., Wulf, V. (eds.) End-User Development, pp. 1–8. Springer, Dordrecht (2006). https://doi.org/10.1007/1-4020-5386-X_1
3. Norman, D.A.: Why interfaces don't work. In: Laurel, B. (ed.) The Art of Human-Computer Interface Design, pp. 209–224. Addison-Wesley, Reading (1990)
4. Krishna, G.: The Best Interface is No Interface: The Simple Path to Brilliant Technology. Pearson Education, Harlow (2015)
5. Imire, P., Bednar, P.: Virtual personal assistant. In: Martinez, M., Pennarolaecilia, F. (eds.) ItAIS 2013. Proceedings of 10th Conference of the Italian Chapter of AIS, pp. 98–105. ITHUM srl, Roma (2013)
6. Barricelli, B.R., Cassano, F., Fogli, D., Piccinno, A.: End-user development, end-user programming and end-user software engineering: a systematic mapping study. J. Syst. Softw. 149, 101–137 (2019). https://doi.org/10.1016/j.jss.2018.11.041
7. Petre, M., Blackwell, A.: Children as unwitting end-user programmers. In: Proceedings of VL/HCC 2007, pp. 239–242. IEEE (2007)
8. Costabile, M.F., Mussio, P., Parasiliti Provenza, L., Piccinno, A.: Advanced visual systems supporting unwitting EUD. In: Proceedings of the Working Conference on Advanced Visual Interfaces, pp. 313–316. ACM, New York (2008)
9. Barricelli, B.R., et al.: BANCO: a web architecture supporting unwitting end-user development. IxD&A 5, 23–30 (2009)
10. Tetteroo, D., Markopoulos, P., Valtolina, S., Paternò, F., Pipek, V., Burnett, M.: End-user development in the internet of things era. In: Conference on Human Factors in Computing Systems, pp. 2405–2408 (2015)
11. Sammet, J.E.: The use of English as a programming language. CACM 9(3), 228–230 (1966). https://doi.org/10.1145/365230.365274
12. de Souza, C.S.: The Semiotic Engineering of Human-Computer Interaction. The MIT Press, Cambridge (2005)
13. Tondl, L.: Problems of Semantics. Reidel Publishing, Dordrecht (1981)
14. Valtolina, S., Barricelli, B.R., Dittrich, Y.: Participatory knowledge-management design: a semiotic approach. J. Vis. Lang. Comput. 23, 103–115 (2012). https://doi.org/10.1016/j.jvlc.2011.11.007
15. Barricelli, B.R., Valtolina, S.: Designing for end-user development in the internet of things. In: Díaz, P., Pipek, V., Ardito, C., Jensen, C., Aedo, I., Boden, A. (eds.) IS-EUD 2015. LNCS, vol. 9083, pp. 9–24. Springer, Cham (2015). https://doi.org/10.1007/978-3-319-18425-8_2
16. Barricelli, B.R., Valtolina, S.: A visual language and interactive system for end-user development of internet of things ecosystems. J. Vis. Lang. Comput. 40, 1–19 (2017). https://doi.org/10.1016/j.jvlc.2017.01.004

Transforming Meta-design from Paradigm to Working Theory

Daniel Tetteroo^(✉)

Eindhoven University of Technology, Eindhoven, The Netherlands
d.tetteroo@tue.nl

Abstract. In a traditional product lifecycle, the design of the product typically predates its use. Meta-design is a paradigm rooted in end-user development research that aims to address this issue, by proposing a shift from the traditional design-time vs. use-time separation, towards a model where designers meta-design open ended systems that allow for future changes by end-users.

Meta-design has existed as a paradigm for almost 20 years, but is still not widely adopted in practice. The application and study of meta-design has been mostly limited to retrospective analyses, rendering the paradigm descriptive instead of prescriptive. The challenge remains in understanding the factors impacting the adoption of meta-design, and in predicting and explaining the factors that determine successful meta-designed environments. This paper proposes an approach towards building this understanding, in order to connect conceptual notions related to meta-design with knowledge obtained from studying its implementation.

Keywords: Meta-design · Theory building

1 Introduction

User-centered design [1] and participatory design [2] describe how users' needs and desires can be taken into account during the design phase of interactive products and services. Nevertheless, during most product and service development, the phase in which an interactive product or service is being designed (the design time) usually predates the phase in which it is used (the use time) [3]. Accounting for changing tasks, contexts and needs is difficult in models where design happens before use. Finally, a model that separates design from use is ill-suited for cases that require a high level of personalization, such as personalized healthcare solutions.

The paradigm of *meta-design*, within the context of designing interactive artifacts, was introduced by Fischer and Scharff almost two decades ago as "*activities, processes, and objectives to create new media and environments that allow users to act as designers and be creative*" [4]. Meta-design proposes a shift from 'design for use before use' towards 'design for design after design' [5]. Its premise is that designers should, instead of designing 'closed' products or services, become meta-designers who create socio-technical environments that empower users to engage actively in the continuous development of systems, rather than being restricted to the use of existing systems [4]. Central to meta-designed environments are both a technology and a

© Springer Nature Switzerland AG 2019
A. Malizia et al. (Eds.): IS-EUD 2019, LNCS 11553, pp. 217–220, 2019.
https://doi.org/10.1007/978-3-030-24781-2_18

community of stakeholders. These stakeholders take on roles that may vary between passive consumers (of the technology) all the way to meta-designers.

Meta-design has been strongly linked to the end-user development (EUD), end-user programming (EUP) and end-user software engineering (EUSE) communities [6]. In a recent publication, Fischer et al. provide a comprehensive overview of meta-design as a framework for EUD, in terms of, amongst others, application domains and conceptual relationships that have been explored in a research context [5]. While meta-design has existed as a paradigm for almost 20 years, as Fischer et al. acknowledge, it is in need of a strong underlying, holistic theoretical framework. Although the meta-design paradigm has been applied successfully in some cases, the challenge remains in predicting and explaining the factors that determine successful meta-designed environments. In the remainder of this paper, I will briefly unpack this challenge, and outline a potential approach for addressing it.

2   Transforming Meta-design into a Working Theory

As Fischer et al. discussed previously, there are several frameworks that conceptually relate to meta-design, considering the framing of meta-design as a transformation from *closed systems* to *open systems* [5]. Furthermore, several concrete applications of meta-design have been reported upon, often pertaining to specific technology developments and application contexts. What is currently missing, is an intermediate layer that translates the conceptual notions of meta-design and its related frameworks into design-oriented theory that might help to further the development of meta-designed environments in context specific application areas. Two approaches towards this matter that have been proposed by others are Semiotic Engineering, rooted in the field of Social Communication [7], and the Hive-Mind Space model [8], rooted in the Software Shaping Workshop approach [9]. While both approaches provide valuable contributions in developing a theoretical understanding of meta-design, I argue that such an intermediate layer theory should not only help us understand cases of meta-design, but also help us in predicting when the application of meta-design is appropriate, and what the factors are that determine the success of applying meta-design in a particular context.

The challenge of developing such an intermediate layer can be approached from different perspectives. For example, one could attempt developing such theory by capturing key notions of meta-design into actionable models, and validating these models through studies of meta-design in both artificial, lab-based settings, as well as through field studies involving implementation of meta-design in real-world cases. The downside of such an approach is the risk of addressing various aspects of meta-design in isolation, potentially ignoring crucial factors arising from the interaction of these aspects and rendering the theory only useful for describing and explaining artificial cases.

Alternatively, one might attempt to construct such theory through a bottom-up approach, by studying existing cases of meta-design and attempting to generalize findings pertaining to factors that impacted the development and implementation process. In relation to EUD, the latter approach might become somewhat problematic, given the limited number of field deployments that have been documented in scientific literature, and the lack of common frameworks used for their analysis [10]. In addition, such an approach might end up describing a fragmented and limited subset of what meta-design conceptually entails, depending on what implementations have been studied, and how these implementations might have developed.

The approach I propose, in an attempt to overcome the limitations of both approaches, is to combine aspects of both top-down and bottom-up theory development.

2.1 Dissecting Meta-design into Core Components

A first, top-down step towards developing a working theory on meta-design concerns distinguishing the elements of which meta-designed environments are typically composed. The nature of meta-designed environments can be viewed as being threefold: (1) at the core of the environment, there exists a technology (or a collection of technologies); (2) there are individuals who interact with the technology, each having their own reasons and intentions, engaging in a for them relevant way with the technology; (3) finally these individuals form a community of (meta-) designers, domain experts and end-users (i.e. a 'rich ecology of participation' [5]) interacting with each other and with, or through the technology. The individuals making up the community might take on different roles over time, depending on their needs, interests and capabilities.

2.2 Transitioning Towards Theory Development

Considering the threefold nature of meta-designed environments, we can make good use of established, generic theories that provide us with different 'lenses' to look at meta-designed environments. For example, the Unified Theory of Acceptance and Use of Technology (UTAUT [11]), allows us to study meta-designed environments from a human-computer interaction perspective, predicting behavior of individual users. In contrast to the individualist perspective of UTAUT, Actor-Network Theory describes complex socio-technical networks, by posing that actors (both human and non-human) are connected with each other through relationships, and nothing exists outside those relationships [12]. This theory allows studying meta-design environments from a networked perspective, taking into account the roles of both technology and humans.

While these theories are merely examples, the general principle of using generic theories connected to the core elements of meta-designed environments in the analysis thereof, helps us overcome the drawbacks associated by strict top-down, or bottom-up approaches. By applying such theories as frameworks for the analysis of existing meta-designed cases, we can collect bottom-up knowledge on the factors that influence the successful design and implementation of meta-designed environments in a structured way, allowing for generalization over application domains. At the same time, by selecting adequate theories that correspond to the three core elements of the meta-design paradigm, we can obtain a more holistic understanding of the factors pertaining to successful meta-designed environments, beyond e.g., a purely technological perspective.

3 Conclusion

Meta-design is a strong paradigm for EUD, promoting a culture change from 'design for use before use', towards 'design for design after design'. Even though the paradigm has existed for almost two decades, it has remained rather conceptual in nature, and its application to real-world cases has remained a challenge. The contribution of this paper is in proposing a first step towards the development of a working theory that incorporates both the conceptual aspects of meta-design, as well as knowledge obtained from studying existing implementations of meta-design in a real-world context. Such a working theory could, eventually, help transcend the status quo and facilitate meta-designers in the successful development and implementation of future meta-designed systems.

References

1. Norman, D.A.: The Psychology of Everyday Things. Basic Books, New York (1988)
2. Bødker, S., Iversen, O.S.: Staging a professional participatory design practice: moving PD beyond the initial fascination of user involvement. In: Proceeding of NordiCHI 2002, pp. 11–18. ACM, New York (2002)
3. Maceli, M., Atwood, M.E.: From human crafters to human factors to human actors and back again: bridging the design time – use time divide. In: Costabile, M.F., Dittrich, Y., Fischer, G., Piccinno, A. (eds.) IS-EUD 2011. LNCS, vol. 6654, pp. 76–91. Springer, Heidelberg (2011). https://doi.org/10.1007/978-3-642-21530-8_8
4. Fischer, G., Scharff, E.: Meta-design: design for designers. In: Proceeding of DIS 2000, pp. 396–405. ACM, New York (2000)
5. Fischer, G., Fogli, D., Piccinno, A.: Revisiting and broadening the meta-design framework for end-user development. In: Paternò, F., Wulf, V. (eds.) New Perspectives in End-User Development, pp. 61–97. Springer, Cham (2017). https://doi.org/10.1007/978-3-319-60291-2_4
6. Fischer, G., Giaccardi, E.: Meta-design: a framework for the future of end-user development. In: Lieberman, H., Paternò, F., Wulf, V. (eds.) End User Development. Human-Computer Interaction Series, vol. 9, pp. 427–457. Springer, Dordrecht (2006). https://doi.org/10.1007/1-4020-5386-X_19
7. de Souza, C.S.: Semiotic engineering: a cohering theory to connect EUD with HCI, CMC and more. In: Paternò, F., Wulf, V. (eds.) New Perspectives in End-User Development, pp. 269–305. Springer, Cham (2017). https://doi.org/10.1007/978-3-319-60291-2_11
8. Zhu, L., Mussio, P., Barricelli, B.R.: Hive-mind space model for creative, collaborative design. In: Proceedings of the 1st DESIRE Network Conference on Creativity and Innovation in Design, pp. 121–130. Desire Network, Lancaster (2010)
9. Costabile, M.F., Fogli, D., Mussio, P., Piccinno, A.: End-user development: the software shaping workshop approach. Informatica 9, 1–23 (2006)
10. Tetteroo, D., Markopoulos, P.: EUD survival "in the wild": evaluation challenges for field deployments and how to address them. In: Paternò, F., Wulf, V. (eds.) New Perspectives in End-User Development, pp. 207–229. Springer, Cham (2017). https://doi.org/10.1007/978-3-319-60291-2_9
11. Venkatesh, V., Morris, M.G., Davis, G.B., Davis, F.D.: User acceptance of information technology: toward a unified view. MIS Q. 27, 425–478 (2003)
12. Latour, B.: Reassembling the Social: An Introduction to Actor-Network-Theory. Oxford University Press, Oxford (2005)

End-User Development for the Wolly Robot

Gianluca Bova[2], Davide Cellie[2], Cristina Gioia[2], Fabiana Vernero[1,2],
Claudio Mattutino[1], and Cristina Gena[1,2(✉)]

[1] Department of Computer Science, University of Turin, 10149 Turin, Italy
{fabiana.vernero,cristina.gena}@unito.it
[2] School of ICT, University of Turin, 10124 Turin, Italy
{gianluca.bova,davide.cellie,cristina.gioia}@edu.unito.it
http://www.unito.it

Abstract. In this paper we describe the co-design and implementation of an educational robot called Wolly. We iteratively involved kids as co-designers helping us in shaping form and behavior of the robot, as well as the set of commands to control its actions and behavior.

Keywords: Educational robotics · End-user development · Co-design

1 Introduction

Educational robots can play different roles, such as helping children to learn basic algorithms by programming the robots themselves [1]. In our HCI lab, we carried out a co-design activity with children aimed at devising an educational robot called Wolly [4]. The main goal of the robot is acting as an affective peer for children: hence, it has to be able to execute a standard set of commands, compatible with those used in coding, but also to interact both verbally and affectively with students. We are now working on controlling Wolly by means of a standard visual block environment, Blockly[1], which is well know to many children with some experience in coding. However, we would also like to have a simpler set of instructions, specifically designed for Wolly, so that children can use basic commands to control its behavior.

The idea of developing tools that allow children to build structures, mechanisms and behaviors dates back to the Resnick's project on programmable bricks [9], which allow children to build and program even robots and served as an inspiration for commercial products such as LEGO MindStorms [6]. Another very common approach to robot programming for kids is the use of block-based visual programming languages, such as Scratch[2], Blockly, and others. Graphical and visual environments for programming the behavior of robots are also

---

[1] https://developers.google.com/blockly/.
[2] https://scratch.mit.edu/.

We would like to thank the 4A class of Falletti Primary School, Turin.

A. Malizia et al. (Eds.): IS-EUD 2019, LNCS 11553, pp. 221–224, 2019.
https://doi.org/10.1007/978-3-030-24781-2_19

proposed as end-user development solutions for humanoid commercial robots [8], retail contexts [5], social therapies [3], and more. In order to investigate a children-centered solution for the end-user programming of Wolly, we have organized a co-design session with children, which will be described in Sect. 2.

2   Background and Experiment

As a first step in the development of the robot, in November 2017 we conducted a co-design session with 25 children, described in detail in [4]. All children were in the third grade, 8 to 9 years old, and with no experience in educational robotics. Following a co-design methodology, they were asked to provide suggestions for some features of the robot: its name, physical appearance, facial expressions, personality and character. Based on the insights drawn from the co-design process, we designed the robot appearance and structure (see Fig. 1(a)). In particular, the robot -built using a common hobby robotic kit- is able to move through its four independent motorized wheels and can be controlled through either a web application or a set of Android apps that contact its REST APIs. Its body has been almost completely 3D printed, while its head consists in an Android-based smartphone able to show and perceive emotions[3], to produce verbal expressions and to understand voice commands.

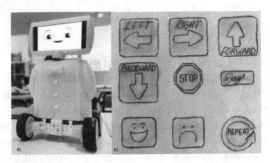

Fig. 1. (a) the Wolly robot; (b) the most frequent children command proposals

As far as interactive features are concerned (see [7] for details), Wolly plays the role of an educational robot that helps kids in coding exercises, giving them suggestions on how to reach their goals and write their code, at the same time being able to execute instructions such as moving on a chessboard, as other educational robots can do. However, since Wolly is also able to interact with kids in a verbal and affective way, we would like to enable children to program its basic behaviors and social interactions, in order to teach them the basis of social robot programming.

Thus, in April 2019 we carried out another co-design session with 24 children (10 females and 14 males) belonging to the same class involved in the first robot

---

[3] The smartphone shows the robot's face and its expressions, while the emotion recognition functionality is based on Affectiva software.

co-design, with the aim of eliciting suggestions on the design of Wolly's basic behavior commands. Children were in the fourth grade of elementary school, 9 to 10 years old. The command co-design activity lasted one hour and was organized in the following phases.

Introduction (10 min): the coordinator presented the activity, introduced three facilitators and answered the children's questions. Children were asked to draw their proposals for the following robot commands: move forward, move backward, turn right, turn left, stop, repeat a command a number of times, say something, express an emotion (happiness, fear, surprise, disgust, anger, sadness, plus a neutral one).

Ideation (30 min): the kids could draw their proposal with the help of the facilitators, which went around the desks and answered any questions.

Recreation (15 min): the children, in turn and in groups, were invited to interact with Wolly, so that they could appreciate the progress of the robot that they had helped to create.

Results and Discussion. The analysis of the proposed symbols was inspired by observational studies from Bakeman and Gottman [2], adapted to this context of analysis. In particular, we borrowed the idea of *coding schemes*, used to categorize the different proposals. Then, we computed the *percentages of agreement* among children as follows:

$$Pa = \frac{Na}{(Na + Nd)} * 100 \tag{1}$$

where Pa refers to the percentage of agreement, Na refers to the number of agreements, Nd refers to the number of disagreements. We found the following percentages of agreement among children's proposals (see Fig. 1(b)):

- **move forward:** arrow ($Pa = 85.7\%$), upwards ($Pa = 62.2\%$), containing written direction ($Pa = 57.14\%$);
- **move backward:** arrow ($Pa = 65.1\%$), downwards ($Pa = 65.0\%$), containing written direction ($Pa = 52.17\%$);
- **turn right:** arrow ($Pa = 80.0\%$), to the right ($Pa = 95.8\%$), containing written direction ($Pa = 48.00\%$);
- **turn left:** arrow ($Pa = 90.0\%$), to the left ($Pa = 95.5\%$), containing written direction ($Pa = 60.00\%$);
- **stop:** stop symbol ($Pa = 37.5\%$), stop textual instruction ($Pa = 31.3\%$), hand up ($Pa = 18.8\%$)
- **repeat:** repetition of the symbol of the command to be repeated ($Pa = 43.8\%$), textual repeat instruction ($Pa = 31.3\%$), cycle block ($Pa = 18.8\%$). Numbers for repetitions were present not as much as expected ($Pa = 31.3\%$), while the most frequent symbol was the arrow ($Pa = 37.5\%$), often used as final part of a block;
- **say something:** textarea ($Pa = 44.4\%$), balloon ($Pa = 33.3\%$), microphone ($Pa = 22.2\%$);
- **express an emotion:** emoticon ($Pa = 89.5\%$)

Although children have been coding for two years, results show that they have not always proposed typical coding instructions, e.g., they seem to prefer directional arrows to express movement commands instead of simply writing the desired direction in a block (as Blockly does), thus confirming some already encountered orienteering difficulties (e.g., problems in recognizing the left and the right side, especially when the robot to command was not turned from their point of view, see [7]). Another surprising result is that almost 20% of them represented the repetition through a cycle block, while 44% proposed to use the repetition of the same command symbol. Although in fourth grade, children have often proposed solutions typical of the pre-school age, preferring symbols (often containing the textual instruction) to blocks containing textual instructions, thus showing that they have not completely internalized abstract concepts.

As future work we will re-propose the same co-design approach to children with no or little experience in coding, to compare the results. Then we will implement the most shared and suitable command proposals in a drag and drop interface, and we will test the approach in the wild. We will also add other commands as moving the robot head, changing the voice volume and its utterance, etc. in order to provide an increasingly refined control over the robot social behavior.

References

1. Alimisis, D., Moro, M.: Special issue on educational robotics. Robot. Auton. Syst. **77**, 74–75 (2016). https://doi.org/10.1016/j.robot.2015.12.006
2. Bakeman, R., Gottman, J.M.: Observing Behavior: An Introduction to Sequential Analysis. Cambridge University Press, Cambridge (1986)
3. Barakova, E.I., Gillesen, J., Huskens, B.E.B.M., Lourens, T.: End-user programming architecture facilitates the uptake of robots in social therapies. Robot. Auton. Syst. **61**(7), 704–713 (2013). https://doi.org/10.1016/j.robot.2012.08.001
4. Cietto, V., Gena, C., Lombardi, I., Mattutino, C., Vaudano, C.: Co-designing with kids an educational robot. In: 2018 IEEE Workshop on Advanced Robotics and its Social Impacts, ARSO 2018, Genova, Italy, 27–29 September 2018, pp. 139–140 (2018). https://doi.org/10.1109/ARSO.2018.8625810
5. Oishi, Y., Kanda, T., Kanbara, M., Satake, S., Hagita, N.: Toward end-user programming for robots in stores. In: Proceedings of the Companion of the 2017 ACM/IEEE International Conference on Human-Robot Interaction, HRI 2017, pp. 233–234. ACM, New York (2017). https://doi.org/10.1145/3029798.3038340
6. Paterno', F.: End user development: Survey of an emerging field for empowering people. ISRN Softw. Eng. **2013**(532659), 1–11 (2013). https://doi.org/10.1155/2013/532659
7. Perosino, G., Trainito, M., Vaudano, C., Mattutino, C., Gena, C.: Design and development of Wolly, an educational affective robot. In: Under Submission (2019)
8. Pot, E., Monceaux, J., Gelin, R., Maisonnier, B.: Choregraphe: a graphical tool for humanoid robot programming. In: RO-MAN 2009 - The 18th IEEE International Symposium on Robot and Human Interactive Communication, pp. 46–51, September 2009. https://doi.org/10.1109/ROMAN.2009.5326209
9. Resnick, M.: Behavior constrction kits. Commun. ACM **36**(7), 64–71 (1993). https://doi.org/10.1145/159544.159593

PAC-PAC: End User Development of Immersive Point and Click Games

Filippo Andrea Fanni[1], Martina Senis[1], Alessandro Tola[1], Fabio Murru[2],
Marco Romoli[2], Lucio Davide Spano[1(✉)], Ivan Blečić[2],
and Giuseppe Andrea Trunfio[3]

[1] Department of Mathematics and Computer Science,
University of Cagliari, Cagliari, Italy
davide.spano@unica.it
[2] Dept. of Civil, Environmental Engineering and Architecture,
University of Cagliari, Cagliari, Italy
[3] Department of Architecture, Design and City Planning,
University of Sassari, Sassari, Italy

Abstract. We present a tool supporting end-users in the development
of point-and-click videogames based on 360° videos. It aims specifically
at people without previous experience in game development and coding.
Users can easily create scenes, add simple objects such as transitions or
switches, connect scenes to each other and define the game rules. The
tool is developed as a part of PAC-PAC, a project for promoting cultural
and environmental heritage through videogames.

Keywords: Point-and-click games · Authoring environment ·
End-user-development · Virtual Reality

1 Introduction

In the PAC-PAC project (an acronym for *"Point-And-Click - Patrimonio Ambi-
entale e Culturale"*, Point-And-Click - Environmental and Cultural Heritage) we
aim at fostering the promotion of tourist location through videogames. Its goal is
developing an authoring environment for people working in tourism promotion
for creating Point-and-Click (PaC) games set in real-world locations, for dis-
tributing them on the web as entertaining promotion material. The tool should
require the same effort and knowledge needed for creating web or social network
contents. The developed games exploit web technologies that work on desktop,
mobile and Virtual Reality (VR) devices. We use 360° videos for supporting
immersive virtual visits, which are relatively simple to create with consumer
hardware.

© Springer Nature Switzerland AG 2019
A. Malizia et al. (Eds.): IS-EUD 2019, LNCS 11553, pp. 225–229, 2019.
https://doi.org/10.1007/978-3-030-24781-2_20

2   Creating Games in PAC-PAC

The authoring environment represents a PaC game as a graph of 360° videos
nodes (*scenes*), connected by arcs implementing the *transition* from a location to
another. The interface for editing the game recalls familiar multimedia content
editing applications, such as e.g., MS Power-Point (see Fig. 1). All the scenes
are available in the left bar (Fig. 1-C), which supports ordering and searching
in the list. The main part (Fig. 1-D) contains the current scene. It displays the
unwrapped video and the position of the interactive objects included in the scene.
The top-level menu (Fig. 1-A) has four elements: (i) *Game* for adding new scenes
and/or modifying game-level properties (e.g., background music, scene groups),
(ii) *Objects* for adding new interactive objects in the current scene, (iii) *Assets*
for managing the game assets (videos, overlay images, music, sound files etc.)
and (iv) *Play* for testing the game by playing it. When creating a new scene, the
user selects a regular or 360° photo/video from the asset collection, or uploads
it from her own files. It is possible to group related scenes using semantic tags,
which define macro-locations (e.g., all the scenes related to the same dungeon).
Each tag is associated with a specific colour.

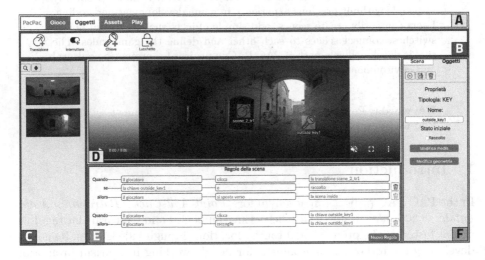

Fig. 1. The PAC-PAC game authoring interface

The authoring environment provides a set of objects helping the user in
defining the game behaviour, displayed in the top bar (Fig. 1-B). Each object
represents a tool that, added to the scene, introduces an interactive element.
For inserting an object into the scene, the user presses the corresponding button
in the upper bar. Once inserted, the user modifies its configuration filling the
properties panel in the right bar (Fig. 1-F). Each object has an interaction area,
which receives the player's clicks for activating the object. For instance, the
interactive area of a transition is the surface the user clicks for changing the scene.

The tool supports creating it by clicking the contour points in the 360° video. In addition, each object has an optional property for animating the interactive area at the object activation through a video (e.g., opening a door when triggering a transition as in Fig. 2-A).

The tool includes different types of interactive objects besides the *transition* we already discussed. For instance, the *key* allows unlocking another object when collected, the *switch* allows changing the current scene configuration according to its status (e.g., a light turns on/off), the *counter* counts the clicks on the specified interactive areas, the *timer* triggers an action after the specified time, the *locker* requires clicking a set of interactive areas in a specified order for triggering an action etc.

Similarly to other EUD tools in different domains [1–3], our authoring environment uses rules for defining the behaviour of each object in isolation and their interactions for creating the game puzzles. Rules define the dynamic behaviour of a scene, supporting the user in inspecting and controlling the game logic. The rule editor is located in the bottom part of the interface (see Fig. 1-E). It contains a list of Event-Condition-Action (ECA) rules expressed in natural language (Italian) according to the following the pattern (elements in angular brackets are required, the ones in square bracket are optional):

```
when    ⟨subject⟩ ⟨action⟩ ⟨object|value⟩
[if     ⟨condition⟩*]
then    (⟨subject⟩ ⟨action⟩ ⟨object|value⟩)*
```

A *subject* is either an interactive object in the game or the player. Each subject has a set of pre-defined *actions* that work on specific *objects* or require specific *values*. Updates and events are (*subject, action, object—value*) triples. They define an event if included in *when* or an update in the *then* part. Therefore, user-defined updates may trigger events having the same triple in the *when* part. The editor supports a guided rule editing, suggesting admissible values while the user types the part name. The editor reports both the type and the name for the selected interactive object (e.g., if we have a *door1* transition object in our game, the object rule part indicates it as *the transition door1*). The *conditions* are simple or composed boolean predicates on the interactive object state. The editor supports their authoring suggesting the proper predicates for the selected object, in order to avoid errors. In addition, the editor adds default rules at the object creation (e.g., an on-click rule when creating a transition), for supporting the behaviour inspection and automating repetitive user's actions.

Figure 2 shows two sample game behaviours and the correspondent definition rules. In the first one, we want to connect the *outside* scene to the *inside* scene through a door. The player has to collect a key for opening it. We need to insert a transition (*door1*) and to create an interactive area around the door in the video. The editor inserts automatically a rule for managing the transition click and moving the player. The user specifies only the target scene, *inside* in our sample. After that, the user inserts a key object (*outside-key*) specifying the image to overlay on the 360° video. The editor automatically adds a rule for collecting the key when clicking the associated area. Finally, the user connects

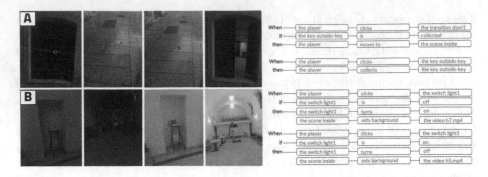

Fig. 2. Game interaction and the associated rules in two examples: modelling a door and the associated key (part A) and a switch for turning lights on or off (part B).

the two objects adding a condition in the first rule (if part), for testing whether the player collected the key before triggering the transition. Figure 2-A shows the final interaction result and the associated rules.

In the second example, we want to create a switch that turns on and off a light in the scene *inside*. We add a switch object in the scene and we create its interactive area. The environment adds two rules defining the switch behaviour: when the user clicks the *light1* switch, it turns on if it was off and vice versa. The user adds an action to both rules that change the scene background video according to the state: *h7.mp4* for the light on and *h5.mp4* for the light off (Fig. 2-B). A video showing the complete procedure for defining the two sample behaviours and the resulting game is available at http://youtu.be/P13c1-kIt-g.

Once the user completes the game definition, she can publish it on the web. Both the authoring environment and the game engine exploit web-based technologies, so players can access games using mobile phones, tablets and personal computers. In addition, the engine supports immersive experiences through Virtual Reality Head Mounted Displays, adapting the input modality to the current device.

3   Conclusion and Future Work

In this paper, we introduced an end-user-development authoring environment for creating point-and-click videogames. Our main goal is producing a tool suitable for users without experience in game development and coding. The authoring environment allows users to create scenes and defining the game logic exploiting simple objects and rules. In the future, we want to expand the game logic further by implementing a broader range of objects for supporting more complex puzzles. In addition, we are going to implement a game debugging mode and to evaluate the tool with users.

References

1. Dey, A.K., Sohn, T., Streng, S., Kodama, J.: iCAP: interactive prototyping of context-aware applications. In: Fishkin, K.P., Schiele, B., Nixon, P., Quigley, A. (eds.) Pervasive 2006. LNCS, vol. 3968, pp. 254–271. Springer, Heidelberg (2006). https://doi.org/10.1007/11748625_16
2. Manca, M., Santoro, C., Corcella, L., et al.: Supporting end-user debugging of trigger-action rules for IoT applications. Int. J. Hum.-Comput. Stud. **123**, 56–69 (2019)
3. Mi, X., Qian, F., Zhang, Y., Wang, X.: An empirical characterization of IFTTT: ecosystem, usage, and performance. In: Proceedings of the 2017 Internet Measurement Conference, pp. 398–404. ACM (2017)

End-User Development in Industry 4.0: Challenges and Opportunities

Daniela Fogli[1(✉)] and Antonio Piccinno[2]

[1] Dipartimento di Ingegneria dell'Informazione,
Università degli Studi di Brescia, Brescia, Italy
daniela.fogli@unibs.it
[2] Dipartimento di Informatica, Università di Bari "Aldo Moro", Bari, Italy
antonio.piccinno@uniba.it

Abstract. This position paper aims to discuss challenges and opportunities related to human-computer interaction technologies for Industry 4.0 and to explore the role that end-user development can play in new industrial scenarios. The paper highlights the gap between what Industry 4.0 and related enabling technologies promise and how the Operator 4.0 will be called on to change his/her work practice. End-user development and meta-design are here proposed as suitable methods to fill this gap and improve operators' quality of work.

Keywords: Industry 4.0 · End-user development · Meta-design

1 Introduction

The fourth industrial revolution, also called Industry 4.0, is transforming industrial manufacturing with the introduction of cyber-physical systems, industrial internet, collaborative robots, and advanced human-computer interaction technologies [14]. Collaborative robots will work in direct cooperation with humans, by also requiring to be (re-)programmed easily to cope with quick changes in production batches; and smart and mobile technologies, including virtual reality (VR), augmented reality (AR) and wearable devices, will be used to perform daily work in novel and more efficient ways. However, if not properly managed, this scenario risks to have a negative impact on operators' quality of life, also considering that demography is changing, shortage of skilled workforce is observed in most of European states [5], and health-related problems may be brought about by new technologies. Therefore, designing and evaluating novel interaction modalities between operators and machines to support the different facets of the Operator 4.0 [13] will become fundamental in the next years.

End-user development (EUD) [12] might represent a possible answer to shape such interaction modalities and help operators tailor tools and workplaces to their needs and preferences. The EUD definition has been recently refined in [2] to comprehend the shaping, on behalf of end users, of both hardware and software technologies in order to accommodate them to different uses and preferences. Most of the enabling technologies foreseen by Industry 4.0 involve novel interaction devices that should be integrated in daily work without worsening the quality of work, in terms of security, mental effort,

A. Malizia et al. (Eds.): IS-EUD 2019, LNCS 11553, pp. 230–233, 2019.
https://doi.org/10.1007/978-3-030-24781-2_21

visual difficulty, physical fatigue, discomfort, disorientation, and so on. Studying suitable EUD methods and techniques for the Industry 4.0 and framing the intervention through meta-design [6] is a challenge to address in the next years.

2   The Operator in the Industry 4.0 Era

Technologies fostered in the frame of Industry 4.0 aim at providing industrial manufactures with several opportunities for increasing efficiency, flexibility and production capability. Promoters of Industry 4.0 claim that human operators will be better supported to prevent errors, recognize machine failures, change production, perform maintenance activities, and avoid repetitive tasks. Work environment themselves promise to change providing operators with greater autonomy and problem-solving capability, enriching the quality of work with an engaging user experience, fostering novel ways for collaboration and knowledge sharing, and ensuring security of the workplace.

Romero and colleagues [13] identified and discussed eight types of operator in Industry 4.0, which reflect the above changes in the factories:

1. The *super-strength operator*, that is a worker empowered by a human-robotic exoskeleton that increases strength and endurance.
2. The *augmented operator*, who uses augmented reality devices to transfer digital information in the physical world in a non-intrusive way.
3. The *virtual operator*, who uses an immersive multimodal environment for simulating interventions or training in some specific tasks.
4. The *healthy operator*, that is a worker endowed with devices (e.g., wearable trackers) for monitoring physical and cognitive workload and scheduling work-shifts accordingly.
5. The *smarter operator*, who interacts with intelligent personal assistants and Internet of Things (IoT) solutions to receive reminders and instructions.
6. The *collaborative operator*, that is a worker operating in direct cooperation with a robot that helps him/her perform repetitive and non-ergonomic tasks.
7. The *social operator*, who uses mobile devices and social networks to connect with other operators and smart things to access, share and manage knowledge.
8. The *analytical operator*, who analyzes data collected in the smart factory and processed by machine learning algorithms to monitor factory performance and predict relevant events.

In this scenario, human operators will be called on to do fewer manual activities in favor of problem-solving tasks that require information and knowledge management [9]; complexity thus may increase, but operators might not have the background and competences necessary to deal with such complexity [10]. The engaging user experience offered by AR, VR or wearable devices might require more flexibility and adaptability on behalf of end users, who may also be called on to evolve rapidly as the work environment evolves. Operators' mental model of tasks and machines will need to be modified; advanced technologies will mediate the interaction with traditional machines and provide huge amount of data to be processed for decision making.

In order to keep the human in the loop and really support human workers by improving their quality of life, enabling technologies for Industry 4.0 must be properly deployed and managed.

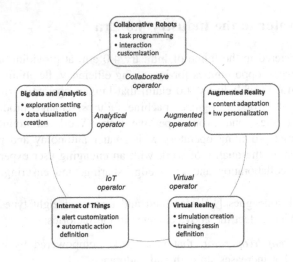

Fig. 1. EUD for the operator 4.0.

3   Filling the Gap with EUD and Meta-Design

We claim that the integration of EUD methods and techniques with the above enabling technologies might help human workers evolve more smoothly into the different types of Operator 4.0. For instance, Beschi et al. [4] propose a new approach to collaborative robot programming, by providing users with a natural interaction to define simple tasks and allowing them to gradually learn new possibilities for complex task creation. Several initiatives in the cultural heritage field show how AR solutions could become sustainable in the long term only if domain experts can be supported with EUD environments that allow customizing contents and presentation [8]; at the same time, hardware technologies employed in AR solutions, such as head mounted displays and smart glasses, might need to be easily tailored to the operators' preferences and physiology in order to limit cognitive efforts and fatigue [11]. Simulations and training sessions to be carried out with the help of VR might require to be created by end users not knowledgeable in computer programming to support context-dependent practices and specific operators' characteristics. Design environments for IoT behavior control and management could be necessary as well; they might be inspired to those ones proposed for smart environments, which are usually based on the rule-based paradigm that proved intuitive for the majority of people [1, 7]. Finally, the definition of data visualizations customized to users' interests, preferences and skills might need to be supported in the context of big data and visual analytics.

Figure 1 synthesizes the opportunities offered by EUD to support the different types of operator. The *super-strength operator* in [13] has been included in the *augmented operator*, by assuming exoskeletons as a form of augmentation that must be (physically) personalized to the user; whilst, the *smarter operator, healthy operator* and *social operator* have been comprised in the *IoT operator*, which is able, through EUD, to manage the entire IoT ecosystem, as conceived in [3].

In summary, enabling technologies for Industry 4.0 should be tailored to the work context and type of operator by the users themselves; this means providing them with one or more EUD environments conceived within a meta-design framework, which not only focuses on enabling technologies, but also and above all can sustain the cultural transformation [6] necessary to address the future complexity of work and workplaces.

References

1. Ardito, C., Buono, P., Desolda, G., Matera, M.: From smart objects to smart experiences: an end-user development approach. Int. J. Hum.-Comput. Stud. **114**, 51–68 (2018)
2. Barricelli, B.R., Cassano, F., Fogli, D., Piccinno, A.: End-user development, end-user programming and end-user software engineering: a systematic mapping study. J. Syst. Softw. **149**, 101–137 (2019)
3. Barricelli, B.R., Valtolina, S.: Designing for end-user development in the internet of things. In: Díaz, P., Pipek, V., Ardito, C., Jensen, C., Aedo, I., Boden, A. (eds.) IS-EUD 2015. LNCS, vol. 9083, pp. 9–24. Springer, Cham (2015). https://doi.org/10.1007/978-3-319-18425-8_2
4. Beschi, S., Fogli, D., Tampalini, F.: CAPIRCI: a multi-modal system for collaborative robot programming. In: Malizia, A., et al. (eds.) IS-EUD 2019. LNCS, vol. 11553, pp. 51–66. Springer, Cham (2019)
5. Caprile, M., Palmén, R., Sanz, P., Dente, G.: Encouraging STEM studies: labour market situation and comparison of practices targeted at young people in different member stages. European Parliament's Committee on Employment and Social Affairs (2015)
6. Fischer, G., Fogli, D., Piccinno, A.: Revisiting and broadening the meta-design framework for end-user development. In: Paternò, F., Wulf, V. (eds.) New Perspectives in End-User Development, pp. 61–97. Springer, Cham (2017). https://doi.org/10.1007/978-3-319-60291-2_4
7. Fogli, D., Lanzilotti, R., Piccinno, A.: End-user development tools for the smart home: a systematic literature review. In: Streitz, N., Markopoulos, P. (eds.) DAPI 2016. LNCS, vol. 9749, pp. 69–79. Springer, Cham (2016). https://doi.org/10.1007/978-3-319-39862-4_7
8. Fogli, D., Sansoni, D., Trivella, E., Arenghi, A., Passamani, I.: Advanced interaction technologies for accessible and engaging cultural heritage. In: Guidi, B., Ricci, L., Calafate, C., Gaggi, O., Marquez-Barja, J. (eds.) GOODTECHS 2017. LNICST, vol. 233, pp. 364–373. Springer, Cham (2018). https://doi.org/10.1007/978-3-319-76111-4_36
9. Kaasinen, E., et al.: Mobile service technician 4.0 – knowledge-sharing solutions for industrial field maintenance. Interact. Des. Archit. J. **38**, 6–27 (2018)
10. Kusmin, K.-L., Tammets, K., Ley, T.: University-industry interoperability framework for developing the future competences of industry 4.0. Interact. Des. Archit. J. **38**, 28–45 (2018)
11. Murauer, N., Pflanz, N.: A full shift field study to evaluate user- and process-oriented aspects of smart glasses in automotive order picking process. Interact. Des. Archit. J. **38**, 64–82 (2018)
12. Paterno, F., Wulf, V. (eds.): New Perspectives in End-User Development. Springer International Publishing, Cham (2017). https://doi.org/10.1007/978-3-319-60291-2
13. Romero, D., et al.: Towards an operator 4.0 typology: a human-centric perspective on the fourth industrial revolution technologies. In: Proceedings CIE46, Tianjin, China (2016)
14. Ruppert, T., Jasko, S., Holczinger, T., Abonyi, J.: Enabling technologies for operator 4.0: a survey. Appl. Sci. **8**(1650), 1–19 (2018)

A Browser-Based P2P Architecture
for Collaborative End-User Artifacts
in the Edge

Rodolfo Gonzalez[1], Sergio Firmenich[1,2(✉)], and Gustavo Rossi[1,2]

[1] LIFIA, Facultad de Informática, Universidad Nacional de La Plata,
La Plata, Argentina
{sergio.firmenich,gustavo}@lifia.info.unlp.edu.ar
[2] CONICET, Buenos Aires, Argentina

Abstract. The Web is a natural platform for end-user development given the amount of services and contents that users may require to adapt, automate, etc. Transcodings, mashups, Web augmentation, and other techniques have emerged to allow end users to improve their Web experiences. In this context, the use of Web browser extensions is a very common strategy for these EUD environments. Sharing information about the same artifact among different users is still a challenge, since these artefacts are created to work standalone, or they are designed to centralize information in a back-end application in the cloud. This paper presents, Browser.ver, a novel P2P architecture for the creation of EUD environments in Web Browsers. Our aim is that it can be used for developing and deploying end-user tools that hosts services and applications for other users, without an intermediate server.

1 Introduction

End-user tools have emerged to improve end users' Web experience. Task automation, adaptation of content and functionality and support for non-functional requirements are some domains that have been addressed by extending the behavior of Web browsers. Aldalur et al. [1] describe dimensions to analyze these kinds of extensions. One is the underlying architecture (Client-Side, Server-Side, Client&Server-side or Proxy). A second category describes collaborative features (Collaborative Development, Sharing and Personal Use). So far, most approaches to Collaborative Development or Sharing require Client-Server architectures. This shows a limitation of Web browsers-based tools: they are not able to communicate with each other without an intermediate server application. Then, if a user that created an artifact using an EUD tool wants to offer her creation as a service, she must "share" the artifact (as it actually happens) to be installed and run in other user's Web browser. Collaborative features in the end-user artifact (e.g. to share annotations, to support collaborative interaction, etc.) must be synchronized through a server component deployed in the cloud or in an intranet. This strong dependency on back-end technology is a bottleneck for the advance of EUD in this area, because end users are required to have more advances skills if they want to contribute to the development and maintenance of these back-end counterparts.

A. Malizia et al. (Eds.): IS-EUD 2019, LNCS 11553, pp. 234–238, 2019.
https://doi.org/10.1007/978-3-030-24781-2_22

In this paper, we present an architecture for the creation of EUD environments supporting collaborative features (during the development stage and in use) without requiring an intermediary server. Our approach is based on a P2P platform that makes possible to perform browser-to-browser communication. It is inspired in the idea of Web browsers in the edge [4]. However, instead of just hosting Web applications to reach a decentralized Web, as in [4], our philosophy is to use this P2P to create a Web browser able to serve edge applications and services created by end-users, through the use of in-browser EUD environments, using existing content and services from the Web.

2   A P2P Architecture for EUD Tools in Web Browsers

There are dozens of works that describe EUD approaches based on Web browser [1]. In general terms, these approaches provide mechanisms for exporting and importing end-user artifacts for sharing. Sharing is usually achieved by uploading artefacts to public repositories; collaboration between end users is achieved using an intermediate server when needed. Our approach is based on the idea that there is not server involved, and artifacts may directly communicate with each other. This implies that the artifacts may act as servers or clients in different moments, according to the collaborations performed in a given moment. There are also some promising projects for creating a P2P Web, where the Web browser may act also as a Web application server. For instance, Beaker Browser [6] allows end users to make a copy of any Web page and store all the content locally, to be served later to other Web browsers. Very interesting scenarios are described in a recent work [4]; using this P2P architecture based on the Web browser as a strategy to provide a decentralized Web is promising. In this paper, we propose new scenarios focused on the domain of end-user tools for Web browsing.

2.1   Browser.ver: Approach and Prototype

The Browser.ver architecture (Fig. 1) aims to provide Web browsers with capabilities for P2P message passing. End-user tools created on top of this architecture (Browser. ver applications) are the final responsible of managing these messages. Each application may act as server (red in Fig. 1) and as a client (green in Fig. 1). The end-user tool *Browser.ver application 1* is installed in Web browser 1 and 2. At a particular moment, *Web browser application 1* acts as a server in Web browser 1, after a request from Web browser 2 (Point 1). Its behavior as a server implies retrieving Web contents, and parsing them for creating a mashup application (Point 2). The mashup application is delivered directly to the Web browser 2 (Point 3), where the client counterpart of *Browser.ver application 1* (green) renders the result (Point 4). At the same time, the same Web Browser 2 may have another end-user tool acting as a server (*Browser.ver application 2* in red). In this case, the behavior of this application in the role of server for the request from Web browser 3 (Point 5), is to interact with an API deployed in the cloud and construct a UI with the retrieved data (Point 6). This new Web page will be served to Web browser 3 (Point 7). Note that Web browser 3 is now rendering a Web page without requesting any content or service from the Web, but from another Web browser in the network of peers that conform this edge Web (Point 8).

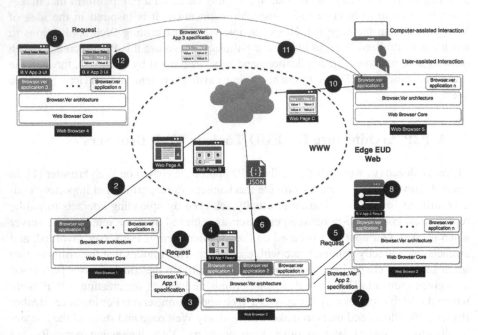

Fig. 1 Browser.ver approach for building an Edge EUD Web (Colour Figure Online).

What is sent as a specification between a server peer and its client counterpart will depend on the kind of application and the moment of interaction. We foresee two main categories for shaping these responses:

– *Complete Web Pages:* In both scenarios so far described (Points 1–8 form Fig. 1), what is sent as a response is a *complete Web page*, containing traditional resources such as JavaScript, CSS, media resources, with the corresponding HTML document. This kind of response is useful for serving mashup applications, for serving Personal Web sites [6]. These complete may be built dynamically in different ways, corresponding to the kind of end-user tool. The simpler is to have a predefined template that is filled of Web contents. A second way is that the Web browser acts as a proxy server that only apply certain changes over an existing Web page, which is important in cases where it is important not to load the final Web browser where the application is used). Note that the client counterpart could be a generic Web page renderer provided by Browser.ver, then end users that have not installed all the some Browser.ver applications, may either way to use these services.

– *Domain Specific Model:* Some tools will depend on the final execution context. For instance, automating a Web task usually requires having a program where the task is being performed, because it must be aware of end-user interaction events. This category helps to this purpose, and more generally, to any other EUD tool based on a *domain specific meta model*, such as Sticklet [3]. Sharing artifacts specifications to be executed in another Web browser that has installed the required Browser.ver application, is a trivial consequence of the P2P service platform. However, domain-specific responses may be applied during the development and the use of the end-user tool, allowing real-time and asynchronous collaboration. For instance, imagine a Browser.ver application that is designed to fill a layout with information provided (and obtained under demand) from other peers. This is the case of the last example in Fig. 1. Point 9 shows the main UI of *Browser.ver application 3* in the Web browser 4. When it is opened, it requests the connected users (peers that have the same application installed and are online) to send a particular information (images, Web pages snippets, etc.). The server counterpart reacts by obtaining any Web page/content from the Web, select a particular piece of this content (Point 10: this step may be assisted manually/semi-automatically by users or automatically by Browser.ver applications) and send it (Point 11). The client counterpart processes the response and visualizes the provided information (Point 12). This kind of real time collaboration is useful in different domains and situations. It could be applied for obtaining accessibility help, for defining distributed interaction behaviors, for the creation of crowdsourcing based applications, etc.

In our current implementation, Browser.ver is a Web browser extension. It is based on WebSockets as a signaling support to allow P2P connection through WebRTC. The content of the responses travels internally through the connection between a particular Browser.ver application and Browser.ver. The full functionality of Browser.ver is executed as an extension in background in Web browsers, so it forwards messages (requests and responses) that receives and sends the data to the corresponding Browser.ver application. Currently, we are using our prototype in Mozilla Firefox Web browser.

3 Conclusion and Future Works

We presented an architecture for easily achieving P2P collaboration in Web-based EUD environments, creating an end-user driven Web in the edge. The prototype architecture has been used for building specific end-user tools, demonstrating the feasibility of the approach. The first prototype required a server for initiating the signalization among peers, but currently we are testing a second prototype not requiring any central server at all, but instead using a distributed signal service such as those in several P2P applications. Currently we are working on the adaptation of an EUD environment for the Personal Web, in order to provide it with P2P capabilities. Further works includes the adaptation of other EUD environments as well as to investigate how P2P collaboration can be defined using also EUD tools, which basically implies to define the shape of messages, and the moments when these messages should sent as a server and as a client.

238   R. Gonzalez et al.

References

1. Aldalur, I., Winckler, M., Díaz, O., Palanque, P.: Web augmentation as a promising technology for end user development. In: Paternò, F., Wulf, V. (eds.) New Perspectives in End-User Development, pp. 433–459. Springer, Cham (2017). https://doi.org/10.1007/978-3-319-60291-2_17
2. Ennals, R., Garofalakis, M.: Mashmaker: Mashups for the masses (demo paper). In: Proceedings of the 2007 ACM SIGMOD International Conference on Management of Data (SIGMOD 2007). Web Augmentation (2007)
3. Díaz, O., Arellano, C.: The augmented web: rationales, opportunities, and challenges on browser-side transcoding. ACM Trans. Web (TWEB) 9(2), 8 (2015)
4. Jannes, K., Lagaisse, B., Joosen, W.: The web browser as distributed application server: towards decentralized web applications in the edge. In: Proceedings of the 2nd International Workshop on Edge Systems, Analytics and Networking, pp. 7–11. ACM, March 2019
5. Beaker Browser. https://beakerbrowser.com. Accessed 9 May 2019
6. Firmenich, S., Bosetti, G., Rossi, G., Winckler, M.: End-user software engineering for the personal web. In: 2017 IEEE/ACM 39th International Conference on Software Engineering Companion (ICSE-C), pp. 216–218. IEEE, May 2017

An End-User Semantic Web Augmentation Tool

Cristian Sottile[1,2]([✉]), Sergio Firmenich[1,3], and Diego Torres[1,2,4]

[1] LIFIA, Facultad de Informática, UNLP, La Plata, Argentina
cristian.sottile@lifia.info.unlp.edu.ar
[2] CICPBA - Comisión de Investigaciones Científicas de la Provincia de Buenos Aires,
Tolosa, Argentina
[3] CONICET - Consejo Nacional de Investigaciones Científicas y Técnicas,
Buenos Aires, Argentina
[4] Departamento de Ciencia y Tecnología, UNQ, Bernal, Argentina

Abstract. Web Augmentation is usually applied to add, remove and change Web sites' functionalities, content, and presentation. Content-based Web Augmentation is commonly performed by integrating content from an external Web site into the current one. In this article, we explore the use of the Semantic Web as a source of information to be incorporated to any Web site, aiming to simplify the development of Web Augmentation based on Semantic Web data. Our approach allows end-users without any programming skills to build Web Augmentation scripts that takes some information from the current Web page, and produce new related information gathered from the Semantic Web. This article introduces a pipeline process for building Semantic Web Augmentations and an end-user development tool called SWAX to create augmentation layers without the need for any programming or Semantic Web skills.

Keywords: Semantic Web · Web Augmentation · User interface

1 Introduction

The Semantic Web [1,7] (SW) provides sources of semantic information useful to be interchanged among computer systems with a standard model called RDF. Most of RDF data sources allow being queried through a SPARQL endpoint.

Web Augmentation (WA) is an approach to improve Web applications by incorporing new functionalities. A common strategy is to enhance them on the client side [2], after they are received from the server.

Semantic Web Augmentation (SWA) is a particular type of WA where the SW provides the new information. The SW is accessed via a SPARQL endpoint or RDF API to extract information pieces, which are then adapted and inserted into the DOM structure on the client side. The Website ends up including the original contents plus the new ones from the SW. In this article we tackle with a

© Springer Nature Switzerland AG 2019
A. Malizia et al. (Eds.): IS-EUD 2019, LNCS 11553, pp. 239–243, 2019.
https://doi.org/10.1007/978-3-030-24781-2_23

kind of SWA where the new information is related to the content of the Website. SWA developers need to be skilled in client-side and SW technologies [6].

This article introduces both a pipeline process for building SWAs and an end-user development tool called SWAX to create augmentation layers without the need for any programming or SW skills.

Section 2 describes the pipeline process for building SWAs. Section 3 introduces the end-user development tool designed as a Web browser extension. Related work is analyzed in Sects. 4 and 5 details conclusions and further work.

2   The Process

This section explains the process for building Semantic Web Augmentations. It is a pipeline process where each component receives as input the output of its predecessor, and consists of three main steps:

- **Data extration:** We stated that our kind of SWA will involve the information present in the desired Website. In this step, these data are extracted from the DOM.
- **Data fetching:** Given a generic SPARQL query and the *extracted data*, this step fills the generic query with the data, producing a specific query for each one, and then run these queries against a SPARQL endpoint, obtaining new information from the Semantic Web.
- **Insertion:** Given an HTML template and the *fetched data*, this step generates specific HTML elements by filling the templates with the data, and inserts them into the Website, performing the Web Augmentation.

3   An End-User Development Tool for SWA

This section introduces an end-user development tool for building SWAs, which we called SWAX[1]. It is a Web browser extension whose functionality is based upon the process described in Sect. 2, and allows to build a WA script based on the current Website. It can be enabled in any Web page, initiating a wizard-like UI to configure the augmentation in a sequence of intuitive steps. The result is a script that is general enough to augment all Web pages whose DOM structure and semantics are similar to the original one. One configuration, several executions. Additionally, the script can be executed to test its results.

As a guide example, we will take the IMDb[2] website, and we will aim to improve the films pages by adding the amount of Oscars every cast member won. The *"The Godfather II"* Website on IMDb[3] could be used to produce a script to augment this and every IMDb film page. In the following, we introduce the tool's sequence of steps using this example.

---

[1] Source code and video-tutorials at https://github.com/cfsottile/swa-extension.

[2] IMDb stands for Internet Movie Database. http://imdb.com.

[3] https://www.imdb.com/title/tt0071562/.

1. **Extraction:** First, the user selects what DOM elements from the Web page will be used as data input for the semantic augmentation, by enabling the selection mode and clicking them. Continuing with our example, these would be actor's and actress' names. Then, the user defines how to extract the information contained in the selected DOM element (e.g., the text content or the HREF) and the tool shows the value extracted from it.

2. **Querying:** The semantic query that will retrieve the new information from the SW must be defined. There are different ways to help the SPARQL query building using visual tools. We delegate it to Visual SPARQL Builder (VSB) [3], which provides an intuitive interface to assist users in vocabulary and properties detection. Our tool provides an augmentation layer also on VSB for communication purposes. The resulting SPARQL query will be executed against the DBpedia SPARQL endpoint, obtaining the augmentation data.

3. **Building:** This step involves the definition of the HTML template that will be used to insert the augmentation data to the Web page. The user must write the HTML code including references to the augmentation data; however, the template may consist of only references, thus it is not mandatory for the user to know HTML. The tool presents the references as buttons that, when clicked, insert the corresponding reference into the template input.

4. **Insertion:** This step configures the weaving of the HTML augmentation elements built in the previous step. The user must choose the desired places in the Web page to inject them. This is done similarly to the Selection step, by selecting HTML elements from the DOM.

5. **Saving:** The user will define a set of URLs where the augmentation should be applied. In our cast example, this would be https://www.imdb.com/title/*. Then, the user can save the augmentation script, which will be applied every time a URL within the set is opened, or try it in the current page for testing purposes. Figure 1 shows the cast section of the *"The Godfather II"* page before and after the augmentation.

Fig. 1. Case study: Oscars

4   Related Work

Rico et al. [6] introduced a tool to allow Web developers with no SW skills to create templates capable of handling semantic data. WOA [4] presents an approach for the creation of WA layers by firstly annotating Web contents with semantic tags. Most SW improvements of non-SW applications are based on the *semantification* of Web pages from social efforts [5,8]. For the best of our knowledge, there exist no end-user tools for defining the weaving of information extracted from the SW in the current context of Web browsing.

5   Conclusions and Further Work

The SW is in a mature state since many years. However, it is not common to see tools for allowing Web users communities to consume all this infrastructure. In this paper, we present a pipeline process for building SWAs, and an end-user development tool based upon it called SWAX to create augmentation layers. The approach allows end-users without any programming skills to produce generic WA scripts that allow for enriching the contents of groups of Web pages.

The first future work is the need for an exhaustive evaluation. The prominent prototype demonstrated well behavior and easy to use augmentation tasks in laboratory tests. Nonetheless, we are designing usability tests with a group of developers. Additionally, more extraction and insertion strategies are in development, as well as user experience improvements. Also, there are several SPARQL query builders like VSB that could be adapted for SWAX.

References

1. Berners-Lee, T., Hendler, J., Lassila, O.: The semantic web. Sci. Am. **284**(5), 28–37 (2001)
2. Bouvin, N.O.: Unifying strategies for Web augmentation. In: Proceedings of the Tenth ACM Conference on Hypertext and Hypermedia: Returning to Our Diverse Roots, pp. 91–100. ACM (1999)
3. Eipert, L.: Metadatenextraktion und vorschlagssysteme im visual sparql builder. In: Cunningham, D.W., Hofstedt, P., Meer, K., Schmitt, I. (eds.) INFORMATIK 2015, pp. 1925–1936. Gesellschaft für Informatik e.V., Bonn (2015)
4. Firmenich, S., Bosetti, G.A., Rossi, G., Winckler, M., Barbieri, T.: Abstracting and structuring web contents for supporting personal web experiences. In: Bozzon, A., Cudre-Maroux, P., Pautasso, C. (eds.) ICWE 2016. LNCS, vol. 9671, pp. 77–95. Springer, Cham (2016). https://doi.org/10.1007/978-3-319-38791-8_5
5. Kahan, J., Koivunen, M.R.: Annotea: an open RDF infrastructure for shared Web annotations. In: Proceedings of the 10th International Conference on World Wide Web, WWW 2001, pp. 623–632. ACM, New York (2001)
6. Rico, M., Corcho, O., Macías, J.A., Camacho, D.: A tool suite to enable Web designers, Web application developers and end-users to handle semantic data. In: Semantic-Enabled Advancements on the Web: Applications Across Industries, p. 123 (2012)

7. Shadbolt, N., Berners-Lee, T., Hall, W.: The semantic web revisited. IEEE Intell. Syst. **21**(3), 96–101 (2006)
8. Torres, D., Diaz, A., Skaf-Molli, H., Molli, P.: Semdrops: a social semantic tagging approach for emerging semantic data. In: 2011 IEEE/WIC/ACM International Conference on Web Intelligence and Intelligent Agent Technology (WI-IAT), vol. 1, pp. 340–347. IEEE (2011)

Improving Tools that Allow End Users to Configure Smart Environments

Carmelo Ardito[1(✉)], Maria F. Costabile[1], Giuseppe Desolda[1],
Marco Manca[2], Maristella Matera[3], Fabio Paternò[2],
and Carmen Santoro[2]

[1] Università degli Studi di Bari Aldo Moro, via Orabona 4, 70125 Bari, Italy
{carmelo.ardito,maria.costabile,
giuseppe.desolda}@uniba.it
[2] HIIS Laboratory, CNR-ISTI, Via G. Moruzzi 1, 56124 Pisa, Italy
{marco.manca,fabio.paterno,carmen.
santoro}@isti.cnr.it
[3] Politecnico di Milano, Milan, Italy
maristella.matera@polimi.it

Abstract. The widespread introduction of the Internet of Things into people's daily lives calls for approaches that allow even unskilled end users to autonomously configure their own smart environments. Various tools, either research or commercial, are available, which allow end users to combine smart objects and services for creating applications that meet their needs. However, challenging issues do persist, including interaction paradigms adequate to end users, as well as the ability to control that the created applications will do what they are intended to. This work-in-progress proposes the integration of two recently developed tools, in order to overcome some limitations of the existing solutions.

Keywords: End-User Development · Internet of Things · Debugging

1 Introduction

The design and development of flexible software able to satisfy the many possible users' needs is still a difficult challenge. The identification of all the requirements at design time might be too complicated, and such requirements would not be definitive because user needs are likely to change and evolve over time. Moreover, a wide variability of possible contexts of use should be considered, since the explosion of mobile and Internet of Things (IoT) technologies has made it possible for people to access their applications from a variety of contexts of use that differ in terms of available devices, smart objects, and services [1]. Thus, it is not possible to guarantee a complete fit between the initially designed system and actual user needs at any given time. The fundamental challenge is to empower end users to configure smart environments able to exploit several interconnected devices and objects, which will enable many possible interactions in a user's surrounding.

As largely recognized in the literature, End-User Development (EUD) approaches fit very well the requirement of letting end users customize systems for their situational

© Springer Nature Switzerland AG 2019
A. Malizia et al. (Eds.): IS-EUD 2019, LNCS 11553, pp. 244–248, 2019.
https://doi.org/10.1007/978-3-030-24781-2_24

needs [2–5]. This provides a significant advantage also to professional software engineers, because the software they create will have broader adoption, impact and diffusion. EUD approaches can enable people, who are not technology-savvy or do not know programming, to tailor applications for managing smart environment. In the last years, the authors of this paper have been developing tools that exploit new abstractions, concepts, languages, in order to support end users in creating and tailoring IoT context-dependent interactive applications capable to satisfy their needs. The tools have some specific features and we are working to integrate them, in order to take advantage of the features of both tools.

2 Some Limitations of Current Tools

Some recently proposed tools support non-technical users to configure smart object behavior. Through Web editors, users can synchronize the behavior of smart objects by either: (a) graphically sketching the interaction among the objects, for example by means of graphs that represent how events and data parameters propagate among the different objects to achieve their synchronization, or (b) defining *event-condition-action* (ECA) rules [7], a paradigm largely used at both the commercial (e.g., Tasker, IFTTT) and research level (e.g., [8, 9]) for the specification of active systems. The idea underlying ECA rules is to specify an operation by using a number of if-then statements expressing how the system should behave when specific situations occur.

Such tools have some limitations on how they support end users to specify the behavior of smart objects. Specifically, the graphical notations for rule specification do not match the mental model of most users [11]. Another limiting factor is that the expressive power of the ECA rules created with some tools, such as IFTTT, Zapier and Atooma, is rather low, permitting to only specify very simple synchronized behaviors [12, 13].

An interesting aspect is how a user can test and possibly assess whether the behavior of the application they created or modified actually results in the expected one. This need is especially relevant in IoT domains, where incorrect behavior of applications or actuators can eventually have safety-critical consequences (e.g., in the elderly assistance domain, in the home domain, etc.). This issue is relevant both in single-user and in multi-user scenarios. For instance, conflicting rules can occur with a single user who might not realize that some rules can conflict under specific circumstances. In other situations, multiple users might define rules attempting to influence the status of devices or physical objects belonging to the same environment in a conflicting manner, based on contrasting preferences. In both cases, a debugging feature could be beneficial to highlight potentially conflicting rules or provide the reasons why a rule will not be triggered in specific situations. This aspect is scarcely addressed in the EUD area and most EUD tools do not include debugging aids also because end users find debugging especially difficult [14]. Debugging mechanisms that are adequate for end users are of great importance [15].

The next section describes two tools that support EUD of IoT applications, providing good solutions to the two issues described above, that we aim at integrating in a single smart application configuration tool.

3 The Proposed Solution

EFESTO-5W is a web-based platform that, by means of a visual composition paradigm, allows non-technical end users to synchronize the behavior of multiple smart devices [16]. The platform inherits some modules for service invocation and management already developed in the EFESTO mashup framework [17]. The behavior is defined by creating Event-Condition-Action (ECA) rules. With respect to other tools, EFESTO-5W provides a richer set of operators for the definition of ECA rules, which are characterized by multiple events and actions [18], as well as by temporal and spatial constraints on event detection and action execution. Thus, their expressive power is much higher. In addition, the adopted visual paradigm better accommodates the end users' mental model. End users may also define custom attributes, a conceptual tool to transfers domain-specific knowledge to smart-objects, thus simplifying and empowering the creation of an ecosystem of ECA rules [19]. The EFESTO-5W architecture fosters its customization to different domains. For instance, the decoupling of UI layer promotes the lightweight development of further UIs implementing visual metaphors more adequate for specific domains [20].

A platform for the specification and execution of trigger-action rules has been introduced in [21]. It supports people without programming experiences to select the relevant elements for their personalization rules through a logical classification of the possible triggers and actions, which can be dynamically configured taking into account the actual smart objects and applications available. The execution of the rules is obtained with the support of a context manager, which is able to communicate with the available sensors, appliances and devices in order to inform the platform when the triggers of the created rules are verified. At that point the associated actions are sent to the corresponding objects and applications for their execution. A solution for integrating end user debugging features in such approach is presented in [15]. It supports the possibility of simulating specific contextual states, and check whether in those cases the rules indicated would be executed or not, also providing some explanations to understand the results motivations. It also includes conflict detection features concerning when there are rules requesting conflicting actions (e.g. light off and on) at the same time.

The overall architecture integrating the two tools is summarized in Fig. 1. The Smart Application Configuration Tool, created by professional developers, allows end users to define the ECA rules that determine the smart application behavior (see the user interface at the top left). The defined rules are interpreted and managed by a Personalisation Engine, which will subscribe to the underlying middleware to be notified when the relevant triggers occur. A Debugger allows users to debug the created ECA rules using the user interface shown at the top right of the figure. The middleware is composed of a server and various delegates that receive information from the different sensors. The information gathered from the devices available in the real context is collected and logically organized by the Context Server.

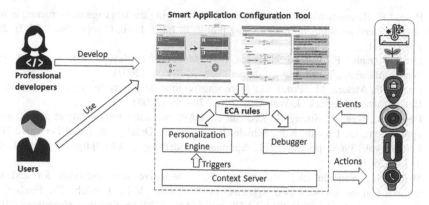

Fig. 1. Schema of the integration of the two EUD tools for configuring IoT applications.

4 Conclusion

Our research aims at proposing tools that, by exploiting EUD techniques, allows people who are not technology-savvy or do not know programming, to tailor applications for managing smart environment. The work in progress presented in this paper is about the integration of two recently developed tools. We are confident that this work will provide important results, in order to overcome some limitations of the existing solutions.

Acknowledgments. This work is partially supported by the Italian Ministry of University and Research (MIUR) under grant PRIN 2017 "EMPATHY: EMpowering People in deAling with internet of THings ecosYstems".

References

1. Atzori, L., Iera, A., Morabito, G.: The Internet of Things: a survey. Comput. Netw. **54**(15), 2787–2805 (2010)
2. Fischer, G., Giaccardi, F., Ye, Y., Sutcliffe, A., Mehandjiev, N.: Meta-design: a manifesto for end-user development. Commun. ACM **47**(9), 33–37 (2004)
3. Lieberman, H., Paternò, F., Klann, M., Wulf, V.: End-user development: an emerging paradigm. In: Lieberman, H., Paternò, F., Wulf, V. (eds.) End User Development. Human-Computer Interaction Series, vol. 9, pp. 1–8. Springer, Dordrecht (2006). https://doi.org/10.1007/1-4020-5386-X_1
4. Ardito, C., Buono, P., Costabile, M.F., Lanzilotti, R., Piccinno, A.: End users as co-designers of their own tools and products. J. Vis. Lang. Comput. **23**(2), 78–90 (2012)
5. Barricelli, B.R., Cassano, F., Fogli, D., Piccinno, A.: End-user development, end-user programming and end-user software engineering: a systematic mapping study. J. Syst. Softw. **149**, 101–137 (2019)
6. Costabile, M.F., Fogli, D., Mussio, P., Piccinno, A.: Visual interactive systems for end-user development: a model-based design methodology. IEEE Trans. Syst. Man Cybern. - Part A: Syst. Hum. **37**(6), 1029–1046 (2007)

7. Pane, J.F., Ratanamahatana, C.A., Myers, B.A.: Studying the language and structure in non-programmers' solutions to programming problems. Int. J. Hum.-Comput. Stud. **54**(2), 237–264 (2001)
8. Ceri, S., Daniel, F., Matera, M., Facca, F.M.: Model-driven development of context-aware Web applications. ACM Trans. Internet Technol. **7**(1), 2 (2007)
9. Daniel, F., Matera, M., Pozzi, G.: Managing runtime adaptivity through active rules: the Bellerofonte framework. J. Web Eng. **7**(3), 179–199 (2008)
10. Dey, A.K., Sohn, T., Streng, S., Kodama, J.: iCAP: interactive prototyping of context-aware applications. In: Fishkin, K.P., Schiele, B., Nixon, P., Quigley, A. (eds.) Pervasive 2006. LNCS, vol. 3968, pp. 254–271. Springer, Heidelberg (2006). https://doi.org/10.1007/11748625_16
11. Wajid, U., Namoun, A., Mehandjiev, N.: Alternative representations for end user composition of service-based systems. In: Costabile, M.F., Dittrich, Y., Fischer, G., Piccinno, A. (eds.) IS-EUD 2011. LNCS, vol. 6654, pp. 53–66. Springer, Heidelberg (2011). https://doi.org/10.1007/978-3-642-21530-8_6
12. Caivano, D., Fogli, D., Lanzilotti, R., Piccinno, A., Cassano, F.: Supporting end users to control their smart home: design implications from a literature review and an empirical investigation. J. Syst. Softw. **144**, 295–313 (2018)
13. Fogli, D., Lanzilotti, R., Piccinno, A.: End-user development tools for the smart home: a systematic literature review. In: Streitz, N., Markopoulos, P. (eds.) DAPI 2016. LNCS, vol. 9749, pp. 69–79. Springer, Cham (2016). https://doi.org/10.1007/978-3-319-39862-4_7
14. Coutaz, J., Crowley, J.L.: A first-person experience with end-user development for smart homes. IEEE Pervasive Comput. **15**(2), 26–39 (2016)
15. Manca, M., Paternò, P., Santoro, C., Corcella, L.: Supporting end-user debugging of trigger-action rules for IoT application. Int. J. Hum.-Comput. Stud. **123**, 56–69 (2019)
16. Desolda, G., Ardito, C., Matera, M.: Empowering end users to customize their smart environments: model, composition paradigms, and domain-specific tools. ACM Trans. Comput.-Hum. Interact. **24**(2), 12 (2017)
17. Desolda, G., Ardito, C., Matera, M.: EFESTO: a platform for the end-user development of interactive workspaces for data exploration. In: Daniel, F., Pautasso, C. (eds.) RMC 2015. CCIS, vol. 591, pp. 63–81. Springer, Cham (2016). https://doi.org/10.1007/978-3-319-28727-0_5
18. Desolda, G., Ardito, C., Matera, M.: Specification of complex logical expressions for task automation: an EUD approach. In: Barbosa, S., Markopoulos, P., Paternò, F., Stumpf, S., Valtolina, S. (eds.) IS-EUD 2017. LNCS, vol. 10303, pp. 108–116. Springer, Cham (2017). https://doi.org/10.1007/978-3-319-58735-6_8
19. Ardito, C., Buono, P., Desolda, G., Matera, M.: From smart objects to smart experiences: An end-user development approach. Int. J. Hum.-Comput. Stud. **114**, 51–68 (2018)
20. Ardito, C., et al.: User-driven visual composition of service-based interactive spaces. J. Vis. Lang. Comput. **25**(4), 278–296 (2014)
21. Ghiani, G., Manca, M., Paternò, F., Santoro, C.: Personalization of context-dependent applications through trigger-action rules. ACM Trans. Comput.-Hum. Interact. **24**(2), 1–33 (2017)

Research on Making Nature Smart with Children

Rosella Gennari[1], Maristella Matera[2], Alessandra Melonio[1],
and Eftychia Roumelioti[1](✉)

[1] Free University of Bozen-Bolzano, Piazza Domenicani 3, 39100 Bolzano, Italy
gennari@inf.unibz.it, eftychia.roumelioti@stud-inf.unibz.it,
alessandra.melonio@unibz.it
[2] Politecnico di Milano, Piazza Leonardo da Vinci, 32, 20133 Milan, Italy
maristella.matera@polimi.it

Abstract. Recent research invites children to be the protagonists of the design of novel smart nature ecosystems for them. Games and card-based workshops can help engage them in co-design and serve as a tool for generating ideas and designing new concepts. The SNaP game is a collaborative card-based board game that aims at engaging 11–14 years old children as protagonists in the design of novel smart nature ecosystems. This paper outlines the main features of the game, the workshops it was used in and the resulting reflections.

Keywords: Smart nature · Children · Board game · Co-create

1 Research Area and Motivations

Children are included more and more in the design of new technology, in different stages and with various roles (e.g. [4,10]). Recently, a complementary perspective on children's role has emerged: the role of protagonist [8]. According to it, children guide the design process and thus are given the means to develop skills in designing and reflecting on technology and its role in their lives [9]. In addition, numerous generative toolkits and techniques have also been used to make children's participation interesting and enjoyable, including the use of visual materials, storytelling, playful activities and prototyping kits in making activities. Studies have highlighted, in particular, the value of games and card-based workshops to serve as a stimulus for participation and a tool for generating ideas and designing new concepts [2]. Sets or decks of cards, such as the IoTT Card Set [1] and the IoT Design Deck [3], are considered a long-established type of tool for co-designing. Tiles Cards, for example, have been used for the design of IoT applications with children in co-design workshops [7,11]. At the same time, research from HCI communities indicates an increasing interest in facilitating children's engagement in the design of novel smart nature ecosystems, enhanced with technology for them.

© Springer Nature Switzerland AG 2019
A. Malizia et al. (Eds.): IS-EUD 2019, LNCS 11553, pp. 249–253, 2019.
https://doi.org/10.1007/978-3-030-24781-2_25

This research aims to continue this line of investigation by co-designing and co-creating smart nature ecosystems with children through play. To this end, this paper presents the SNaP game. Specifically, it presents its main design features and reflects on results of game-play sessions in workshops with children.

2   The SNaP Game

The *Smart Nature Protagonists (SNaP)* game is a collaborative card-based board game for co-design workshops, with ideas taken from traditional board game design [13,14]. It considers children as co-designers in the design practice of augmenting outdoor environment objects. Its main parts are its cards, the scaffolding map and the game board. They are detailed in the following.

2.1   Nature Cards

Nature Cards (see Fig. 1) have been created to inspire the design of augmented environment objects. They are addressed to children aged from 8 years old and aim to include them in the design process. The idea and layout of the cards is based on the Tiles Ideation Toolkit [12]. Currently, they are composed of three categories: (1) Environment Cards, representing

Fig. 1. Nature Cards: blue Input Cards; green Environment Cards; yellow Output cards (Color figure online)

objects that can be usually found in a park or an outdoor non-urban environment; (2) Input Cards, representing sensors and buttons that trigger an interaction; (3) Output Cards, representing actuators that react to the interaction.

2.2   Scaffolding Map

The *Scaffolding Map* is the warm-up part and its purpose is to familiarise players with the tools and the concept of the game. The map consists of elements, which correspond to Environment Cards, that are connected trough QR codes to a website that shows video examples of related smart nature objects. These elements in the map can be "opened" like windows; they hide tags that, read with a smartphone or a tablet, link to the video examples. Players are challenged to play and guess what input and output cards are needed for making such smart objects. Once they think they are done, they ask the moderator whether they have guessed correctly by checking the correct combination of cards on the smartphone or tablet.

2.3 Game Board

The game board of SNaP is designed for 2–4 players from 8 years old onward. See Fig. 2.

During the game-play, players have the role of *Designers*. The game is facilitated by a moderator, with the role of *Mayor*. Each player has a mission to accomplish in order to make the park interactive. Players win the game collaboratively: if each of them has designed at least an interactive object and fulfilled his/her mission in order to make the SNaP park interactive.

Each player places his/her token at the corners of the board and tries to reach the central circle by throwing the dice and moving his/her token. Depending on the space the token reaches, the players may be entitled to get one or more cards from the piles of cards, get coins, try to combine the cards and take notes, exchange roles, exchange or buy a card. During the game-play, the players should have a discussion round; they have to discuss in turn about their ideas with the rest of the team and the Mayor. In the end, the players should present their final interactive objects with the corresponding cards to the Mayor.

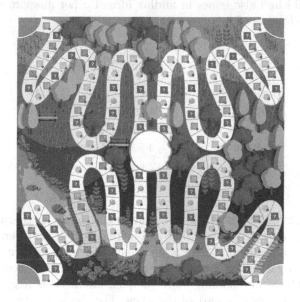

Fig. 2. Game board

3 Reflections and Future Work

The SNaP game is an attempt to foster children's participation as protagonists in the co-design of smart interactive nature ecosystems for them. It adopts domain-specific cards, related to concrete elements of a given domain (namely, a natural environment), within a game play that structures children's ideas and promotes shared reflections.

The game evolved by playing it with HCI experts and in 4 main workshops with children, from 10 to 14 years old. See Table 1. Data related to children's ideas and engagement, the interactions among them and their experience of the game play were collected and integrated with results from expert evaluation rounds. Results of specific workshops with children are reported in [5,6].

In general, during their game play with SNaP, all players collaborated and helped each other, e.g., by suggesting others ideas during the discussion, albeit children tended to stick to their cards and were not willing to exchange them.

Therefore, it is likely that the final ideas were rich not only because of the creativity of each single participant, but also because of the numerous stimuli they received from each other. Overall ideas were evaluated feasible by experts of HCI albeit rather simple, e.g,, they used few inputs or outputs. In general, children's engagement was high, albeit it seems to be higher with younger children (11 years old) than with older children (14 years old). When probed, all children complained that the game was "too short" and hence they could not collect sufficiently many cards.

As for specific cards, some players seemed to have found some missions too difficult. A child had also issues in finding ideas for her mission, and hence she needed the scaffolding of peers to carry on her ideas.

Table 1. Workshops with SNaP

Version	Moderators	Players	Age
SNaP 1.0	2	4 female	10–13
SNaP 1.0	2	2 female + 2 male	11
SNaP 1.0	2	2 female + 2 male	14
SNaP 2.0	2	2 female + 2 male	11

Future work will be devoted to improve the game, by iteratively designing and evaluating new features that can increase children's overall experience. For example, the scaffolding map will be enriched with further examples that show how a person can interact with environment cards to accomplish different missions. Cards for enabling more complex interactions (e.g., services) may be introduced in a specific part of the game. For the same reason, for ideating higher quality interactive objects for nature ecosystems, novel role cards will be added, which will enable children to play the role of experts and better reflect on their ideas and other players' ideas. Novel game mechanics elements will be introduced to further foster the collaboration among players and the exchange of cards, e.g., traps that require all to collaborate so as to solve a mission.

Acknowledgements. Our thanks go to all participating children, as well as to the financial support of GeKI and SOfAA from the Free University of Bozen-Bolzano.

References

1. Angelini, L., Mugellini, E., Couture, N., Abou Khaled, O.: Designing the interaction with the internet of tangible things: a card set. In: Proceedings of the Twelfth International Conference on Tangible, Embedded, and Embodied Interaction, TEI 2018, pp. 299–306. ACM, New York (2018). https://doi.org/10.1145/3173225.3173288
2. Brandt, E.: Designing exploratory design games: a framework for participation in participatory design? In: Proceedings of the Ninth Conference on Participatory Design: Expanding Boundaries in Design, PDC 2006, vol. 1, pp. 57–66. ACM, New York (2006). https://doi.org/10.1145/1147261.1147271
3. Dibitonto, M., Tazzi, F., Leszczynska, K., Medaglia, C.M.: The IoT design deck: a tool for the co-design of connected products. In: Ahram, T., Falcão, C. (eds.) AHFE 2017. AISC, vol. 607, pp. 217–227. Springer, Cham (2018). https://doi.org/10.1007/978-3-319-60492-3_21
4. Druin, A.: The role of children in the design of new technology. Behav. Inf. Technol. **21**, 1–25 (2002)
5. Gennari, R., Matera, M., Melonio, A., Roumelioti, E.: A board-game for co-designing smart nature environments in workshops with children. In: End-User Development. Springer, Cham (2019)
6. Gennari, R., Melonio, A., Matera, M., Roumelioti, E.: A board game and a workshop for co-creating smart nature ecosystems. In: Methodologies and Intelligent Systems for Technology Enhanced Learning. Springer, Cham (2019)
7. Gennari, R., Melonio, A., Rizvi, M., Bonani, A.: Design of IOT tangibles for primary schools: a case study. In: Proceedings of the 12th Biannual Conference on Italian SIGCHI Chapter, CHItaly 2017, pp. 26:1–26:6. ACM, New York (2017). https://doi.org/10.1145/3125571.3125591
8. Iivari, N., Kinnula, M.: Empowering children through design and making: towards protagonist role adoption. In: Proceedings of the 15th Participatory Design Conference: Full Papers-Volume 1, PDC 2018, pp. 16:1–16:12. ACM, New York (2018). https://doi.org/10.1145/3210586.3210600
9. Iversen, O.S., Smith, R.C., Dindler, C.: Child as protagonist: expanding the role of children in participatory design. In: Proceedings of the 2017 Conference on Interaction Design and Children, IDC 2017, pp. 27–37. ACM, New York (2017). https://doi.org/10.1145/3078072.3079725
10. Kinnula, M., Iivari, N., Isomursu, M., Kinnula, H.: Socializers, achievers or both? Value-based roles of children in technology design projects. Int. J. Child-Comput. Interact. **17**, 39–49 (2018). https://doi.org/10.1016/j.ijcci.2018.04.004
11. Mavroudi, A., Divitini, M., Gianni, F., Mora, S., Kvittem, D.R.: Designing IOT applications in lower secondary schools. In: 2018 IEEE Global Engineering Education Conference (EDUCON), pp. 1120–1126, April 2018. https://doi.org/10.1109/EDUCON.2018.8363355
12. Mora, S., Gianni, F., Divitini, M.: Tiles: a card-based ideation toolkit for the Internet of Things. In: Proceedings of the 2017 Conference on Designing Interactive Systems, DIS 2017, pp. 587–598. ACM, New York (2017). https://doi.org/10.1145/3064663.3064699
13. Salen, K., Zimmerman, E.: Rules of Play: Game Design Fundamentals. The MIT Press, Cambridge (2003)
14. Schell, J.: The Art of Game Design: A Book of Lenses. Morgan Kaufmann Publishers Inc., San Francisco (2008)

Author Index

Printed in the United States
By Bookmasters